Toward Sunrise

BY

Alexis Roeckner Ferri

Copyright © 2021 Alexis Roeckner Ferri

All rights reserved. No part of this book may be reproduced, distributed or transmitted in any form or by any means, without written permission from the publisher, except in the noncommercial uses permitted by copyright law.

For permission requests, contact Permissions Coordinator, sealofterspress@gmail.com

Printed in USA
All rights reserved.

ISBN-13: 978-0-9994562-0-0

DEDICATION

For Jim, who believes in second chances

And for the horses, who gave me mine

A NOTE FROM THE AUTHOR

This book is a depiction of real life events involving real people. With the exception of Jim and Jean Gath, all of the individuals described in my book have purposefully been left nameless-or else given a nickname or initial-in order to protect their privacy.

DEDICATION

For Jim, who believes in second chances

And for the horses, who gave me mine

A NOTE FROM THE AUTHOR

This book is a depiction of real life events involving real people. With the exception of Jim and Jean Gath, all of the individuals described in my book have purposefully been left nameless-or else given a nickname or initial-in order to protect their privacy.

CONTENTS

CHAPTER	TITLE	PAGE
	FOREWORD	i
ONE	MASHES	1
TWO	RHYTHM	4
THREE	WHAT DO YOU DO?	8
FOUR	CREATING TIERRA MADRE	12
FIVE	THE ORIGINAL TWENTY-NINE	16
SIX	HORSEMANSHIP 101	27
SEVEN	JAZZ	31
EIGHT	VOLUNTEER ORIENTATIONS	37
NINE	S.P.E.R.M.	41
TEN	ON	47
ELEVEN	MEDICINE	50
TWELVE	THE WALK AROUND	55
THIRTEEN	KEEPING HOUSE	59
FOURTEEN	EVERY TIME	65
FIFTEEN	STUDLEY	66
SIXTEEN	LOOSE HORSE	71
SEVENTEEN	THE CRAZIER ONES	74
EIGHTEEN	ALL IS WELL	81
NINETEEN	DANCING	88
TWENTY	MONEY	90
TWENTY-ONE	THE FIRST BENEFIT	93

CHAPTER	TITLE	PAGE
TWENTY-TWO	THE AWAKENING	101
TWENTY-THREE	RESOURCES	104
TWENTY-FOUR	STORYTELLING	108
TWENTY-FIVE	MIRACLE	111
TWENTY-SIX	SIMPLE JOYS	114
TWENTY-SEVEN	RECORDS AND MINDSETS	116
TWENTY-EIGHT	TEAMWORK	119
TWENTY-NINE	DEAR RANDOM VISITOR	123
THIRTY	CHANCE	126
THIRTY-ONE	FAIR	134
THIRTY-TWO	SURVIVAL MODE	136
THIRTY-THREE	WE WIN THESE	138
THIRTY-FOUR	THE TALE OF THE DONKEYS	147
THIRTY-FIVE	HOW BAD AND HOW OFTEN?	158
THIRTY-SIX	RINGING SILENCE	160
THIRTY-SEVEN	HOW?	162
THIRTY-EIGHT	SONORA	163
THIRTY-NINE	OUT	172
FORTY	SEASONS	175
FORTY-ONE	ON BEING A LEADER	181
FORTY-TWO	HORSES AND HUMANS	185
FORTY-THREE	RAIN	188
FORTY-FOUR	MY FEAR	196

CHAPTER	TITLE	PAGE
FORTY-FIVE	THE MOOSE	197
FORTY-SIX	THANK YOUS	201
FORTY-SEVEN	SUNNY	206
FORTY-EIGHT	CORNERS	212
FORTY-NINE	EVERY ONCE IN A GREAT WHILE	214
FIFTY	MY FAVORITE GIFT	219
FIFTY-ONE	THE AUCTION	220
FIFTY-TWO	A FAVOR	227
FIFTY-THREE	IF NOT US	230
FIFTY-FOUR	DETAILS	233
FIFTY-FIVE	ONE MORE THING	235
FIFTY-SIX	THE GATE	240
	EPILOGUE - CIRCLES	244
	ACKNOWLEDGEMENTS	247

FOREWORD

June first of 2009 dawned pretty much like it did every day, with the Great Herd pulling Father Sun across the eastern horizon to light our brand new day.

By about eight o'clock, with my self-imposed daily chores just about complete - feeding the horses their breakfasts, mucking about half the ranch and cleaning and refilling a dozen or so water tubs and buckets – I heard the front gates open.

Who was coming? Oh, wait – it's that high school kid that's supposed to help out and write about her experiences for some class project. Great. Now, I'll have to spend a bunch of time showing her around. Like I needed somebody following me around on a busy morning.

As I was ruminating on all this, a car drove almost all the way up the lane toward me, past the area where people parked their vehicles.

A window came down.

"Where should I park?"

"Darlin', you just drove past the parking area – the place where the other cars are parked. See?"

"Oh. Okay."

Jesus, this was going to be worse than I thought.

Once parked, the girl came up to me and introduced herself. "I'm Alexis." And I put on my best smile and welcomed her to Tierra Madre Horse Sanctuary.

She seemed nice enough and, after a few minutes, I realized that her earlier "Where should I park?" faux pas was not thickness of skull, but rather a desire to do things right. Maybe she'd thought those other cars were 'official' Tierra Madre folks' cars and here she was, just a student, and maybe she was relegated to some lower class parking spot.

I decided to give her a chance.

And that decision, right then and there, was probably just about the best decision I've ever made at Tierra Madre. No. Check that. Not 'probably'. Definitely.

Over the next days and weeks, Alexis showed up every day. Every single day – Saturdays and Sundays included. And she learned quickly and she learned well. And she was eager and she was smart and she busted her butt around here, doing anything and everything that was asked of her. And she always asked for more.

Most of all – best of all – she loved the horses. She got to know each and every one of them as the individual spirits they are. She began to know their quirks and their needs and their personalities. She learned which horses required special medicines and supplements. She learned how to interact with each of them and how to halter and walk them and turn them out into the arena. She learned how to truly care for them.

Honestly, over that long, hot summer, she became what can best be described as my apprentice. She took over a number of my daily morning duties and I trusted her to do so. We lost a couple of horses that summer, too. And Alexis was right there to help send them to the Great Herd. And that is something that's harder than hell - for anybody, let alone a young woman who was only entering her senior year in high school. But she did it.

As the summer began to wane, it was time for school to start. And Alexis' school project was finished, at least from the physical aspect of it. She still had to write it and all, but her duties were complete.

Except they weren't.

Late every weekday afternoon, when I would be giving big Suze her afternoon mash, I'd see Alexis coming around the arena, walking toward us. And, every day, I'd have to laugh to myself. Because Alexis would be sporting her school uniform – a plaid skirt, a white blouse and black knee socks. The incongruity got me every time. I never did get used to seeing her in anything but jeans.

We'd talk for a few minutes and I'd regale her with tales of that morning and she'd walk around the ranch and spend a little time with each of her friends.

And, bright and early every Saturday and Sunday morning - and every day during school breaks – Alexis would be here.

This is was special.

This was different.

This wasn't your basic volunteerism.

This was a mission.

Her mission.

And, because I realized that this was her mission, Alexis became my mission.

I would teach her everything I knew. I would give her all the responsibility she could take on. I would give her the leeway to make mistakes and make decisions – because there was one thing in her heart that was unmistakable: her undying love for - and dedication to - our horses.

Alexis graduated from high school. And she went on to college. But, just like always, she'd be here every time her schedule allowed. For four years.

And then she graduated from college. And then she got her Master's degree.

And she was still here.

She was still here for the horses.

And, I might add, for me.

Over the years, Alexis became not only my right hand, she became my partner.

First, she became the ranch manager. Then, she became the ranch director. Then, she became the Executive Director of Tierra Madre Horse Sanctuary.

And now, she sits on the board of Tierra Madre Horse and Human Sanctuary.

Since that day back in 2009, Alexis has gotten married. And she and Alex bought their first home. And added cats and a wonderful dog. And then, they welcomed little Aurora into the world.

And, even with all of that going on in her busy life – including a current 'second' career at a major charity – Alexis is still here, at least one day a week. And she's still my partner. Nothing major happens around here without Alexis' input and guidance.

Anyway, that's how I see it.

And I'm thrilled that you're about to see it all through Alexis' eyes.

Alexis – my best friend, my partner.

Jim Gath

President and Founder of Tierra Madre Horse & Human Sanctuary

"The weakest step toward the top of the hill, toward sunrise, toward hope, is stronger than the fiercest storm."

~ Joseph Marshall III, *Keep Going*

CHAPTER ONE
MASHES

During one of my first days as a volunteer at Tierra Madre Horse Sanctuary, in June of 2009, Jim led me into the tack room and showed me how to make mashes.

The tack room was actually the Everything Room, back then. We didn't have any sheds outside of the barn yet, so the little room off the breezeway in the barn was crammed with everything from saddles and bridles to bags of grain and medicine.

A florescent light lit up the small space overhead, not that we needed it with the early morning sun spilling across the floor. Every now and then a spider or two skittered around on the ceiling, weaving their webs, and later, Jim told me that the tack room was just as much their home as it was his, so they had every right to stay.

An old, small fridge sat on the blue counter against the wall with the sink. By the following week, I was bringing Gatorades to stick in there next to bottles of medicine with names that went over my head. A whiteboard containing words like 'SMZs' and 'Bute' and 'MGM' and 'Pergolide' hung just outside, with a checklist next to each day to mark whether or not the medicine had been given to the corresponding horse.

Jim dipped a scoop into one of the food bags on the floor.

"Not all the horses get a mash this time of day, but each one that does, gets something a little different," he told me. He tossed grain into one of the waiting buckets on the floor while scooping a whiter, pelleted substance from a pail at the same time. "Everyone here has a diet, and some have got some problems. But they're not problems, really, just medical stuff we deal with. That's what we do here."

I nodded as I watched him put different amounts of horse food into different buckets. Ten minutes earlier, I'd asked him if horses had four stomachs, like cows (spoiler alert: they don't) so I wasn't feeling particularly confident in saying anything. I was so inexperienced about caring for horses that I didn't know the right questions, let alone their answers. But something about Jim's confidence steadied me, and I asked questions anyway.

"What's that?" I said, pointing to a bag that contained what looked like flakes of rubber and fingernails.

"That's beet pulp. This bag has a little molasses in it. Makes it sweet, see? Helps the horses keep weight on, and it's also good for the stomach. King John will get some of this in a minute, and little Rusty."

He filled seven or eight buckets. Some of the horses got the gross-looking beet pulp. Some got the little white pellets. Some got a small pill or two. All got grain, but in different amounts. There was a tub of electrolytes, made with salt from the grocery store, and a sweet-smelling substance that looked like corn flakes. I didn't know what anything was much less into which buckets they went, but Jim looked like he could have mixed everything together with his eyes shut.

Jim put the scoop down and took a few of the buckets over to the sink. He showed me how to stir in the right amount of water to make the contents just sloppy enough to make a mash. Then, I accompanied him out into the morning to deliver them. It was very important, I learned that day, that each horse got the correct mash. And they all knew the mashes were coming. John and Hudson and Heighten and Mr. Steve Vai and Mistah Lee and CharlieHorse were all front and center at their stall gates waiting for us at the same time. Not Little Rusty so much. I brought his yellow bucket to him to where he stood in his stall.

Eventually, I made the mashes on my own.

Lost in the throes of depression at seventeen, I didn't feel much those days. But the bliss of being able to help the ranch run by completing one small task was one of the first breaks in my wall of non-feeling, of emptiness.

Each morning, I usually met Jim in the tack room while he was making a Mooseshake, a concoction of bute, water, and pancake syrup that he'd give to the Moose, who struggled with a hoof problem I'd later learn was called laminitis. Jim would leave to go deliver it while I proudly scooped bran and grain and sweet feed and beet pulp and Neigh-Lox and other substances together, mixing in water and stirring them together in their buckets and pausing to admire my work. Then I'd stride out into the sun, buckets on my arms, blue sky overhead, calling out to the horses and reveling in the soft nickers I got back as they saw me approach with their food.

I had no idea then that over my next ten years at the ranch, I would balance far more than buckets on my arms.

I had no idea then that someday, I would be responsible for far more than getting the right mix of food into the right container, and to the right horse.

I had no idea then that I would eventually step into roles that needed to be filled as they came up and blunder through the crazy, whirling dance that was running Tierra Madre.

All I knew during those early mornings was that the horses needed their mashes, and I got to make them and dole them out and watch the horses eat.

And the balance of those mash buckets swinging on my arms, during those golden summer days of 2009, is where it all began.

CHAPTER TWO
RHYTHM

When the chain rattles on the front gate as it opens and it creaks as it swings wide, the transformation starts.

As I step onto the dirt road as I've done hundreds-thousands-of times over the years, I step into the shoes of someone I never knew I could be.

Rain or shine, night or day, frost or blistering heat. Good mood, bad mood, joy, or despair. It matters not. The sound of the gate opening stirs me, calls me.

When I enter the gates, I enter my domain. My territory. 2.98 acres of heaven, every square inch of which I know like the back of my hand. The place I feel most safe, and most myself.

When the gate opens, a new day begins, and I am home.

"This place does something to you," someone once told me back during my first summer. I never forgot those words.

This place does something to you.

This place, which Jim founded as a horse sanctuary in 2005 (and which gained nonprofit 501(c)(3) status in 2008), is nestled between a string of horse properties and a residential street in unincorporated Cave Creek, Arizona, just north of Phoenix.

Jim named it Tierra Madre Horse Sanctuary. *Tierra Madre* is Spanish for Mother Earth. And at Tierra Madre, we take our commitment to Mother Earth very seriously. Everybody-from the horses to the birds to the bunnies to the mice to the friendly snakes to the bees-is welcome. Except flies. We try to get rid of those.

The dirt road curves to the left after the gate has been cleared (and shut, for it must remain shut at all times), and volunteers park their cars in the clearing of desert just beyond where the driveway bends.

Most days, I took the curve and drove up the driveway toward the house and the barn, swinging my car out to the right halfway down to park by the poop dumpster directly next to the big field. Lee, Jim's ranch dog, met me at my car each and every day, tail swinging, and he accepted pats before we'd walk up to the barn together.

Across from the big field and the driveway upon which we'd walk lay the big turnout arena. The barn is just north of it. To the west is the round pen (north of the wash by the front gate) and a shed row that stretches to the northwest corner of the property, about twelve stalls total. The barn, green roofed, perpendicular to the shed row, has five in-and-out stalls, with three on the west side of the breezeway and the other two, the tack room, and a small house in which Jim lives on the east.

Wild desert lies beyond the field to the east, all the way up till the edge of the property. A wash weaves its way through the land and comes out by the poop dumpster. Bunnies scurry over the terrain, and birds too, though they usually would scatter as Lee and I trotted up to the barn and I headed through the breezeway to my office-a large gray plastic shed-to drop off my things.

Most days, I carried my laptop and binders full of fundraising outlines, or medical folders, or receipts, or donuts for the volunteers. During the summer, I was armed with water and sunscreen and extra bandanas. During the winter, I carried extra coats and gloves, and god help me if I forgot my rain jacket with the hoodie. Always, I had on a hat and carried my knife at my hip. One of our old farriers once told me to never be without a knife around horses.

Most days, Jim and I met in the breezeway and stood together for ten or fifteen minutes, talking about anything and everything under the sun as it itself rose in the east, catching up about the kids or our plans for the week or what was going on in our lives at the time. Other days, he was already hustling or had already left for the store or just hadn't come out of the house yet. And I jumped into the fray: the mucking of stalls, the cleaning of water buckets, the dolling of medicines, the changing of leg wraps or hoof booties, the switching of horses in the turnout arena, the directing of volunteers, the greeting of vets or farriers or deliveries, preparing to meet groups, setting up the projects for the day.

The rhythm of the ranch.

The rhythm started with buckets balanced on my arms. And over the years

I learned how to balance more than a handful of mashes at the same time.

The sun would chase me as it rose, chase me as I walked all over the ranch, a halter swung over my shoulder, a hoof pick in one back pocket and Derma-Vet ointment in the other, thrush buster on my shirt, silver spray on my arms, bran dribble on my shoulder, and my hands holding a fly spray bottle or a wound care bucket or leg wraps or a muck rake. Sometimes there was a small piece of carrot in my pocket that would go quietly to someone who gave me a knowing look and a soft nicker.

Back when I first began in 2009, I strode out across the ranch solo, with only Jim and the man who once lived on the property as a ranch hand for company. As the years flew by and the volunteer team blossomed into a family fifty, sixty, seventy, at one time eighty people strong, each day found me answering questions, looking over my shoulder to talk to one person while headed toward another, haltering horses, leading horses, giving medicine, mucking stalls, scrubbing buckets, pulling poop carts, throwing hay, haltering and leading horses again, opening gates, closing gates, scrutinizing limps, picking up hooves, wrapping legs, cleaning out feeders, feeding hay, sweeping mats, giving baths, doing groundwork, all done while supervising every person on the ranch at the same time.

The running of the ranch was a dance of great complexity and of enormous magnitude. The stronger the ranch became over the years, the more beats there were to the rhythm to which we all moved. And just like getting the right mash to the right horse, knowing each step was crucial.

Everything came down to details. Jim had a saying: "How you do anything is how you do everything."

I became the ranch director of Tierra Madre when I was 23 years old.

It was the end of October, 2014. I was over five years into my life at the sanctuary, fresh out of college, and had spent nearly every morning of that previous summer at the ranch while I applied everywhere for a full-time job. That summer of 2014, I volunteered with a small group of incredible volunteers, all of us working under a big-hearted, amazing woman who held the place together while Jim was away for a few months. When he returned, the woman, who was pregnant, needed to step down to focus on her growing family. And it became clear that going into the future, the ranch needed help.

Jim was tired. He'd run Tierra Madre solo for over ten years at that point, day in and day out, with fluctuating volunteers who helped him with the day-to-day running of things. Due to Jim's love and watchful eyes and because he lived on site to care for them, and because of the dedication of the few volunteers we had, the horses were all happy and healthy. But the ranch had to run, and Jim couldn't do it alone.

And when I couldn't find a job, Jim gave me one: the director of his ranch.

Tierra Madre was a blank slate when I officially moved from volunteer to director that October. One might even argue that the slate was smudged a bit. We struggled financially. There were no real ground rules or policies or systems for getting chores done. We had no acting board of directors, no committees, no reports, no programs, no schedules, only a few consistent donors, and a handful of amazing volunteers that had no formal training but a hell of a lot of heart.

As it happened, I had no formal training either. I liked to think I had a hell of a lot of heart, though.

And my heart belonged to what guided me through it all.

The horses.

They relied on me to get it right. They needed me to rise up, to figure it out, to watch and listen, and to work with people of all different personalities to form the semblance of a functioning nonprofit.

And so, as I started my journey to helping Jim recreate Tierra Madre, to find the rhythm that would someday reveal a thriving organization, I went into it thinking that the horses needed me.

What I didn't know during those early days was that I couldn't have been more wrong.

I was the one who needed them.

CHAPTER THREE
WHAT DO YOU DO?

Sometimes, when I told people what I did for a living or introduced myself to visitors at the ranch, I got asked a question I never quite knew how to answer.

"What do you do?"

Usually, because most people asked out of politeness, I smiled and responded with, "Oh, I take care of the horses!" or something smart like, "I make sure everyone stays out of trouble!"

Sometimes, people were genuinely curious. And those answers weren't enough.

I still hadn't figured out how to accurately respond one May morning, when I was three and a half years into running Tierra Madre, and Jim had a visitor come out around noon for a quick tour of the ranch. When she arrived, I was finishing up with our vet and our therapeutic farrier, both of whom were around to do checkups and trims, so Jim showed her the horses while I finalized medicine dosages and put halters away and wrote a check and tidied up the tack room and did the walk around.

After all was said and done, our vet and farrier were gone, and I had been introduced to our visitor and we had all made pleasant conversation for a while, Jim's friend turned to me and asked the question.

"What do you do?"

I had a mouthful of my lunch at the time and Jim answered for me.

"She runs the place," he said proudly. "She's our executive director."

"But what do you *do*?" his friend pressed me.

I swallowed. "Everything," I replied, laughing a little. "Behind the scenes work, and everything that needs to be done around here every day."

"Like what?"

And I honestly, truly, had no idea what to say.

Some days, everything was so mingled together in my head that untangling the madness into tangible, coherent thoughts required a herculean amount of effort. Sometimes, the chaos of each morning at the ranch blended into the afternoon, when I did office work from home, and each day blurred into the next.

What did I do?

Besides planning the ranch's events and fundraisers? Besides watching every dollar we spent? Besides investing in our donors and helping to create our programs and doing community outreach? Besides training and supervising the volunteers on a day-to-day basis? Besides making reports and addressing envelopes and designing flyers and researching grants and writing posts for our social media accounts?

I watched the sun rise in the morning in the breezeway while I planned each day's turnout and projects.

I greeted the volunteers as they arrived one by one while the horses wandered in the arena or munched on breakfast.

I mucked stalls and scrubbed buckets and filled waters. I could clean stalls and have three hoses running at the same time without any water overflowing or missing any scrap of poop in the dirt.

I scheduled hay deliveries and dirt deliveries and vet visits and farrier visits. I signed checks for hay deliveries and dirt deliveries and vet visits and farrier visits. Actually, the vet came so often they just had our card on file at the clinic.

What did I do?

I wiped eyes and noses and lips. I treated cellulitic legs and Habronema summer sores and corneal ulcers and hoof abscesses and called the vet when I couldn't fix the problems hurting my kids. I put medicine in runny eyes and hurting hooves and protesting mouths. I knew who wouldn't take a needle to the neck and who would fight to the death rather than take a syringe to the mouth and who would smell medicine in a mash a mile away.

I stood on ladders in stalls to unscrew mister jets so they could be soaked in CLR, then went around the ranch and put them all back up before summer came. I washed fly masks and put fly repellant on legs, necks, chests, faces.

I pushed carts through the mud, rain, wind, dust storms, and blazing heat. I tossed eighty pound bales out of trucks and lifted fifty pound bags of bran over my shoulders. I was on my feet, walking, bending, lifting, throwing, pulling, pushing, for hours.

I calmed thousand pound animals who were bucking and rearing in fear, or made them back up without stopping for thirty feet with nothing but a lead rope and a hand on their chest if they got ornery.

I could open boxes of Elastikon and reorganize the hoof care bucket and wage war with the mice in the tack room and text a picture of a wound to the vet and answer a volunteer's question all at the same time.

I haltered horses, walked horses, trained horses, brushed horses, fed horses. I knew who couldn't eat alfalfa and who was allergic to Bermuda and who needed less at lunchtime and who needed a bit more. I made sure they didn't get too many treats, which was a challenging feat when six volunteers each brought a ten-pound bag of carrots on the same day and wanted to dole them out all at once.

I knew where each horse liked to eat and where each one liked to be scratched and where I could find each one napping during the afternoon. I knew who liked baths and who just might attempt to run me over if I came near them with the hose. I could be standing anywhere on the ranch and know which of them just whinnied, and why.

I knew with a single glance when something was wrong.

Likewise, I knew with a single glance who just stole Kiss's hay or who just knocked over the food cart or who just made Sunny squeal at the top of her lungs. I hollered at bickering horses to knock it off without looking up. I bribed and scolded and threatened, often all in one breath.

I knew the difference between stubbornness and pain and the varying degrees of uncertainty and downright fear. I soothed and comforted and consoled. I hugged and patted and kissed worried foreheads.

I told the horses everything: my plans for the day, my frustrations, and my fears. My dreams for the ranch, for them, for myself.

I made mistakes. Every single day, I made mistakes. Every single day, I learned something new.

And every single day, the horses never gave up on me.

What did I do? I ran a ranch where the horses stepped on my feet, nipped at my arms, threw me into gates in their excitement, tore food out of my hands, dumped out their water tubs after I filled them, ripped my clothing, dribbled bran and slobber in my hair, knocked over mashes I made, and took every ounce of my energy. Each and every one of them was a part of me. And of all the things I did, I loved those horses with everything I had.

"What do you do?" Jim's friend pressed me.

I smiled.

"Where should I start?"

CHAPTER FOUR
CREATING TIERRA MADRE

"Who here knows the difference," I asked the group of new volunteers in front of me, "between a rescue and a sanctuary?"

Everyone looked back at me, faces politely inquisitive. I was leading a small group, maybe ten people or so, down the shed row toward Iron Man's stall to begin our tour. Sometimes when I asked this question during volunteer orientations, somebody knew the answer. This time I got to go into my entire pitch.

"A rescue," I said as we walked, "takes horses, or any kind of animal, and rehabilitates them. They rehome them after a certain period of time, to a good owner. A sanctuary, what we are, takes horses for life. Once every single horse here walks through these gates, they're forever home."

"So every single horse that's here will stay here?" someone asked, and I nodded.

"Yep. That's the commitment we make to them: that all they have to do in life is just be horses. That they'll be happy and safe forever."

This was the perfect transition to Iron Man's story, a beautiful black ex-racer who had stopped dead in the tracks during his 112th race many years before and refused to keep running. Self-retirement, if you will. And there he stood nibbling alfalfa while my group ooed and ahhed over him.

When Tierra Madre was founded in 2005, Jim was running the ranch as a boarding facility. One by one, he began to accept horses that had nowhere else to go. They would trickle in after a frantic phone call from someone out of options or from a rescue who had a horse no one would adopt: a horse blind in one eye, a horse who'd broken down at the local racetrack, a horse so abused by humans he'd bite and kick anyone who approached him with a bridle. Sometimes, some of the owners keeping their horses at the ranch would lose interest and leave the horses there.

Jim took them all.

Then one day, he realized he had more of his own horses than he did boarders. He stood by the arena talking to a friend of his on the phone, lamenting that he'd gotten upside down.

And his friend said five words that changed the course of the ranch's history.

"Jim," she said, "you're all they've got."

Jim says those words hit him like a godshot.

And Tierra Madre Horse Sanctuary was born.

The closure of equine slaughterhouses in the United States in 2007, plus the recession that began in 2008, launched an unprecedented epidemic of unwanted horses. Far from ending the cruel and horrific industry of horse slaughter, the closing of U.S. slaughterhouses just dispersed it. Horse slaughter plants still operate with regularity in Canada and Mexico, and every year, tens of thousands of horses are shipped over our borders to them.

This path that a horse takes from safety to horror is called the slaughter pipeline. When a horse is abandoned or surrendered by their owner, they run the risk of falling into the wrong hands: individuals who are looking to make a profit by acquiring horses at a low cost then selling them to slaughterhouses who pay for horse meat by the pound. These people are called kill buyers. For a horse, being purchased by a kill buyer is a death sentence.

Once they are purchased by kill buyers, horses often live in cramped, high-stress, and inhumane living conditions-called kill pens-for a time while the kill buyers try to sell them through using emotional blackmail. If the horses are bought, the kill buyer spends that money on more horses to sell, and they ship. If the horses are not bought, they ship.

Then, horses are crammed into trailers-with no food, water, or medical care-and transported. If they survive the trip over the border, they reach the end of the slaughter pipeline.

They die. Brutally. Violently. Inhumanely.

They die scared and alone.

The role of equine rescues and sanctuaries is to intercept horses in the slaughter pipeline and get them to safety. Our mission is to get to the horses before the kill buyers do by taking them from owners who need to rehome them, going to livestock auctions, or buying them directly from kill pens. We take in a large amount of them, but each ranch's finances and available capacity will limit the amount of horses each can take.

That is why a huge component of the equine rescue industry is advocacy work. Horse slaughter is a symptom of larger problems: overbreeding, owners' lack of resources, and the fact that some parts of the world consider horse meat a delicacy. But through the work of rescues and sanctuaries, thousands of horses are saved from the slaughter pipeline each year.

The great reality of the rescue world is that rehoming animals is essential to its survival. If one horse is adopted out to safety from a rescue, another in need can fill its place. But sometimes, a horse can't be rehomed. That's where sanctuaries like Tierra Madre come in.

A sanctuary has horses that have low adoptability potential due to some behavioral, medical, or physical issues. Every horse that called Tierra Madre home fell into one of the categories of sanctuary material: they had been abused, or severely neglected, or injured, or abandoned, or otherwise surrendered due to age and medical challenges. Because many-if not most-couldn't be ridden or would otherwise not tolerate being ridden, the likelihood of them finding a safe home and escaping the slaughter pipeline was next to zero.

So Jim took no chances. He knew from the very beginning that he wanted to keep his horses safe within his gates. They had been surrendered for a reason. He would not operate a rescue, he decided. He would not rehome his kids. He would run a ranch where each and every horse could live out their days in peace.

On my group and I walked through the shed row. Across from the stalls, Hollywood and Tater and Tommy were playing in the arena, and the group paused to admire the breathtaking sight of three chestnut horses galloping, kicking up dust, and throwing their heads as they pranced.

We said hi to Slayer, Iron Man's neighbor, then Sunny, and Annie, and Buddy, and Jani. I told their stories. How Slayer had been surrendered by a sweet old lady who'd been into heavy metal. How Sunny arrived in Rain's belly, when we'd saved her from slaughter the day before she was to ship.

How Annie and Buddy had shown their age, and outlived their use. How Jani had done barrels and gymkhanas and trail rides and lessons all her life and lived with chronic laminitis as a result. Each horse at the ranch had a different history, a different way of viewing the world. They all had one thing in common: against all odds, despite the hardships they'd seen, they'd found home.

"This isn't just a sanctuary for horses either," I mentioned as we watched Heighten and Hudson playing through the bars of the fence separating their pens. "Many people who come here to volunteer find the same thing our horses did. A safe place. A happy place. And I hope you always remember that. This is your sanctuary as much as it is the horses'."

"How long have you been here?" someone asked.

"Since June of 2009," I answered. Feet from me, Bella reached her nose out to nudge my hand, and I reached out to rub her face. "And I knew on my first day I was never going to leave."

CHAPTER FIVE
THE ORIGINAL TWENTY-NINE

I was seventeen years old during the summer of 2009.

It was the summer before I began my last year in high school, and my school required all seniors to complete a hundred hours of community service in order to graduate. I'd chosen to begin my hours prior to the school year, thinking it would be a good idea to get a head start.

We were given suggestions like libraries, homeless shelters, offices, food banks. I chose horses.

My first real experience with horses began when I was fifteen, when I was desperate to finally get close to the animals I had spent my entire life loving and was allowed to sign up for riding lessons. I spent a year and a half riding at a show barn where my instructor bred Arabians and trained her pupils to get into the show ring. The students showed up in expensive, professional English riding gear and wanted to learn how to expertly control the animals upon which they rode. I showed up in jeans and wanted to feel horse nuzzles in my hair.

I didn't know it at the time, but getting a head start on completing service hours at Tierra Madre was the best thing I ever did to not just get plenty of horse nuzzles in my hair, but to begin lifting the fog of depression that had consumed me for three years at that point. I didn't know that I was about to spend every summer morning at the ranch, learning, watching, doing, and slowly reentering a world in which I thought I deserved to live.

I got lost on the way to Tierra Madre that first morning. The directions were so confusing. I finally figured out where the front gate was among all the horse properties and that I had to get out of my car, open the gate, drive through, then get out and close it again. I didn't know where to park. The ranch hand who was there at the time waved at me to come back when I drove up the wash.

When I finally figured out parking and got out of my car, a black and gray shepherd greeted me at the end of the driveway, and he wasn't friendly. He snarled and barked at me and I immediately took the advice of the gray-haired man standing up by the barn, who called: "Don't look at him-just ignore him!"

The man, Jim, introduced himself and smiled as he shook my hand. I didn't know then that he took one look at me and figured I wouldn't last more than a week.

I didn't know then that over the next few weeks and next few months and next few years, Jim would become my best friend in the world.

He showed me around. He introduced me to the horses, the herd that I refer to as the Original Twenty-Nine. They were the horses who lived at Tierra Madre when it all began for me, horses who astonished me that first day and every day since with their different personalities and stories and likes and dislikes. Some of them liked to have their faces scratched. Some of them looked at me with trepidation. Many of the horses looked excited and eager to play while others moved around with a mature, calm air. A few had wise, ancient eyes.

Even all these years later, I still remember where everyone lived, whom got along with whom, whom all went to the arena together during that first summer.

Right of the driveway, in the big open field to the east, was John's herd.

John was the king. A big black Thoroughbred, with a small, misshapen white star on his forehead, he ruled the horses in the field unquestioningly. He had showed up in a trailer with another horse Jim had agreed to take some years ago, and the driver had stated he had no idea who the horse was but that he had nowhere to go. Jim accepted him on the spot.

I didn't have to know horses all that well to know that John was the leader of his herd. One look into his eyes was all it took to know he was *intancan*, the Lakota word for leader that Jim used.

John's second-in-command was Solo. A brown Saddlebred with an attitude, Solo liked to chase around the other horses because he knew he could get away with it with John at his back. He was John's wingman, and after John joined the Great Herd in 2014, Solo fell in rank of the herd, particularly when Spencer came to Tierra Madre and became the herd's *intancan*. Actually, when Solo was hit with a series of abscesses in his front feet a year later, he became really sad. Lonely, even.

So, we decided to let Solo wander for a little bit each morning. After he was turned out in the arena, instead of putting him back in the field, we would release him and he'd casually spend the next hour or so wreaking havoc on the ranch. He'd knock over the treat can, mess up the hay in the shed, and have a blast taunting all the horses in their pens before going home. It cheered him up immensely.

Next came Suze, and Suze was the queen. In those early days, she was absolutely bat-shit crazy. A huge, beautiful Thoroughbred, Suze had been a show horse before being rescued by Jim from an insane woman who wanted to get rid of her because she had a hairline sesamoid fracture in one of her front hooves that required something like six weeks of stall rest. Always wild eyed, she sent the herd scattering when she charged anxiously back and forth, tossing her head and looking around as though expecting a mountain lion attack any second. Over the years, though, she calmed down. Eventually the wildness was replaced by regality and confidence. She ruled the field horses with authority, despite battling cellulitis in her hind leg for the last year and a half of her life.

Next of John's herd was Bentley, or B, as we called him. Next to Charlie, who lived across the hallway north of the field, B was the biggest horse on the ranch. A jet-black Thoroughbred, B had perhaps the most expressive eyes of any horse I've ever met. Within them I saw gentleness, or fire, or whatever he was feeling in the moment. He was quick to tell us when he wasn't happy, and just as quick to show us softness when he was. He joined Solo in the ranks of wanderer for some time, having the run of the ranch for a while in the morning, quietly going about saying hi to all the volunteers and mowing down fallen hay on the ground (which was good, because as big as he was, he could never eat enough).

Then, Venture and Jericho. Those guys were the best of friends, and always together. Both Arabians, Venture was a light bay and Jericho, a flea-bitten gray. I only knew Jericho for four months, before colic took him in October of that year. He used to happily hold his head high out of my reach when I went around doing the NoFly. Just a gentle boy who loved life and everything in it.

Venture became the Mayor of the Breezeway after Jericho died. Midmorning, we'd open the field gate and let him out where he'd wander up to the breezeway for some sweet feed and carrots. Sometimes, we'd get up and ride him bareback around the ranch. When his time came almost five years to the day we lost Jericho, he left us with happiness in his eyes, as though he knew his best friend would be waiting for him on the other side.

Last of John's herd was Kiss. Kiss was the low man on the totem pole. He quietly walked away when the other horses told him to move and waited patiently for the others to receive their meals before getting his. A red Saddlebred with a pretty white star, he had apparently been introduced to the field to his ultimate bewilderment. *But I'm a show horse*, he had said. He'd been used to a life of being pampered, and all of the sudden he was being told what to do by a lot of scruffy-looking horses.

"Humans tend to associate *leader* with being good, and *follower* with being bad," Jim said on that first day. "Horses don't think about it that way. Either you're a leader, or you're not. And it's okay either way."

Across the hallway, in the first stall closest to the house where Jim lived, were Charlie and the Min.

Big Charlie was a bay Thoroughbred, eighteen hands at the withers, with hooves that were almost the size of dinner plates and a head that weighed several hundred pounds. He was thunder and lightning when he galloped in the arena, but he was the gentlest soul. His stall mate, Min, was not. A gray Miniature Horse, Jim referred to him as the resident terrorist. He had a bad patella tendon and walked a little stiffly, but it sure didn't stop him from charging at people and biting them.

Next over was M'Stor (pronounced *Mister*), a stunning chestnut Thoroughbred. He was young and vibrant and kept sticking his head through the bars of his pen to nudge Jim as Jim told me his story. Jim had saved him after he broke his knee in a race. It'd been a horrific slab fracture, and the person who called Jim from the local racetrack said if he couldn't find a place to live that day, he'd be put on the slaughter truck the next morning. After two years of rehabilitation-during which he had a series of terrible abscesses in one of his front hooves-he was the fastest horse on the ranch.

Slayer was the Thoroughbred that lived next to M'Stor. A bay beauty with a white star, he stole my heart almost at once. His previous owner had been an elderly, proper English woman who surrendered him when she could no longer care for him. And she loved the band Slayer! Jim said she'd had another horse named Poison who went somewhere else.

Little Rusty lived behind Slayer.

The first time I saw Little Rusty I think something in my heart shattered. He was so skinny I thought I could have put my arms around his girth and almost have them touch. Jim was angry when he told his story: his owner had surrendered him after saying she couldn't care for him any longer, but had pulled in behind the trailer in a spanking new BMW, dressed to the nines. Out came a horse that was skin and bone, a crooked back, messed up hooves, and countless bedsores on his body.

Jim told her to get the hell off his property and never return.

Little Rusty, or my baby as I lovingly referred to him that summer, was the recipient of one of the mash buckets that I made every single morning. The other horses got their mashes in buckets hanging at their gates, but I always crawled through the bars into Little Rusty's stall and put his mash directly in front of him so he didn't have to move. Sometimes, I'd go in there and take his flymask off and let him scratch his face on me. He loved that.

After Jim had done all he could do make his last few months comfortable, Little Rusty joined the Great Herd in August, just two months after I began. He was one of the sweetest boys I ever knew, who got dealt a cruel hand in life.

The farthest pen east of the barn was Tarzan's home. T was missing an eye, and he had supposedly been blinded in a trailer accident before coming to live at Tierra Madre. As Jim introduced us, he told me that that version of the story had been made up. If T really had been blinded in a trailer accident, Jim said, T would have never gone in a trailer again. But he'd gone in and out of one, cool as you please, to come to the ranch.

"But when we went to muck his stall the first day, he saw the rake and bolted," Jim said as we stood in front of the chestnut Quarter horse. "Tarzan told me that he had been blinded by a human. With a rake. And I believe Tarzan, not the human. Horses don't lie, you see. Humans lie all the time. But not horses."

Sweet Boy and Sedona lived next to each other in the barn, in the two stalls nearest to Jim's house. Sweet Boy had his own bell outside his stall, and he rang it by nudging it with his nose as we walked up to them. Jim showed me that when Sweet Boy rang his bell, it meant he wanted treats. "And if you're standing anywhere in this space," Jim said as he reached into the nearby treat bucket to oblige him, "it's fair game."

Sweet Boy had been abused by his last humans. Jim had given his owner riding lessons there at the ranch, and whenever he was saddled up, Sweet Boy reacted with fury and fear. Jim supposed that based on Sweet Boy's reaction to being cinched, someone had kicked him in the belly to keep him from bloating, so the cinch would be as tight as possible. Further, he would not tolerate a bit. There was simply no getting one in his mouth.

Not that a horse needs a bit to be ridden. Sweet Boy rode beautifully with just a halter and reins, but after his owner fell off of him when she didn't put her heels down during a lesson (her fault-not Sweet Boy's) she angrily took Sweet Boy away, citing Jim's "hippie methods" as unsatisfactory. As the trailer pulled out of the gates that day, Jim turned to the person standing next to him and said, "He'll be back."

Sure enough, a few weeks later, the woman brought Sweet Boy back through the gates. She'd purchased another "normal" horse, and wanted to be rid of Sweet Boy. Would Jim take him off her hands?

Jim put Sweet Boy back in his stall, and told him he was home for good.

Sedona lived next to Sweet Boy. A big Warmblood, he was purchased to be a dressage horse and the lady who bought him realized she'd been duped when he demonstrated no experience in dressage whatsoever. When she brought him to board at Tierra Madre and realized Sedona was a bit of a doofus with no training and a bad tendon, she panicked and wondered what to do. Jim, laughing, told her to leave Sedona at the ranch. And so she did, and Sedona was home.

Across the breezeway and across from the tack room lived the Moose.

So many others have lived in that stall since my first summer-Chester, Ted, Bourbon, Sonora, Rain and Sunny, Bentley, Jazz, Journey-but to me it will forever be Moosie's stall.

Moose was the Medicine Man: a horse with an ancient soul, with infinite wisdom, with quiet dignity and eyes that pierced me through to my soul.

Jim said that when you looked into the Moose's eyes, you saw a thousand generations of horses.

Moosie had a chronic hoof condition called laminitis. I didn't know anything about the disease then, and in fact I had no idea then that years later, I would become obsessed with learning everything about it. All I knew then was that Moosie walked tenderly, and needed lots of medicine and veterinary care. Not that he ever complained about it. Moosie was one of the strongest, most accepting, wisest horses I ever knew.

Ted lived next to the Moose. Playful, in-your-face, and forever banging on the bars of his stall door for food, he was my special favorite that summer. He loved rubbing his face up against me and nibbling my hair. He'd been surrendered with a horrible back, one that needed chiropractic work, and he couldn't be ridden despite the work that had been done to correct the damage. In fact, he'd been labeled a "dangerous" horse by his old owner due to how he acted up whenever anyone came near him. Until he came to Tierra Madre, he had been in pain for well over a decade.

CharlieHorse was the little old gentleman who lived at the end of the barn, nearest to the shed row. I fawned over him the entire summer. He was in his late twenties or early thirties, with a sway back, which happened to some older horses as the ligaments and muscles along the spine weaken with age. Jim told me when he'd received the phone call, CharlieHorse's person essentially told Jim it was no problem if Tierra Madre couldn't take him, because they were going up to Montana some time later and could use the horse as bear bait.

"What??" I yelped.

"Yep. He was here the next day," Jim said.

Perpendicular to the barn, running parallel to the west side of the big arena, was the shed row of horses.

We've since added two stalls to the north that stretch to the corner of the property, but the original shed row started with Guess.

Guess and Jim went way back. Years ago, she was taken in at a horse rescue run by Jim's friend, who asked him if he would work with some of the horses in the hopes they would become good trail horses. He and Guess developed a strong bond, but one thing led to another and Jim had to move briefly back to Los Angeles and Guess eventually had to go to a new home. He cried when they parted. Three years later, the owner called up Jim and asked if he remembered Guess.

"Remember her??" Jim had yelled into the phone. "She's one of the great loves of my life!"

"Well, her human can't keep her anymore and she needs a home. Would you be interested in taking her?"

"When can she be here?"

Two hours later, the trailer had pulled up to Tierra Madre and Guess was led out. Upon seeing Jim, she made a beeline for him and buried her face in his chest.

"And I told her, 'You're home for good, baby girl,'" said Jim, stroking Guess's nose as she reached out to him. "And here she is."

Next door to Guess was Bella, another Thoroughbred. Like M'Stor, she was a former racer who'd broken her knee in a race and had had a back so bad that when she arrived at Tierra Madre, the chiropractor who worked on it said she must have fallen off a truck for it to be as bad as it was. Bella was also featured in the Tierra Madre logo, which was a silhouette of her and Jim reaching out to each other. Calm, gentle, with just enough fire in her to cause her to fight whenever anyone tried to groom her belly, Bella hated being ridden but was perfectly content to buck and run in the arena as fast as she could.

Jani was next. An older chestnut mare with a pretty white blaze save for a circle just above her right eye, Jani had bad feet from decades of doing barrels, gymkhanas, trail rides, lessons, and just about everything else. She blinked at me a few times during our introduction then returned to her hay. Something I loved about Jani right from the start was that she didn't particularly care about pleasing anyone. She'd put in her time with humans, and wanted to be her own owner.

Heighten was a huge chestnut Thoroughbred who leaned against Jim in greeting when we stopped at his stall. "He was bleeding like a stuck pig when we first met," Jim said. "He'd cut himself against some fallen roofing or something over his stall. I got the doc out quick and he fixed him up right away, but Jesus, right? He had an awful back, too, actually. His owners said he bucked like crazy under saddle and I realized he was in pain."

His owners had asked Jim if they could leave him at the ranch-then still a boarding facility-when they decided they didn't want Heighten anymore. "Sure," Jim had said, "if you pay to have his back fixed first." They did.

Jim said that he and Heighten had known each other in a past life. Long, long ago, Jim said, in the 1860s, in the badlands of the Dakotas, he believed that he had been the horse and Heighten had been his rider. "And I know that may sound fucked up but I believe it. I believe it with all my heart and all my soul. And so does Heighten. Right, my Bruvva?"

Hudson was chewing and nibbling the air, good-naturedly goofing off as we walked up to him. Another Thoroughbred, he had one of the best pedigrees on the ranch, with bloodlines tracing back to famous racers like Bold Ruler (Secretariat's sire), Foolish Pleasure, and Raise a Native. He'd been started on the track at a young age only to disinterestedly wander out of the starting gates on his own terms. After it became clear that he didn't want to race, his owners rehomed him. He'd come in with Bella to be boarded only to eventually be left at the ranch when his owners couldn't commit to caring for him anymore. He was the goofiest horse I'd ever met. Jim called him the Big Galoot.

Mr. Steve Vai was a cute Arabian bay next door to Hudson. It's been well over ten years since I last saw this beautiful horse and I can remember his eyes so well: liquid, inquisitive, and softer than anything. I knew him for a few months before he rapidly declined due to laminitis. Rather than let him suffer, Jim sent him to the Great Herd.

Next was Akira, an elderly paint mare with a kind but reserved air about her. She had been broken-hearted when she first arrived at Tierra Madre, Jim said. Something had happened to her late in life-whether it was being surrendered, or treated unkindly, or whatever-that had left her sad almost beyond all repair. Jim had made it his mission to make her happy again. She was one of the oldest on the ranch, and had bad teeth, which meant we had to give her lots of soft foods and break up her hay for her.

"Little Miss Akira Jones," Jim said fondly as he introduced us. "And every night, I give her the twenty-one-kiss salute." He planted seven kisses on her face and said, "Seven-" then gave her another seven, "-fourteen-" then a final few kisses, "-twenty-one. Twenty-one kisses for my little girl."

I didn't know much about horses, but looking at Akira, I could tell right away that she was no longer the sad horse Jim had met. Her eyes sparkled and snapped and she looked after Jim when we left. A few months in to volunteering, Jim occasionally let me ride her in the arena when all the chores were done. Akira loved giving lessons, and was a wonderful teacher.

Mistah Lee lived next to Akira. Another horse close to his thirties, he was a beautiful, handsome gray gelding with a hip so arthritic that when Jim had radiographs done to get a better idea of how to treat it, the arthritis had shown up significantly on the x-rays. That summer, one of my duties was give him a walk each day, to gently stretch his hip and build muscle. He adored his walks. I spent many a summer morning wandering the ranch with him, letting him take in the freshness of the mesquite trees and desert brush, watching him look around him with happiness.

I melted when I met RustyBob. A chestnut Quarter horse with the softest eyes and cutest nose on the planet, Rusty nickered when he saw me and offered his nose for me to pet, which I did at once. He had bad stifles, which meant he couldn't be ridden but had no problems moving around at his own pace. His former owners actually still gave a monthly donation for him, which was almost unheard of when it came to owner surrenders. One of the sweetest horses in the universe, I loved Rusty right away. By day two I was crawling into his stall to give him hugs and whisper secrets in his ear.

Diamond, or Little D as we called her, lived next to Rusty. She was a small Arabian mare, a liver chestnut with a white blaze who was precious in every way, but with a sassy streak that showed itself if her neighbors ever tried to cozy up to her. If I remember correctly, she belonged to a very kind woman who gave Jim a donation every month for her to live there. Jim never particularly cared about who technically owned a horse, so long as the horse was bound to his property and was safe. Little D's strength came shining through in the last few months of her life, when she heroically fought acute laminitis then gracefully surrendered at the end.

The very last horse, at the south end of the shed row nearest the round pen and the front gate, was Chance.

Back in those days, he was unapproachable.

A palomino Tennessee Walker, Chance was the newest addition to the ranch and had arrived just a few months before. He had been horrifically abused: beaten, kicked, whipped, and god knows what else through the gate of his pen. He'd been locked in a stall with no windows and thrown food every few days. Terrified and angry and unable to run from danger, he naturally began to respond to anyone near his pen by violently attacking them. At his last home before coming to Tierra Madre, he had supposedly picked up a young boy near his stall by the coat and thrown him.

Jim's ranch hand at the time could halter him for turnouts without losing too much blood. But otherwise, Chance was left alone. Jim said however long it took for him to get comfortable with people again, Chance would have that time. "But stay away from him while you're here," he told me sharply. "He'll hurt you."

As though to reiterate this fact, Chance, watching us with fire in his eyes, pinned his ears to his skull, blew air out of his nostrils, and banged on his stall bars with his hooves as hard as he could. The message couldn't have been any clearer: *Stay away from me.*

And in those moments that I can't explain, I fell hard. In an instant, I was head over heels in love.

Oh, I loved all those horses I met that day. I still do, and always will.

But as Chance and I looked and looked and looked at each other, I saw so much in his eyes that I saw every day in mine. He pulled me back to the ranch the next day, and the day after that, and the day after that until I was going to the ranch almost every day that summer just to see him. I didn't get close to him, like Jim told me. But I sat outside his stall for long periods of time at a safe distance away and just talked to him, watching him, trying to decipher him.

So many horses have come through our gates since my first summer, of course. Many of the Original Twenty-Nine have galloped into the Great Herd. But they will forever hold some of the dearest space in my heart.

They showed me what it meant to go through hell and still stand looking toward the horizon at the start of each day. They showed me what it meant to be strong.

They showed me that if they could live after trauma and abuse, then maybe-just maybe-so could I.

CHAPTER SIX
HORSEMANSHIP 101

"And he said unto the horse, 'Trust no man in whose eyes you do not see yourself reflected as an equal.'" ~ Anonymous

Those words were written on a wooden plank and hung high in the breezeway, over the whiteboard, for everyone to see. They drove our every interaction with the horses. They drove our purpose, our vision, our mission. They were the beating heart of Tierra Madre, and we lived by them.

In every decision that we made at the ranch came the question: "Is it best for the horses?"

Because with everything we did, the horses came first. Not the people. Not the volunteers. Not the donors or stakeholders or partners or visitors. The horses.

When new people came to the ranch, they needed to not only know a thing or two about how horses thought and acted, but they needed to understand this principle. Seeing horses as equals meant understanding them on a fundamental level, and for each person, that began on day one.

My training was pretty rigorous, and not only because I needed to weed out the people who thought Tierra Madre was a free-for-all for pony rides. Every newcomer went through a safety briefing in which I demonstrated proper approaching, haltering, and walking along with basic knowledge about the dos and don'ts of horses, just like Jim had done for me my first summer. I called the rundown Horsemanship 101, though in later years I started joking with orientation groups that Common Sense 101 was a better name. But because we dealt with people of all experiences, and because I saw far too many preventable accidents and injuries occur over the years, I had to start somewhere. And I couldn't have anyone go into the stalls without training them first.

Horses are prey animals and-perhaps because of this- they are herd animals. In the wild, prey animals group together for protection against predators. So, it is biological instinct for horses to be social creatures and to establish bonds amongst themselves in order to survive. They form herds.

Only two horses are needed to make a herd: a leader and a follower.

When you are doing anything with a horse, I explained to those new to horses on the ranch, in the horse's mind, you are a herd. One of you has to be the leader and the other the follower. And if the human isn't going to be the leader, the horse is going to take charge of the herd.

"Horses don't lie," I would say, echoing Jim's words. "And you can't lie to them. If you're nervous or uncertain about what you're doing, they know. A leader is confident and leads a herd away from danger and toward safety. A leader protects and reassures. If you're not able to do that for a horse, that horse isn't going to listen to you."

Confidence was the key to being a leader in a horse's herd, and knowledge went hand in hand with feeling capable. So, we went over everything when it came to interacting with huge, thousand pound animals. Approach from the side and never sneak up on them. Hand on the butt if you're walking around them. Never stand directly behind or in front of them. Let them see your eyes but try not to make extended eye contact. Halter and walk from the left side. Position yourself at their heads while walking them and don't let them get too far ahead or behind. Make them stop completely before unhaltering. How to pick up feet. How to groom. How to just be with them.

Even after training days, nobody new handled horses unless I was there to watch them for the first few times or another experienced volunteer accompanied them. I matched experience and confidence level to horses. Everyone could walk Buddy or Rusty or Akira or Chiquita or Annie or Tommy or Jani or Jazz or Wild Bill. Those with a little more skill could walk Guess or Slayer or Rain or Studley or Nibzie or Bentley or Solo or Bella or Spencer or Sedona or Sweet Boy or Hollywood or Sunny or Chianti or Spencer or Oliver. And those with lots of experience handled Heighten or Iron Man or M'Stor or Danny or Tater or Bourbon or River or Sonora or Suze. Min wandered where he pleased and somebody would go wave him back to his stall at the end of the morning. Nobody walked

Chance except for me and one or two other ranch managers. And anyone who wanted a boxing match or a forearm workout could walk Hudson.

I knew all their tricks. The horses had different habits or fears or expectations during the time they were walked to and from the arena or leisurely around the ranch, and I could see their actions a mile off when they were being walked by the newbies, or for the first time by experienced volunteers who had earned the right to lead them.

"Bella's about to buck now that she's cleared that gate so keep her moving straight-yep, there she goes. Walk calmly, with purpose, and she'll stop."

"Danny doesn't like that spot right there, that's where the tree branch spooked him a few months ago… okay, good, keep calm and let him go in that tight circle… just like that…okay now lead him straight, eyes ahead…perfect!"

"Tighten your lead, M'Stor's about to drag you to the-okay, pull hard, and make him stop! Okay, now pull his head out of the treat can, with authority… okay, pull *really* hard… M'Stor, get out of there!"

"Make Jani back up a bit before you bring Buddy in, she likes to bite him on the butt as he-okay, yeah, just like that. Just turn him around now that he's in and take his halter off."

Some horses were angels. Like Rusty. There was not a mean bone in Rusty's entire body. I used him for everything: orientations, first grooming sessions, haltering practice, leading exercises. Many a new, timid volunteer spent time in his stall grooming him while he stood with patience beyond anything I asked of him. His kind eyes and sweet face won everybody over, me most of all each and every day.

Some horses saw newbies as personal challenges. Like Bourbon. He didn't suffer fools, as Jim phrased it. When he first came to Tierra Madre, he'd spent most of his time lunging at people over his fence and even years later, he spent about half a second looking people up and down before deciding whether or not to listen to them. If he detected any ounce of apprehension or uncertainty or fear in the human, Bourbon was going to listen to Bourbon, and that was about it. It made sense, though. In horse herds, the judgement of a leader often meant life or death for horse herds. If horses didn't have confidence in their leader, then they took their lives into their own hands…uh, hooves.

Some horses were just beasts. Iron Man and Heighten and Hudson and M'Stor and Suze and Danny were huge Thoroughbreds and weren't badly behaved as much as they simply required extra strength and a calm, nonchalant attitude about their eagerness to get out to the arena to run.

"I can't get over how everyone has such a different personality," a volunteer once told me one day after a tour of the ranch. "I always thought horses were a lot alike. But everyone here is unique."

And they were. Horsemanship 101 was about understanding, fundamentally, that each horse had similar instincts but that each one had their own personality. At Tierra Madre, they were allowed to just be horses.

And with each different personality on the ranch came different lessons to be learned.

CHAPTER SEVEN
JAZZ

I lovingly referred to Jazz as my problem horse.

Oh, he wasn't the one with the problem. He was my problem horse in that *I* had the problem understanding him.

He first came to Tierra Madre under the premise of having some sort of navicular problem in one of his front hooves. His left, I think. His owner-crying and pleading-told Jim she could no longer afford to keep him and was terrified that if she sold him, someone would find out he wasn't rideable and send him over the border. Jim told her to bring him over.

A paint gelding of nine or ten, Jazz had white stockings and a small star on his thin face that was overshadowed by a rather trepidatious look in his eye. Jazz wasn't particular to women back then, but he got along just fine with men. A male volunteer bonded with him almost instantly and had him following him everywhere within an hour, whereas with me, Jazz always had the habit of flicking his ears back a little. He forever studied me with an apprehensive look, as though sizing me up, whenever I was nearby.

He was put in a large pen with Wild Bill, a gentleman of a horse in his thirties with Cushing's disease and a thick coat like a buffalo's. Jazz clung to Wild Bill like a lifeline. Anywhere Bill went, Jazz was there at his flank. He quickly became protective over his friend, particularly during the short time the two of them were moved to the big field with Suze, Solo and the rest. They mainly kept to themselves, staying out of the occasional fights Solo would start with the others. Jazz's anxiety and irritability deepened, even after the two of them were put back in their own pen.

One time, I was taking Wild Bill out to give him his daily mash with Prascend and Equioxx in the breezeway, and Jazz parked himself in front of Wild Bill and refused to let me near him. He kept glaring at me and pinning his ears to show he meant business. Eventually, after a sidestepping battle, I got Wild Bill's halter on him and began to walk him out of the gate. Jazz followed and protectively wedged himself in the foot of space between me and Wild Bill.

Irritated and out of patience, I took the end of my lead rope and swatted it at Jazz's chest to make him back up.

What's kind of funny is that he took great care to aim. In about half a second Jazz looked me up and down, decided which part of my body he'd hit, turned his leg just right, lifted a hoof… and *bam*! He nailed me just above the knee. Hard.

I buckled. Instinct kicked in and I caught the fence before I went down. Get knocked down around an angry horse and you're finished.

Anger pulsating through me, I span around and faced an equally angry Jazz, spitting out words rather than saying them.

"What the *hell*?!"

I took the halter off of Wild Bill and put it on Jazz instead and spent the next ten minutes working with him, making him back up around his pen until he put his head down, glowered at me, and stopped trying to make my other leg into an equally swollen, bruised mess. I yelled at him. A lot. It was only after I sat down sometime later that the pain hit me, since my adrenaline had been pumping so much with fury. The bruise covered the entire upper half of my leg for weeks.

Boy, was I pissed. But looking back, I know I wasn't as pissed as Jazz, whose anger was so great he would have been yelling back at me if he'd had a human voice. Here I was taking his only friend in the world away from him for an uncertain amount of time and then yelling at him for getting upset. His anger was a mask for fear, and he was scared to be left alone.

Still, I thought furiously to myself that night as I iced my leg, not getting it. *Still*.

Wild Bill died not too long after that.

He was well into his thirties and colicked one evening. Tubing him didn't save him. He went peacefully, head in my lap, on his terms.

Jazz was devastated. His only friend in the world was gone, and he was left alone in their pen, miserably keeping to himself, hating the world.

And so, not long after Wild Bill died, we moved him up to the barn. Right away we realized that this was a major turning point for Jazz. Some horses thrive when they have down time to themselves. Others crave-need-more attention.

Jazz definitely perked up when we moved him, but over the next few months, I watched him and began to realize that he didn't look good.

He had a cresty-looking neck, like it was too thick. The rest of his body-from his withers to hindquarters-looked bulky. He was still irritable. And then on a day one February, for the first time, I saw him stumble ever so slightly as he walked.

It was so slight, just barely noticeable. But I took him out of his stall, much to his displeasure, and lifted up his feet to clean them and see if I could find abscesses. He fought me but he begrudgingly let me work on him.

After a few days of cleaning out his hooves and trying to locate the source of a problem to no avail, I told Jim I wanted our vet and therapeutic farrier to come out and look at him. He agreed.

A few days later, standing in the breezeway with the radiograph machine, Jazz was diagnosed with laminitis.

And not just laminitis. Our vet pulled some blood on him, listened to his stomach, and informed us he was insulin resistant and had sand in his gut.

All that time, Jazz hadn't been feeling well. His diet was all wrong. And on top of that, out in the field, he hadn't been receiving the love he needed.

We cut out alfalfa, treats, sweet feed and regular grain from his diet and gave him soaked Bermuda. Thyro-L and psyllium. For a while, he received pain medicine that would take away his discomfort. And almost overnight, he changed. In a matter of days he was walking almost normally. He began to lose weight, and being in the barn, he was able to receive all the attention in the world.

A few weeks after his initial diagnosis our therapeutic farrier came by to trim him again. We'd agreed to do Jazz's trims in stages, as not to drastically change the length of his toes or heels which would have made him abruptly readjust how he walked. As our therapeutic farrier set up his tools and chatted with Jim in the breezeway, I walked over into Jazz's stall to halter him and bring him over.

And the second I walked into the pen, he bolted. Every which way I moved he turned his butt to me defiantly, refusing to let me get near him, threatening me with a kick if I got closer than ten feet.

I was so pissed. I had a thousand things to do that morning; I needed to get Jazz quickly so I could move on to my next tasks. I walked around and around his stall, trying to catch him, and he kept running around in circles. Madder and madder I became as I kept walking around him, telling him to knock it off, to stand still, I was just there to halter him, dammit.

After a few minutes I stopped moving and so did he. And as I stood glaring at him trying to decide what to do, Jazz looked back at me.

And his eyes were wide.

Not only that, I realized as my heart sank upon watching him, he was trembling.

He was scared. He was scared of *me*.

I dropped the halter. Right there in the dirt. Tears came to my eyes as I watched him and looked back at every encounter I'd had with him over the past few days, few months, few years… and I realized that all this time I'd been rushing, rushing, rushing.

And all this time, he was trying to tell me he needed me to slow down. To be calmer. That my hurry wasn't his. *You scare me when you hurry at me, Lex.*

Slowly, the halter still on the ground, I took a step forward and reached out to him. He jumped a little when he felt my hand on his hindquarters. A lump rose in my throat. I felt like a monster.

"I'm so sorry," was all I could choke out. "I'm *so* sorry, baby boy."

Jazz watched me, no longer running or trying to kick me, but quivering. I stood there in silence, feeling wretched, then as slowly as I could I walked up to the side of his face. He let me scratch him for a few minutes. And I heard him speaking to me.

I don't feel well. My feet hurt. I don't know why you were chasing me, in my home. You make me nervous when you rush at me. Why do you rush so much when you're with me? It scares me.

"That's going to change," I whispered to him. "Right now. Today. I'm so sorry. I'm listening now, Jazz. I promise you I'm listening."

I carefully took a few steps back, picked up the halter and approached him again. This time, I side stepped toward his face much more slowly. I patted him and talked to him again before letting him sniff the halter, then put the lead rope over his neck, then finally, slowly, pulled the halter onto his face and fastened it.

Before leading him out, I spent another minute or two praising him, gently explaining that we were going to the breezeway to take a look at his feet and that he would feel much better afterward.

Curious now, and no longer trembling, Jazz contentedly followed me out of his stall.

The next few times I'd go to halter him, he'd still move around his stall uneasily, looking back at me with trepidation. And I deserved every bit of it, and I took it immensely to heart. I started setting aside a good ten minutes to halter Jazz, so I could be slow, take a small treat, spend time to talk to him, until I earned his trust again.

Jazz taught me a lesson I never forgot that day. He taught me to slow down.

He taught me how to listen.

And as the years went on, he blossomed.

With a changed diet, and corrective footwear, and stall rest for six weeks, and medicine for his insulin resistance and the sand in his gut, he became a new horse. His laminitis became a thing of the past. His sand disappeared. His blood levels went back to normal. Living up in the barn, receiving attention, his eyes grew soft and affectionate. He soaked in love and oozed love right back. He became happy.

He taught me more than I could possibly put into words.

Some days even years later, when I went in to halter him, I still got a moment of hesitation when he saw me, a cautious look in his eye.

And I would check myself, and slow myself down, and whisper, "I hear you, baby boy. I'm listening."

And he put his nose in my hair then thrust it into my halter and followed me out to the arena, his eyes filled with joy.

Jazz was my problem horse. He showed me the problems I had and gave me the answers I needed to combat them.

One of the reasons horses are such incredible healers for humans is that they serve as mirrors. They are reactive to what is inside of us and they show us exactly what we need to change. Look closely at the reflection, and you'll see the solution staring right back.

For me, that solution was reflected in two brown, once trepidatious eyes.

CHAPTER EIGHT
VOLUNTEER ORIENTATIONS

Sometime in the late spring in 2015, six or seven months into being the ranch's director, Jim let me start formal volunteer orientations.

Far too often, someone would wander in the gates at some point during the morning-as I and a few others were running around-and express interest in volunteering. If he was there, Jim usually sent them to me. And nothing was worse than having to stop everything and have that person sign a waiver and start the process of showing them everything, introducing them to the horses, explaining what we did and when, the Horsemanship 101 training-

And it was all for nothing anyway. After one or two times, we never saw that person again. Their commitment to volunteering only extended as long as their initial whim to drive out to the ranch.

So I came up with a plan and took it to Jim, who was not yet comfortable with changing how things were, and got rejected. So I came up with another plan and took it back and got rejected again and went back and forth until finally, one hot morning in June, I found myself standing in the breezeway setting out chairs for our first ever volunteer orientation.

Screening volunteers is a necessity in nonprofit organizations. When you're investing resources into people who come to your property to give their time, you need to make sure they are committed and detail-orientated and responsible and respectful. Applications, questionnaires or interviews, and orientations told us everything we needed to know about a person wanting to volunteer.

That morning in June, I greeted my new recruits-twenty or so fresh-faced people-with a stack of papers.

"Y'all are the first group to go through an orientation here," I informed them cheerfully as they smiled back at me politely, "so this will be interesting."

When I first began doing volunteer orientations, I put together a manual that I printed out and gave to everyone. We sat for ten or fifteen minutes while I went through some of the finer points of our morning schedule, some quick facts about the horses (i.e. not to get near Chance under any circumstances), and our basic expectations of them before we took our tour and embarked on Horsemanship 101.

Years later, I started orientations with the manual as a joke.

"I've got a 20-page volunteer manual for each of you," I would say, seriously, to all the new faces, "and we're going to sit down for a half hour or so and go through it. Sound good?"

I always got the diplomatic smiles. Everyone would try to arrange their faces into an agreeable grimace and express how they were willing to do whatever was part of orientation. It always made me chuckle and it always thrilled me to tell them I'd give it to them to read on their own time instead.

One time, a handful of kids were part of the crowd and upon my proclamation that we were going to sit and read what was essentially a textbook, one boy, probably seven or so, looked horrified. "That sounds terrible," he said.

I burst out laughing.

His mother looked embarrassed and started to apologize. But I shook my head.

"You know, I agree," I told him. "That does sound terrible. Let's go play with horses instead."

Beaming, the boy led the way to the arena where Buddy and Jani and Chiquita and Rusty and Jazz were waiting for the group.

I think the beauty of orientations was that I could change them on a dime if I needed. It all depended on my group. A group of fairly experienced adults? Into the arena we went to spend more time with five or six horses off their halters. Lots of kids? I'd bring Chiquita or Buddy or Rusty into the round pen for a one-on-one horsemanship demonstration. A handful of people with lots of questions? We spent more time on the tour going over the finer points of how Tierra Madre worked. Each orientation group had its own vibe, its own personality, and it was fun navigating the best way to teach them.

Over time, I came to love orientation day.

When else could you get a group of excited people together and explain that their lives are about to change?

When else could you teach newbies how to be safe around incredibly dangerous animals while learning why they've sought to be a part of our horses' lives?

When else could you watch someone lead a horse, sometimes for the first time ever, and see them grin ear to ear as they successfully navigate a thousand pound animal through the arena?

When else could you talk with people who had worked with horses longer than I had been alive, and learn new things and perspectives and ideas?

I loved it all. I loved telling everyone about horse herds, about leaders and followers, about Tierra Madre's philosophy of equality. I loved answering questions, building confidence, being the first friendly face that people saw. I loved teaching. I loved getting to know all kinds of people from all walks of life, all wanting to make a difference in the world. I taught individuals and groups as small as two and as big as thirty or forty. I loved it either way.

Most of all, I loved introducing people to the horses.

They laughed at Hudson when he made faces at them. They stood in awe at Rain's miraculous escape from slaughter. They were solemn at Chance's story and marveled at his ability to trust a few people. They squealed over Guess and Bella running in circles in the arena. They loved seeing Sweet Boy ring his bell. Some were drawn to a particular horse right away, just as I had been. And it warmed my heart again and again to see the connections made, the love affairs begun.

Tierra Madre began my lifelong love of working with volunteers. They are the greatest people in the world, in my opinion. They want to give back and make the world a place of beauty, of goodness.

One summer, we were all gearing up a few of the horses to be ridden for a festival in the fall. I was showing one of the new volunteers-who would later become one of my most beloved and trusted ranch managers-how to saddle up Nibzie. I explained how we wanted to get him used to ferrying kids around on his back and walked her through how we wanted to lead him in the arena.

When we were done and Nibzie was munching on a bran mash in his stall, she turned to me and said six words that changed my outlook on volunteers forever.

She said: "Thank you for investing in me."

And it was that day I realized the secret.

Volunteers are an investment. If you want to run a successful nonprofit organization, they are the foundation for everything, the building blocks on which the organization stands.

See, volunteers don't have to show up. But they do anyway.

Explain the rules and tell them why you need them to do things a certain way. Find out why they're there. Learn their names, their stories, their birthdays, their favorite donut, what makes them tick. Learn their favorite horses, and learn why they're drawn to them. Thank them endlessly. Then thank them again. And again. And again.

Give them opportunities to learn new things. Give them structure. And give them gratitude.

And they'll give you everything in return.

Years down the road, when our team was a dozen shy of a hundred people and I needed volunteers for fundraisers, or for the days we were shorthanded, or for posting flyers on mailboxes, or whatever… all I had to do was quietly ask.

And they were there, in a heartbeat, at my back.

I gave them everything I had. And the volunteers gave their hearts and their souls to the ranch, to the horses. And in working with the volunteers, many of whom became my dearest friends, they taught me more than I could have ever imagined.

CHAPTER NINE
S.P.E.R.M.

When I first began managing people back in 2014, everyone who wandered through the gates of Tierra Madre fell into either one of two categories: horse smart, and... well, not horse smart.

It was simple: either people had some common sense and humility about them, or they didn't. Either they knew what they were doing around horses or at least had the capacity to learn, or they insisted they knew everything and wouldn't hear otherwise. That second type didn't last very long.

As time went on and as I gained more experience in volunteer management and people skills in general, I came to find that there are actually five types of volunteers. The volunteers are self-sorting, in a way, and it never took me longer than their first day for me to learn in what category they belonged. After a few years, I got so good at reading people that a lot of the time, I knew which kind of volunteer they would be within a minute or two of meeting them.

It comes down to S.P.E.R.M.

Not *sperm*, mind you. S.P.E.R.M.

Knowing what volunteer was in what category became the secret to everything. It was the internal acronym I used to make daily schedules and determine how many people I needed for certain tasks. It was the system I used to decide who buddied with who, and who shouldn't work together, and how many more people I should recruit for a day when someone called out sick. Events, fundraisers, outreach efforts, projects, and the day-to-day running of the ranch lived and died by S.P.E.R.M.

Not that I ever told anyone. I doubted anyone wanted to hear what kind of S.P.E.R.M. they were. But for my knowledge, everyone had to be in a category.

First were the Solids, the backbone of the ranch.

They were the ones who arrived early to orientation, having paid close attention to the directions. They walked up the driveway with stars in their eyes, soaking in the beauty of horses galloping in the arena, and stood enthralled as they learned about each member of the herd and the history of Tierra Madre.

They came at 5am in the freezing cold to scrub water tubs, pushed hundred pound carts of poop in 120-degree weather, swept the breezeway and stall mats when no one had asked them to, and stayed after the lunch time feeding was over and asked, "Is there anything else I can do?"

They cheerfully rolled up hoses they didn't use, put rakes away they didn't retrieve, and washed out carts they didn't dirty. They were the ones who let me correct them when they were holding lead ropes wrong and thanked me for giving them instruction. They made the dinner mashes while checking the whiteboard forty times to make sure they were making them exactly right. They went with Jim or me when we did medical care on somebody and asked a million questions.

They were the ones who scooped ice cream at root beer float events, sat outside of stores at outreach tables in the scorching heat, helped put baskets together for our silent auctions, and stood at the entrance of the gate to have visitors sign waivers during open ranches. They took home our towels to wash and brought donuts and carrots to share.

Their eyes went first and foremost to the horses. They called me after a particularly nasty vet visit to make sure so-and-so was okay. They crumbled and sobbed when somebody joined the Great Herd.

They were the ones who lead the horses out of their stalls with love in their eyes, the ones I found in the stalls whispering secrets, petting and listening and being.

They were-and are-the pride of the ranch and of my heart.

They were perfectly, solidly part of the family.

And as it happens, the core volunteer team was always composed of Solids.

A lot of the time, though, they didn't start out that way. The beauty of S.P.E.R.M. is that some of the categories are learning stages. And learning how to become a Solid is part of the wonderful, wild process of acclimating to the complex rhythm of the ranch.

The Put-'Er-Theres were next in line to the Solids.

Many Solids started out as Put-'Er-Theres: wonderful people who didn't have quite enough experience to do some of the heavy lifting like turnout of the wilder crews, hoof and wound care, or feeding without supervision, but they made up for it in enthusiasm. Most harbored a great deal of nervous energy that dwindled as they settled in, and I tended to have a lot of gratitude for their eagerness to please.

Put-'Er-Theres were the ones who learned the hard way how to catch loose horses, for in their excitement of taking horses home from the arena, they forgot the crucial step of shutting the gate behind them. They ran back to turn off an overflowing hose they'd stuck in a water tub and forgotten. They didn't wait for me to tell them how much hay the horses get at lunchtime but instead anxiously lifted up flakes and asked me, "Is this enough?" at each feeder.

Often, they were the ones who talked over me and interrupted when I was giving a demonstration or instructions. Sometimes, they wanted to share about their past experience with horses, and it was all I could do to patiently listen to their story while the lunch carts needed to be loaded and Slayer's foot needed to be looked at and two hoses filling waters in the field approached overflowing and Hollywood was pacing in the arena wanting to go home and Studley needed his Habronema medicine and Chianti needed her fly spray and another volunteer was waiting to ask what kind of grain went into Jazz's mash and another wanted to know if she could groom Tater and another wanted an update on a fundraiser happening that weekend.

They wanted to do everything at once and sometimes got frustrated when they saw more experienced volunteers doling out lunch without supervision or walking one of the advanced horses home from the arena. They got impatient with themselves for not knowing every little detail about running the place.

I put them alongside a Solid or had them tail me throughout the morning. I put them to work cleaning buckets in the tack room or wiping down stall bars. I put them in the stalls with grooming kits so they could settle in and get to know the gentler, mellower horses. Buddy. Jani. Rusty. Annie. Chiquita. Tommy. They taught the Put-'Er-Theres more than I ever could.

And over time, they learned. They channeled their enthusiasm into their tasks, and as they figured out the lay of the land, they thrived.

Some of them didn't. And that was okay. A working ranch is not a place for everybody.

Then there were the Extra Extras.

You know how back in the old days, paperboys would wave newspapers and shout in the streets, "Extra! Extra! Read all about it!"?

Well, we had those people too: volunteers who reacted to day-to-day life as though each occurrence was a breaking news story.

Extra Extras came running up to me-in full-fledged panic-because Kiss had a callus on his elbow, or River had a millimeter-long scrape on her forehead, or Jani scratched her flank with her teeth and therefore must be in distress.

Their eyes widened in horror when I told them that Suze had a wrap on her leg because her cellulitic leg was acting up, or that the vet was coming for Studley that day because his summer sores were breeding again, or that Slayer was being treated for an abscess and couldn't go out that day. They were the ones who learned over time just how resilient horses were.

Many of the Extra Extras just had tender, loving hearts, which I loved and appreciated greatly. Not all of them, though. Some of those volunteers were drama queens.

Sometimes, the Extra Extras were the ones who stormed out because they intentionally broke a rule and they didn't like being reminded that they needed to adhere to Tierra Madre policies. They were the ones who didn't like to be told how to lead horses the Tierra Madre way, because they grew up doing it Another Way that was clearly better. They got upset when I told them we were not there to ride the horses, or asked them to go back and rescrub Guess's water because it was still grimy. They were the ones who wanted to show off their equestrian "skills" by unnecessarily disciplining a confused horse they had just met who had done nothing wrong.

Sometimes, the Extra Extras liked to gossip, or they came up to me angrily because they thought so-and-so had offended them and wanted me to intervene. A few times Extra Extras demanded back donations because Jim-who had no patience for what we referred to as "fuckery"-called them out on breaking ground rules which, naturally, showed where their loyalties were, and it wasn't to the horses.

Sometimes, they handed me binders of capital campaign material from multimillion dollar nonprofits, and told me-in explicit detail-everything Tierra Madre was doing wrong, that I was doing wrong. They told me I needed to be doing this, and that, and not that, and not that.

Extra Extras. Some ended up calming down when they realized they were in the wrong. Some just worried about the horses because of their love for them.

But some? They left and never came back, and that was fine by me.

The former three kinds of volunteers were wonderful in their own ways. We would be utterly lost without them. Well, not some of the Extra Extras. But all the rest were keepers.

The last two were not.

Rejects were the people who didn't want to be at the ranch but were forced to be there for whatever reason. They were there for court-ordered community service or were dragged along with Mom and Little Sister for a family outing.

They sat in the chairs by the breezeway and stared at me, bored, when I asked if they wanted to help me make mashes. They pulled out their phones to text and ignored any attempts at conversation. When forced to work, they did a half-assed job of whatever assignment they'd been given and skipped out before the lunchtime feeding.

They showed up late or sometimes not at all, giving excuses the next day.

They were the ones-when their court service was up or their family moved on-that I never saw again.

They were a big freaking waste of my time.

Don't be the person that brings a Reject to a horse ranch.

Last were the Mopes.

They filled water tubs halfway after being told four different times by three different people that they needed to be filled to the top. They spread woodchips in the arena after being shown how they go in the driveway since they're too thick to be under horses' feet. They stared at me blankly when I told them to get on the left side to put on a halter, or would look confused when I showed them again and again how to not wrap the lead rope around their arms.

They were the ones I watched like a hawk with the horses, because who was to say they wouldn't suddenly sit down in an occupied stall?

They didn't last long. Most of them didn't make it past the first day.

Honestly, I was scared of Mopes. All the others I could deal with just fine. But those who were truly, helplessly clueless around the horses made me deeply thankful we had everyone sign waivers.

I've often noticed that volunteers could be combinations of S.P.E.R.M. categories. Some of them were 50% Solid, 50% Put-Er-There. Sometimes a Solid would have just a touch of Extra Extra about them, which came in handy when my eyes didn't catch everything and someone would tell me about a wound or health problem that needed my attention. The best-and the rarest-were the Rejects who slowly, slowly morphed into Solids.

Any and all combinations were fair game. Although you couldn't have a Solid that was any part Mope. There is no such thing as a Solid Mope. Well, I guess there is: it would be a Mope who is really, really good at being a Mope.

CHAPTER TEN
ON

Other than his break during the summer of 2014, Jim hadn't been on a vacation from the ranch since its founding nearly a decade before. Some months after I became ranch director, he and his sister Jean and I all decided that now that someone else was sharing the load of running the place full time, it would be good for him to leave for a week. He would go up to New York City to stay with Jean in her apartment, and Bill and the Solids and I would take care of the kids.

Bill was the operations director of Tierra Madre. He worked for Jim and-of his own accord, despite Jim insisting he take days off-he came to the ranch 365 days a year to feed the horses their breakfasts at 4am then came back in the late afternoon to feed them all dinner. No one knew the ranch or the horses more than Bill. And with our convincing, reassurances that we would be in contact every single day, and many days spent carefully reviewing the medicine and feeding schedules, Jim left for a weeklong vacation.

As usual, I got there first thing in the morning, after Bill fed everybody breakfast and before he left for his other jobs. I stayed at the ranch all day until Bill came back in the late afternoon to feed dinners and to stay the night.

In the mornings, it was business as usual. Turnout. Medicines. Deliveries. Vet and farrier visits. Mucking. Filling waters. Feeding. All done with the help of the volunteers.

At lunchtime, I drove the truck up to the feed store for hay or supplements or to Ace for fly spray or aerosol bandage or Elastikon. Then, in the afternoons, with the volunteers gone and just me on the property, I'd settle in the house with Lee curled up at my feet and get to work on donation receipts or fundraising plans or updating medical records or answering emails or writing social media posts.

More importantly than doing work at the ranch in the afternoons, I was listening.

For pawing.

For banging.

For a whinny that didn't sound right.

Or a crash.

Or a horse going down.

Because when you were at the ranch, even if you were resting in the house, you were always on.

There was no break from being in charge of horses. When you were on Tierra Madre property as someone in charge, lives were in your hands. There was no rest. Diligence was required at all times. When medical emergencies sprang up, there was no time to waste. Minutes-mere minutes of delayed reaction-could mean the difference between life and death.

And it was exhausting. Constantly being on the lookout for signs of distress or illness on a ranch full of horses surrendered for some reason or another, many of those reasons being for medical problems… it was a physical, emotional, mental, psychological drain that never let up, like a slow leak of air from a tire.

I got tastes of being on during those weeks Jim would take desperately needed vacations, when I stayed in the house and occasionally ventured out to glance around and make sure everybody was in their normal spots. I questioned every horse laying down to nap in the sun. I stressed over someone scraping the dirt with a hoof more than once or twice. I panicked when someone didn't take a treat right away.

I had to. I was on.

I had an additional variation of being on at the ranch.

Managing people came with its own set of challenges.

The days I was tired, or not feeling well, or feeling sad or upset or just off… I still had to smile.

I still had to be kind. And patient. And a good teacher, and a good listener, and a good friend. And watchful. And responsible. And respectful. And not too bossy, or snappy, or irritable. For every single person, whether it was two volunteers or two dozen.

I failed, naturally, some of the time. Probably a lot of the time. But I tried my damnedest to be smiling and tranquil and calm, a friendly face for anyone to come to, any time.

That was *my* constant on. Coupled with the on of being utterly responsible for the horses' lives during a week Jim went away was doubly hard.

But Jim and I understood these variations of being on and had an understanding. Jim left for meetings for a good chunk of the morning most days, just to get off the ranch for a few hours, which helped him immensely. And I never had to be always kind and patient and a good teacher and a good listener and a good friend and watchful and responsible and respectful and not too bossy or snappy or irritable around him.

The rhythm of the ranch was constant and ever changing. Things changed every second. The status quo shifted against us on a dime.

And if you were tired and didn't want to dance, it didn't matter.

The rhythm was persistent.

And you were on.

CHAPTER ELEVEN
MEDICINE

"What is *that*??"

I looked down at the bucket I was carrying. To the untrained eye, one might have thought it contained a bundle of cloth with a crusty coating of mud over it. But on that hot summer morning, flies were swarming it and it stank like the pits of hell.

"That's Studley's summer sore cape," I said to the volunteer who was eyeing it like it was a rat carrying the plague. "I have to scrub it out and put it back on him later this morning."

"It's disgusting!"

"Go look at the sore it covers," I said cheerfully over my shoulder as I walked away.

Tierra Madre took in horses that no one wanted or simply couldn't keep anymore-the abused, the injured, the neglected, or those who were older and required extra attention in their twilight years. As a result, the vast majority of the kids had medical challenges or needed special medicines for some underlying condition.

I've never been interested in entering the medical industry, although I have the highest respect for doctors, nurses, surgeons, techs, and the like who take care of people or animals. Over the years, though, and under the guidance of Tierra Madre's official veterinarian and farriers, I learned how to be a bit of a doctor for the horses.

I gave IM (intramuscular) shots, cleaned out wounds with triple antibiotic and betadine, and wrapped cuts and blemishes with gauze and Elastikon. I flushed out eyes with saline and squeezed in goos and drops like Vetropolycin, Atropine, Polymyxin B and Neomycin, Dexamethasone, and other medicines prescribed by our vet for ulcers and infections.

I dug out abscesses in hooves and dabbed them with ichthammol or soaked them in Epsom salts. I treated thrush, wrapped hooves in Elastikon (we went through that stuff like water) and fitted them in booties to keep them out of the dirt and mud until they'd healed.

I treated cellulitis with what Jim christened 'schmoo'-a sticky concoction of gel DMSO and Fura-Zone-and sweat wrapped legs after cold hosing them or scrubbing them with antifungal shampoo.

I took temperatures, prepared and gave oral syringes, and tricked horses into taking medicine in more ways than I can count. I mixed bute into grain and sweet feed, put syrup or applesauce into dissolved SMZs, and injected banamine into apples and carrots. One time I got smart and squeezed an Equioxx tube in between a horizontally cut carrot to give to Solo, who absolutely refused to take medicine in any way, shape, or form and who could detect hidden medicine better than anyone else on the ranch. He got pissed at me halfway through chewing the carrot when he realized I'd snuck in his pain meds. But it was too late. He didn't take carrots from me for a while.

Every horse got something different, for different reasons, and at different times depending on their ailments.

Nibzie got a Saccharomyces Boulardii pill every morning. Heighten got a scoop of Neigh-Lox morning and night and a quarter tube of GastroGard every day for ulcers. Jazz and Rusty needed two scoops of psyllium twice a day. Studley got nine hydroxyzine pills in his dinner mash. Min, Kiss, Tommy, Iron Man, Kiss, Guess, Spencer, and several more of the kids needed a dosage of Prascend, which regulated their Cushing's disease, or Pituitary Pars Intermedia Dysfunction (PPID).

Kids recovering from abscesses were on bute (phenylbutazone), usually two grams a day for a few days, and horses needing long-term pain medicine for arthritis got glucosamine and Equioxx or Previcox. When someone had an infection of some kind, they got SMZs or Equisul or Enrofloxacin along with banamine, our anti-inflammatory medicine we kept in the house by the sink at all times for colic. If someone was dealing with a case of laminitis, usually they were on Thyro-L (insulin resistance often went hand-in-hand with laminitis) along with biotin and Pentoxifyline or Isoxiprine.

Everything had to be just right. We took great pains to ensure each and every horse got exactly the right supplement or medicine, in exactly the right amount. Not that we ever decided who got what medicine. Besides giving bute or Equioxx (similar to aspirin or ibuprofen in humans) or banamine (which we knew was a necessary administration during colic), we never attempted to self-diagnose an illness or serious infection. Medicines were always prescribed by a veterinarian.

Ever since Tierra Madre's founding, Jim used the same veterinarian clinic and was good friends with the founder, Dr. R. Dr. R. was the kids' vet up until the day he retired (and even then, he came to visit Jim and the pair of them would casually walk around and look at the horses together). We've never strayed from our vet's clinic in over a decade, though in the days after Dr. R. retired, we went through a number of different vets before we came across one who became our vet for everything, whom we loved and trusted more than anyone.

Actually, the first time our vet came to the ranch was during an emergency. And nobody was particularly happy we were getting a brand-new vet during an emergency because it was Bentley-who had a medical file the size of a phone book-and he had gone down in his stall one late morning in the dead of summer.

B had a heart murmur and a few times a year, he had fainting spells where he would go down suddenly, lay still for a few minutes, then get back up again and be just fine. By that point he was getting on in years, and though we'd had bloodwork and tests run on him before, nobody ever found anything truly wrong other than his heart murmur. All we could do was call our vet when the fainting spells happened and have a professional assess him to make sure he was okay.

It was toward the end of our morning and I was in the tack room scooping grain when one of the Solids yelled at me to come quick.

I ran out, saw B was down, and rushed over. He was laying still, but in order to assess how perilous the situation was, I would need to try and get him back up.

I quickly ran for the house, calling over my shoulder for one Solid to grab me a halter and another to turn on the hose and drag it toward B's stall. In the house I got ten cc-s of banamine into a syringe while I dialed the vet's office as fast as I could.

The particular vet we had used for the past year had just recently switched clinics, so we were on the hunt for another who would be our go-to. Having one vet was far easier than having anyone from the clinic come out when we needed one. We wanted a vet who knew our horses. But there were no vets we had used available at the clinic during B's emergency, though they told me they had just hired a new one and would send her, ASAP. Okay, I said impatiently, and hung up.

I ran back over and haltered B-who was lying still-and got him up long enough for me to get 10 cc's of banamine in him before he went down again. I quickly hosed his neck and chest then called Jim, who was at his daily meeting.

"Here's what's happening," I said quickly. In times of disaster, Jim wanted all the details in one go. "B went down in his stall. He didn't respond for a minute but he got up for me for a sec then laid down again. The vet's on the way. I got ten cc-s of banamine in him and hosed him down."

"Shit. I'm driving back already. I'll be there soon. What's he doing now??"

"He's still laying down but his head is up. He's breathing kinda hard."

"And the vet's coming? When? Who is it?"

"They estimated twenty to twenty-five minutes. It's a new vet, I didn't remember her name."

"Fuck! That's the last thing we need! She won't know shit about B!"

"She's the only vet they had to send."

"Okay. I'll be there in a few." *Click.*

Jim pulled in only a few minutes before the new vet did. The banamine had started to take effect and B had stood up by then. We monitored him carefully as he stood, steady on his feet, and took a treat or two from Jim and chewed contentedly. All good signs.

The new vet pulled in, parked, walked up to us and introduced herself. Impatient to get to the monumental task of explaining every factoid about B's health conditions, Jim took a deep breath.

"Okay," he said. "This is B, and-"

"Hi, B. Yes, I pulled his file in the truck. Thoroughbred in his mid-twenties, looks like a history of cellulitis in those hind legs and a heart murmur as well as a few episodes of colic over the years. Gets bute regularly, and I also saw he was treated for a wound on his fetlock a year back. That sound about right?"

Speechless. Jim and I were speechless.

New vets had come to the ranch during emergencies before, but never before had we met one who'd so accurately nailed a horse's history in a matter of seconds.

The new vet examined B and I can't remember exactly what she said, but she explained the heart murmur's connection to fainting spells in a way we could understand, and in a way that made perfect sense. She patiently answered our questions and made a supplement suggestion for B along with asking general questions about his diet and exercise. Before long, we were all laughing and joking, B calmly standing in the center of us acting totally normal, and we felt more at ease with this new vet than we had from anyone from the clinic in a long time.

By the end of the visit Jim was asking other questions about some of the other horses, and we tentatively planned to get her on the schedule to come visit again next week, to look at somebody else with a long term medical condition.

After hanging around a bit longer to hear more about Tierra Madre, the new vet and her assistant packed up their gear and headed off to another call. Jim and I looked at each other, grinning, as they drove away.

"I think we found our vet," Jim said finally, and B nudged him, looking for carrots.

CHAPTER TWELVE
THE WALK AROUND

Tierra Madre closed to the public at 11 o'clock every morning. We did this for two reasons: so the horses could nap in peace, and so Jim had some time to just be without anyone on his property. Not to mention, for six months out of the year, it was just too dang hot to do anything in the afternoon.

So, around eleven (or eleven-thirty if we had fewer volunteers that day, or sometimes noon or twelve-thirty if we had vet or farrier appointments that ran into the afternoon), I would do what I called the walk around.

I checked for three things during the walk around: that all the horses were eating their lunches; that all the waters were filled; and that all the gates were latched.

Some days, those fifteen minutes or so was really the only time I got to spend with the kids past doing any necessary medical care or turning them out during the morning. It was something I looked forward to, even if I only got a little bit of time with each horse.

I had a routine. I started with Iron Man at the end of the shed row and began my walk, glancing at waters, usually brushing hay out of Rusty's eyes that got stuck in his forelock, chiding Heighten for splashing out all his water while telling Hollywood not to put all his food in his.

I ended on the field side at the end of the hallway with Chance on one side and Danny and Chianti on the other. As I walked up the hallway, M'Stor was usually sniffing around, looking for more food (he inhaled his lunch), Studley was looking at me waiting for a 30-second withers scratch, and Nibzie was just getting started on a nice, long nap.

One day in the springtime, as I finished the walk around at the hallway in the field ending with Chance, I was starting to head back to the barn to collect my things when Chianti pinned her ears and snapped at me over the fence.

I sighed. Unfortunately, this was not anything new.

Chianti (pronounced key-ON-tee, like the wine) lived in a big pen in the field with Danny at the time, her more dominant and certainly pushy stall mate. He tended to take some of her food at mealtimes, which pissed her off and most likely contributed to her more defensive nature. While certainly happy to live with him, I think because of Danny's assertiveness she sometimes felt overlooked.

Now, the first time Chianti did this to me several months before, I was so bewildered I didn't know how to react, so I walked away. The second time it happened, I got mad and yelled at her to knock it off. She did, but still looked pissed. The third time, I put my arms out and stomped my foot on the ground in an attempt to show assertiveness. I had learned that sometimes making yourself look bigger (i.e. holding out your arms as though they're wings) can be intimidating to an aggressive horse. In a horse herd, a leader will often do this to a pushy herd member. Chianti backed down, but again, she still seemed upset.

By the fourth time, I figured she had become food aggressive and just really, really didn't want anyone around her when she was trying to eat. With Danny always on her case, I started to understand her snarling at everyone else.

But then she'd be defensive even after her lunch was gone. And not just to me, either-the other volunteers often got her pinned ears and angry, flashing eyes.

Maybe she's sleepy and wants to be left alone, I thought. Maybe she's just fed up today. Maybe she's tired of being glanced over.

Now, Chianti was standing at the fence, lunch gone, snapping at me yet again.

I stopped and just glared at her. She glared back.

"Why do you always to that??"

She kept glaring.

"I'm just checking your water. There's no need for that nonsense."

Still glaring. Ears pinned.

I sighed and kept watching her, thinking.

That day, one of the volunteers had had trouble getting Bourbon back to his pen. He'd kept jumping away from her and dancing around rather than walking straight. When I hurried over to see what was wrong, I realized that a feed tub that wasn't usually by the field was sitting in his sight, drying out after being washed, and it was scaring him. We'd moved it, and off Bourbon went to his pen like nothing had happened.

I'd told the volunteer: "Horses aren't assholes for no reason. There's always something they're trying to tell you."

I looked at Chianti for another moment, thinking about this, then-

"Hey, I just gave Studley some scratches. What... what would you do if I came in there and gave you scratches too?"

She didn't do anything, and watched me carefully as I climbed through the fence, quietly walked over to her, and started scratching her neck.

She.

Melted.

Every bit of malice, every bit of anger, every bit of irritability... gone. Gone in the blink of an eye.

She arched her neck slightly as I scratched her and spoke softly, then she brought her head close to mine to nuzzle at my chin, my shoulders, my hair. When I stopped stroking her, she gently put her nose into my hands until I started again.

Danny was over at the end of the pen. And so it was just us. Just us standing quietly together, breathing together, being together. As far as I was concerned, in those moments we were the only ones under the sun.

And I melted too.

I hugged her neck and kissed her and put my face in her mane. And I asked for forgiveness for being so harsh and misunderstanding, for always being in such a hurry to simply get the walk-around done so I could get to the rest of my work, for not taking the time to get to the root of her problem.

She nuzzled me in response, eyes soft and bright.

It's okay, Lex, she said. *I didn't know how else to tell you I just needed some of your time.*

Much later, I climbed out of the pen and stood in front of her as I had before. No more lunging or snapping. Just soft eyes. She followed me as I walked down the hallway and stood at the corner looking after me as left.

I could make sure the waters were full and the gates were safely closed. But I had a responsibility to also make sure the horses' spirits were full, too, that their hearts weren't being latched. No matter how tough the lock could be, sometimes we just had to keep working at prying it open.

CHAPTER THIRTEEN
KEEPING HOUSE

Go to any horse ranch in the world, any one at all, and the people there will tell you that baling twine, duct tape, and chains can fix anything. Tierra Madre was held together by a combination of all three, with a dollop of solid welding work thrown in for good measure.

Things wear down at a ranch. Hoses sprung leaks, water tubs got chewed, and clamps holding up feeders rusted over. Cart wheels came off, muck rake prongs broke, and stall fences needed to be mended. And everything, as Jim reminded everybody daily, cost money. When we couldn't fix the odds and ends with baling twine or duct tape or chains, they had to be bought. One year Ace Hardware mailed Jim a special card that thanked him for being their number one customer.

All the stall doors on the ranch had their own stories. Some had to be lifted up ever so slightly to close properly, or jiggled just right to open, or you had to smack the perpendicular bar to slide the lock down, or twist the handle more to the left than the right. Some had to be chained due to their escape artist inhabitant. A few had gates that only opened outward. We had to drill a new hole into the concrete to make a new opening for another. I always felt bad for the volunteers who-on top of everything else-had to learn the magical ways of each gate. We always worked with chains when fixing gates in an attempt to make them relatively uniform (duct tape or baling twine on a stall door could get chewed and dangerously ingested) but we still somehow always had ornery gates.

Sometimes the stalls themselves were in desperate need of new dirt-which was all we could afford in the early days-or the winter rains had flooded them, or the driveway was almost completely bare of woodchips, or one of the fences in the field was one strong gust of wind away from blowing down. Those times, Jim sometimes let me call in local Boy Scouts. I love the Boy Scouts. They're respectful, hardworking, cheerful, and willing to do just about anything. Eagle Scouts have to complete a community project in order to earn their Eagle Scout status, and we were on the receiving end of the generosity of an Eagle Scout and his troop two or three times. One time, one of the dads called in a media team for the day they were doing projects on the ranch, and I got to be interviewed on TV.

In the springtime, at the first hint of heat from the sun, I broke out the ladder, some pliers, and a bucket and went into every stall to unscrew a hundred mister jets from their sockets. We had seven misting lines that ran through every stall on the ranch: Iron Man's, Heighten's, Hudson's, the west barn line, the east barn line, Studley's, and the field line. I'd flush out the piping by letting the water run for a few minutes on each line, soak all the jets in CLR, then go back around the ranch and screw them all back into place. It took me weeks. Sometimes one of the volunteers would pitch in, either to help me haul the ladder around or else shoo away Iron Man or River or Hudson when I was at work, since those kids particularly enjoyed trying to knock me off the ladder. We usually finished by the first day it hit the high nineties, which was when the misters would be turned on at midday, every day, all summer long.

Also come springtime, we ordered new fly predators. Fly predators are tiny parasitoids that eat fly larva in their cocoon stage, preventing the hatching of thousands and thousands of new flies. We sprinkled them primarily in damp spots and pee holes, since that was where flies tended to lay their eggs, and we noticed a big difference in fly populations afterward.

Flies weren't our worst problem. Back before we had our hay sheds, the bales of Bermuda were stacked on pallets next to the breezeway, behind the tack room and close to Sedona's stall in the barn. When it finally came time to move them, I lifted the pallets off the ground for the first time in several years and I swear we entered a portal to another world.

Maggots. Worms. Roaches. Roly polys. And a fuzzy tarantula we named Terry. Most everything scattered upon being exposed to the world, but one of the volunteers moved Terry out to the wash.

Another time we went to lift up pallets and Henry, the bull snake that lived under them, slipped away. He was five feet long and very friendly, though he wasn't some of the volunteers' favorite. Personally, I preferred seeing Henry over most of the other critters I saw around the ranch: a desert centipede sitting on an alfalfa bale, scorpions curled up on lead ropes, and, once, a tarantula wasp that flew into the tack room, causing me and the volunteers to slam the door shut as fast as we could and declare it time to move properties.

It wasn't all gross. Every week, we had to ensure that we bought enough equine senior grain, low starch grain, wheat bran, beet pulp, sweet feed, psyllium, Neigh-Lox, salt and electrolytes, and whatever additional supplements or medicines we needed at the time. The hay barns were filled every week. We tended to buy Bermuda and Timothy hay every Monday or Tuesday, usually fourteen bales of Bermuda and a bale of Timothy at a time. We ordered alfalfa every three to four weeks from a supplier who delivered it by the squeeze, or 88 bales.

Back before we had the gray sheds (one of which became my office) or the hay barn with the tool sheds attached to them, the tack room was our place for everything from saddles to bags of feed to buckets to medicine. There was barely any room to move and we were constantly tripping over stuff on the floor and walking on top of each other. In the corner behind the door stood a medical cabinet that hadn't been touched in five years and into which no one in their right mind dared to venture. After we got our hay barn and tool sheds and began the Great Tack Room Renovation of '15, we finally cracked it open and recoiled at the mice nests, moldy gauze pads, expired medicine, several years' worth of grime and dirt, and enough maggots to overtake a small country. Fighting nausea, the Solids and I threw the entire cabinet away.

The Great Tack Room Renovation of '15 was our first step toward establishing deep-rooted organization for all of our things, which was an important precedent for the structure that would come to the ranch later. All of the tack- saddles, bridles, reins, saddle pads, and old halters-were to go on the left side of our new hay barn and our tools would go into the right. The first grey shed would house bulk food bags, the second my office and tubs of merchandise and fundraising supplies. The tack room would hold some feed, medicines, and hoof and wound care supplies. And that was it.

Not that the tack room remained spotless every day after the Great Tack Room Renovation. Every so often, I'd walk into it one morning and without warning I would be so incredibly fed up with the clutter that I would decide on the spot that it was time for it to be cleaned out. Usually this happened when I couldn't find my good syringes, or the mice were breeding again, or there was some smell I couldn't identify.

I'd start throwing stuff into the breezeway. Chewed up plastic gloves with mice poop in them. Empty DMSO bottles. Expired eye medicines. Rice bran we hadn't used in years. Crusted-over red blood cell supplement that hadn't seen the light of day in months. As volunteers showed up, some would heroically pitch in and we'd make games out of who could find the grossest item. Afterward, we made an enormous effort to keep the tack room as clean as possible. All of the medicines and supplies had a specific spot. And when multiple people handled the same item throughout the week, it was critical that things remained organized lest we be looking for something needed in an emergency. "A place for everything," Jim would say, "and everything in its place."

A whole lot of pride went in to keeping house at the ranch. Having nice stalls, with working misters, with clean grounds raked of old hay or straw, and washed feeders, and organized tack rooms and sheds made my heart sing. The stalls were mucked once a day and the water tubs were emptied and scrubbed clean and refilled with fresh water every day. We worked hard to keep things as clean and comfortable as possible for the kids, because they deserved it. They deserved nothing but the best we could offer them.

Keeping house wasn't always a pleasant experience. On one occasion, we got two detectives at our gates politely asking to take a look around at the facility. They told Jim there had been allegations of animal abuse and they needed to look at the animals and the property to make sure everything checked out. So Jim walked them around the ranch and introduced them to each and every horse, and they left an hour later with tears in their eyes, telling Jim he was doing God's work.

It's still a mystery as to who called the detectives, but the pool of animal rights activists is-sadly-full of people who draw conclusions based on no evidence or fact, or people whose actions are driven by high emotions and hysterics, or people with nothing to do and who just like to stir up trouble. Our guess is somebody got pissed at Jim for doing something that they didn't agree with (i.e. putting a horse on one kind of treatment and not another) or they saw a picture online of one of our horses who wasn't in the best of health because the horse hadn't spent enough time at Tierra Madre to recover from whatever neglect from which they had been saved.

He wasn't an animal abuse investigator, but I did get a man from the City of Phoenix's Department of Zoning once. He came up the driveway, respectfully showed me his badge, and said he had received a complaint about manure buildup in the horses' stalls and the concerning smell of urine (or something like that) and he needed to look around, if that was okay with me.

I put down the halter, fly spray, Derma-Vet, and god-knows-what-else I'd been carrying and grabbed my clipboard.

"I'll show you around personally," I told him. "I just need to get you to sign this waiver."

Everybody who set foot onto Tierra Madre signed a waiver. We had insurance and a big sign that stated that all activities on our grounds were subject to the Equine Inherent Risk Law (Arizona Revised Statutes s 12-553), but we still never took the chance. After three years or so I tended to say my disclaimer in one breath: "If I could just have you sign this waiver for me right here. This is just a waiver and release of liability that says horses are big animals and if you get hurt you can't sue us."

I didn't say that to the City of Phoenix official. But he signed the waiver and away we went on a tour.

I showed him each and every stall, all freshly mucked that morning like they were every day, and explained that Guess's was a little damp in the corner because she made a game out of splashing her water out of her tub. I showed him the poop carts and rakes and shovels and the pile of dirt we used to refill stall holes when the horses dug them. I showed him the manure dumpster and told him that it was emptied when it gets full, at $350 a pop, and an empty one would last us about three weeks.

"So you're telling me you spend $350 every three weeks just on manure haul?" the official asked.

"Yep," I said. "And as for the urine smell, I'm not sure what to do about that. They're horses. They have to go to the bathroom. They all have pee holes in their stalls, though we try to stay on top of them."

He thanked me profusely and told me he didn't see any problems related to the complaint he'd received, though he did point out a handful of code violations in the shed row stalls. Apparently, we were over our allocated allowed amount of square footage permitted by the state. "Their shade structures," he explained, "can't be more than 200 square feet by 200 square feet." He proceeded to tell me that the way around this would be to go around and take panels out from each shade structure in each stall, so that rather than one big shade structure that showed up as one long skinny rectangle on a satellite, there would be lots of individual tiny ones, all under 200 square feet by 200 square feet.

I cringed, knowing Jim wasn't going to like this unwelcome news, but nodded and assured him we'd take care of it. (We did, by the way, and now all of our shed row stalls have missing panels from their shade structures so we stick to code.)

I walked him back up to the gate and he thanked me again for my time. He gave me his card and told me to call if I had any questions about the panels in the shed row, and that he'd follow up with me in a few weeks.

"By the way," he said casually as he turned to leave. "You have a dead body in your wash."

I about had a damn heart attack. I looked wildly around at the wash, picturing crime scene tape, and flashing lights, and someone being hauled away in handcuffs....

"W-*What?!*"

"No, no, no, not a person," the official said hastily, seeing my face, "I mean like a bird or rabbit or something. It's just something small that's died and it smells."

"Oh."

"It's the smell of decay, I know it all too well. You might just poke around and see if there's a body you can get rid of."

I thanked him, we said our goodbyes, and he left.

I determinedly did not look at the wash as I walked back up to the barn, trying not to reflect on the fact that I had just spent an hour with someone who was intimately familiar with the smell of a dead body.

CHAPTER FOURTEEN
EVERY TIME

Every time I taught a group of people-Boy Scouts or a volunteer orientation or an equine experiential group or a class for a horsemanship program-the alfalfa squeeze truck arrived in all of its screeching, hissing, beeping glory to drown out my every word.

Every time I gave one of the calmest, gentlest horses on the ranch to a newbie who had never walked a horse before, that horse spooked because of the wind or their shadow or because Min dared them to do it.

Every time I tried to give a horse medicine without a halter over my shoulder, just in case, they walked in circles around their stalls and refused to let me near them. And every time I went to them armed with a halter, they stood still as a statue.

Every time I said, "Let's be sure to get the knots down on the alfalfa bales in the food carts," someone inevitably asked me afterward, "Do you want the knots up or down?"

Every time a group of pre-pubescent teenagers visited, one of the male horses really needed to pee and everyone dissolved into laughter during one of my serious discussions about the slaughter pipeline and the importance of our work.

Every time I got my camera out to snap a picture of somebody galloping in the arena, they came to a dead halt.

Every time I stayed a couple of extra minutes after we closed to spend time with somebody, those few minutes turned into an hour.

And every time I had a carrot in my pocket, every single horse on the ranch knew it.

CHAPTER FIFTEEN
STUDLEY

If anyone wants a lesson in shrugging off life's hardships, they need only look at Studley.

Studley came to the ranch with Hollywood and Cadence (who we lovingly nicknamed Tater) in December of 2009. They belonged to a lady who had boarded them at a facility and supposedly not been able to pay their board for some months. The owner of the facility finally threatened to send the horses to a livestock auction and held them hostage until she paid up.

Desperate, the woman turned to Jim for help, and he not only raised the money to bail the horses out, he offered to put them up at Tierra Madre-where he would never threaten to send them to an auction-in exchange for her working off their board. The money was raised, the horses were transferred to Tierra Madre, and once she knew they were safe, the woman came to do volunteer work for us for a few times, then disappeared.

It's important to note here that those kinds of situations weren't always black and white. This woman, though down on her luck, had a heart of gold in getting her horses to safety. Further, she had found Studley as a baby a few years back and had saved him from unimaginable abuse.

Studley had been found tied behind a dumpster outside of a trailer and surviving on scraps of hay that blew over from a barn just over on the next property. He had been gelded with no tranquilizers and a rusty knife and had a nasty infection on his sheath as a result. The woman begged his owners to release him to her and when they finally did, she got his infection treated and cared for him along with Hollywood and Tater, until Tierra Madre took over.

Studley was only two or three when he first walked through our gates, but he'd lived through enough horror to last him a lifetime, not that you could tell at first glance. A handsome dark gray Arabian when he arrived, he faded out to a light gray over the years, keeping his sharply defined face and eyes that always snapped with an unlikely combination of joyful innocence and mischief.

However, the gross abuse and neglect he'd lived through dealt him an unfortunate hand in life in the form of summer sores.

If anyone were to ask me what the nastiest thing I ever had to deal with at the ranch was I would answer, without hesitation: Studley's summer sores.

Every single summer since he came to Tierra Madre, Studley struggled with summer sores that were the result of an equine stomach worm called Habronema. This parasite lays eggs in the horse's stomach which are passed through the body and end up in the horse's manure. The eggs then hatch in the manure and their larvae are eaten by fly maggots who thus grow to maturity carrying the Habronema stomach worm. Because moist areas are hot spots for flies on horses, the lips and mouth are a popular dwelling for them. And when flies carrying the Habronema stomach worm land on a horse's lips or mouth, the horse ingests the worm and the cycle continues all over again.

Flies tend to gather around open wounds as well, which meant that any small nick on Studley's skin turned into a gaping flesh wound almost overnight due to the relentlessness of flies picking it apart and depositing the Habronema larvae into the open flesh. The larvae-although they would never reach full maturity when laid in a horse's skin-irritated any small cut or area of sensitive skin and would very quickly blow up into raging, oozing, bloodied wounds infected with larvae. These wounds are referred to as summer sores, and as you might imagine, they're gross.

We theorized that Studley was taken from his mother at too early an age and he hadn't received all the antibodies he needed from his mother's milk, rendering him with a weakened immune system and an inability to heal from cuts in a normal period of time. Whatever the deal was, despite his annual deworming medicine and the fact that we religiously fly-sprayed him, checked him thoroughly multiple times a day for scratches, controlled our fly population with fly predators, gave him a heavy duty fly mask (and a fly sheet for a few summers the sores were out of control), and cleaned the manure out of his stall a minimum of once a day, the summer sores came back every single summer with a vengeance.

Every spring around the end of February, I would see a small gathering of flies on Studley's mouth or shoulder or hock. Or someone would come up to me and say, "Hey, I noticed there was a bit of blood on Studley's-"

"*No!*" I would sometimes yell without thinking.

"It didn't seem that bad!" the volunteer would say hastily, looking panicked. "Is he okay?"

"Oh. Sorry, it's just that yeah, that happens this time of year. I can't believe it's that time again…"

"What time?"

"Summer sore time. Here, let's go get some stuff from the tack room. Would you grab a halter? Come with me and I'll tell you about Habronema. You haven't eaten recently, have you?"

Treating them was terrible for everyone, Studley most of all. Every day from the beginning of March to the end of October, Jim or a Solid or a ranch manager or I would visit Studley armed with betadine and Derma-Vet and aerosol bandage and triple antibiotic and fly spray and SWAT and a vet-created concoction of liquid Ivermectin and anti-inflammatory oral medicine plus gauze and gloves and a pair of tweezers that we would use to pick out the larvae in his sores. And a carrot. Or two. Or three.

Because did Studley ever complain about the intense treatment his summer sores required?

No. Never.

He stood patiently in his stall or in the breezeway as we stood and doctored him which could be anywhere between five and thirty minutes a day, depending on how bad the sores were. And over the years, we had to doctor his lip, chin, shoulder, forehead, eyes, fetlocks, neck, shaft, and anus- all of which were prime real estate for summer sores. Even when he didn't have active summer sores in those areas, we always had to thoroughly examine him every day, in the hopes of catching a small nick or scratch and pouncing on it before the flies got to it first.

He let me teach volunteers about summer sores and let others doctor him too, with my supervision. He politely pulled back just a bit if he needed a break from the poking and prodding for a minute, or gently turned his head away if it was going on thirty minutes and he was tired.

But he never once tried to get out of it. He'd see us coming with the Studley Bucket full of supplies and a freshly washed fly sheet or mask and blink at us with a casual acceptance.

"Hey, Studs, we gotta do your medicine real quick."

Hmm? He'd respond. *Oh, okay then.*

He put up with itching, bleeding, tenderness, and my bad nicknames for him. He put up with people gathered in his stall to watch him be doctored and many, many months' worth of having to wear fly masks and bandages and a cape-like fly sheet when the sores were really bad. When the sores got totally unmanageable, he put up with our vet debriding the sores and injecting them with a steroid to reduce inflammation (though she always sedated him so the procedures never hurt him). Eventually, when we found the vet who responded to Bentley's emergency and became our regular veterinarian afterward, we decided on weekly visits during the hottest parts of the summer, when the flies were at their worst, to prevent the sores from getting unmanageable in the first place. And so Studley put up with weekly visits.

Jim called him a punkass. In the arena, Studley threw his head and trotted around happily and picked up toys to play and wrestled with Chance and Bourbon and Nibzie. He'd never met a bit of food he didn't like, or a human he didn't like, for that matter. He was thrilled with his life, summer sores and all.

Everyone fawned over him, and rightfully so. He soaked up the attention, and made sure we all knew that his withers were his favorite place to be scratched, and he didn't mind a visit to the treat bucket at all, thankyouverymuch.

And sometimes, if I ever just stood and looked at him for a while, it struck me how odd it was that he was so cheerful all the time.

You have every right, I often thought.

You have every right to be angry and reactive to people. The neglect you went through as a baby-a baby!-was unreal. And not fair. And cruel.

You have every right to be mad that we have to poke and prod at you and put all kinds of goos and sprays on you. You could try and fight us, or not be caught when we came to halter you.

You could not want anyone near you, ever, and no one would blame you.

One morning, when I was in his stall doctoring his sad, bloodied chin, I told him this.

And he looked straight at me with bright eyes.

If I have every right to be miserable, he said, *then doesn't that mean I have every right to be happy, too?*

CHAPTER SIXTEEN
LOOSE HORSE

If I could pin down a motto for Jim, one of the top contenders would be: "Close the goddamn gate!"

We constantly got on people about closing gates. Some of the volunteers, god love them, weren't always so observant in making sure stall doors were properly latched or else would walk horses back into their pens and unhalter them with the gate wide open. One month it got so bad that during volunteer orientations I actually started making people repeat the words after me: "If it isn't latched, *latch* it!"

Some of the Solids and I patrolled the ranch and checked gates constantly. Inevitably though, a chain wouldn't get put on tight enough. Or a poop cart would take too long to cross the threshold. Or someone just made a mistake.

And a horse would bust out of their stall like inmates out of Alcatraz.

We always knew, instantly, when somebody was loose. Every single horse on the ranch made sure of that. At the sight of their freed neighbor, they bucked and kicked and raced to the front of their stalls and screamed, "You're FREE! Go, *go*, GO!"

And the loose horse, full of themselves and immensely proud of their escape, took their encouragement deeply to heart and hauled ass through the ranch as fast as they could go, their shrill whinnies of joy piercing through the property, flying hooves and dirt accompanied by Jim swearing, new volunteers diving out of the way, and me sprinting to grab a halter and yelling directions at the Solids. We usually caught them in one of two places if we cornered them correctly: the narrow stretch of space between the north-most pen and the western end of the barn, and the very end of the hallway that separated the east field from the pens just north of it.

Before orientations, hell, before we started getting structure and proper training and vetting of volunteers down, I got really, really good at catching loose horses. I should list it on my resume as a viable skill.

Sometimes, the loose horse came screeching to a halt in front of another stall to bat their eyes at someone or to personally challenge whoever had looked at them funny and I could slip the rope behind their ears and haul them back. For other horses, I could throw a flake of alfalfa in their path and they'd instantly surrender their newfound freedom in exchange for a few bites of food. Other times they just didn't stop until they were good and ready to be caught, and we all got our cardio for the day.

Because Tierra Madre is enclosed property, and we kept the main gate shut under penalty of death, they never had anywhere to go besides three acres of land. But a loose horse on the property was chaos and to be avoided at all costs.

The chaos ended at one point or another. The loose horse, blowing and snorting, would trot back to their stalls or else be walked back by me or Jim or Bill or a Solid, always looking immensely pleased with themselves. We'd recover, catch our breath, and double and triple check every gate. Someone would apologize over and over and over again, and Jim usually took the opportunity to tell the story of his Grandpa Jake's farm and the time he'd mistakenly let a horse loose, subsequently spent four hours catching him, and how he had learned the hard way to "Close the goddamn gate!"

We had some interesting times over the years, but the funniest to me was one time Chance got out.

It was actually my fault. I'd just brought him home from the arena, closed the gate to his pen but didn't latch it all the way as I was unhaltering him and was about to walk back out. Usually he stood where he was or wandered off after I'd unhaltered him, but that day a volunteer was filling his water and the hose jumped out of the tub and startled him right as I'd gotten his halter off.

He said, *Nope*, then moved past me before I could stop him, pushed open the gate, and trotted off.

At that point, the two of us had been working together for years. That said, hardly anyone else on the ranch was comfortable with him yet and certainly not thrilled with the idea of him being out on his own where he had every opportunity to take a bite out of someone if he pleased.

But I knew him better than that. Someone yelled, "Chance is out!" and as I rounded the end of the hallway after him, I was treated to the sight of six or seven people scrambling into the stalls out of his way while Chance moseyed up to the back side of the barn, cool as you please, sauntering past the alfalfa stack and turning at the hay shed to trot into the breezeway. Laughing, I turned the corner into the breezeway, following Chance as he made a hard left toward Jim's house and his favorite thing in the world.

Sure enough, he'd stuck his head in the treat can and was demolishing it as I walked up behind him, kissing at him so he'd hear me, and slipped the lead rope over his neck.

"Come on, you goofball," I said, putting the halter on him as he chewed. "Back to your stall."

Fine, was his reply. *I'm getting another bite though.*

"You do that."

Chance got his bite of treats and away we went. I put him back in his stall, latching it this time even though it only took a second to unhalter him, walked out, then latched it securely before walking back toward the barn.

Eventually, it became a rare occurrence when a horse got loose, much to the disappointment of the herd. I still drilled it into the heads of my new recruits, each and every month, and checked every gate in my sight whenever I walked anywhere.

"What's the number one rule on this ranch?" I'd ask each group of new volunteers.

"If it isn't latched, latch it!" they'd all chant back.

If there weren't kids present (and hell, even if there were), Jim often chimed in:

"Remember this, if you remember anything today. Just close the goddamn gate."

CHAPTER SEVENTEEN
THE CRAZIER ONES

There are two types of horse people: the crazy ones, and the crazier ones.

The crazy ones are awesome.

As a public, nonprofit horse sanctuary, Tierra Madre got visits from a number of people every year. Hundreds of people came from all over the Phoenix Valley and even from across the country to bring carrots and apples and warm smiles and admiration for all the ranch did. They were horse lovers, passionate equestrians, and some of the kindest, most genuine souls I've ever had the pleasure to meet. Most brought donations, and always left as members of the family. Some of my greatest times have been spent taking visitors around the ranch to introduce them to the herd. The best tours were the ones where those visiting had been following the ranch for some time and were eagerly anticipating meeting their favorites.

Likewise, the vast majority of those who came to the ranch to volunteer were another breed of people. They were angels: hardworking and full of love for the herd.

And we were crazy. The good crazy. Horse crazy. You had to be crazy to want the life of a rancher, the life of somebody who rescued horses. No normal person did what we did.

99% of the people who came to the ranch were wonderful.

Like with everything in life, however, there were exceptions to the rule. And over the years, Tierra Madre saw some real doozies, individuals that I refer to as the crazier ones.

These people tend to stick out, because who on earth could forget the volunteer who liked to stand behind the alfalfa squeeze and eat parts of it, or the one who did drugs in our bathroom?

Certainly everyone remembered the visitor who swung a lead rope into Hollywood's face-scaring the daylights out of him-because of his heinous crime of confusedly walking a half-step ahead of her when she grabbed him from the volunteer walking him. It was for no reason besides wanting to show off her horsemanship "skills." I pulled rank on her that day and told her to give Hollywood to me, immediately. She was banned from the ranch shortly after.

One time, I was walking past another volunteer in the breezeway with a mash for Wild Bill in my hands. "What's that?" she exclaimed, and, before I could answer her, she proceeded to put her finger in the mash for a pinch and taste it.

"Dude!" I yelped. "That has Prascend and Previcox in it!"

"Are those bad?"

"For you? Yes. Very bad!"

I walked in on the same volunteer a few weeks later in the tack room-topless-insisting she'd needed to change her shirt for another and don't mind her, she was cool if I came in. Not that I had a choice. Before the Great Tack Room Renovation of '15, we stored literally everything in the tack room and we bustled in and out of it about twenty thousand times a day.

"Um…" I said as I came in, grabbing a tube of Equioxx and putting down a dirty bucket and searching for Studley's eye meds all at the same time, "you know the bathroom's around the corner, right?"

Another man whom I showed around years back claimed to be an animal communicator. I could smell bullshit a mile away, and it usually began with someone claiming to read animal minds that they would be happy to translate for a small fee of several hundred dollars. Yeah, right.

I played nice and walked him and his friend around and introduced them to the horses. Apart from wanting to be friendly, it was never a good idea to turn away visitors unless we absolutely had to. Otherwise, we risked turning away a potential volunteer, or donor, or connection to something that could help us.

This man did the opposite of help us.

"I'm getting *eleven*," he said when we were in front of Iron Man, who stared back at him with mild interest. "Eleven… the number eleven. Does that mean anything significant to this boy? Eleven? *Eleven?*"

I swear Iron Man glanced over at me for us to exchange a look.

"Uh, not that I know of."

We got to Hudson. I told them how Hudson had been a racer, but after something like six starts his owners had surrendered him due to the fact that he just had no interest in being ridden.

"If he were in with cows that would not be the case. Have you ever considered putting him in with cows?"

I stared at him. "No, we haven't done that."

"He will work beautifully with cows. He wants to be with cows. If you were to ride him with cows, he will do great things for you."

I nodded, of course making a mental note to go get some cows, ASAP. Hudson, who hadn't tolerated a rider on his back for years, snorted as we walked away. Still, there was a chance this guy might give us a donation for our time in showing him around, and I held my tongue.

"This one is telling me something about his lungs," he said when we got to Kiss. "His lungs are bothering him."

"Have you ever had a vet back up what horses tell you?" I asked curiously.

We didn't get a donation.

One time a volunteer came staggering up the lane halfway through the morning, reeking of alcohol and carrying an orange juice bottle that had clearly been spiked, cheerfully asking how she could help. In my outright stupidity that I possessed when it came to managing people in those early days, I watched her uneasily for a time rather than blasting her off the ranch as I should have. She ended up leaving a gate open and after Sweet Boy had hauled ass around the property for several minutes, Jim roasted her to a crisp, and we never saw her again.

Then there was the guy who brought old, rusty saddle racks we didn't need, dumped them on the ranch, and then screamed at me when I politely suggested giving them to a place that would put them to good use. People. Ask ranches what they need before showing up with random crap in your truck. Otherwise, it is junk that we have to pay to get hauled away.

In early January one year, we agreed to take a woman's two horses when no one else in our network of rescues could take them. They were older horses that couldn't be ridden, which usually meant they were sanctuary-bound, and after several weeks of trying to find an alternative solution, Jim and I bit the bullet and told their owner we would make Tierra Madre their forever home. I fell in love with them just by looking at their pictures. I couldn't wait for them to arrive to safety.

But then their owner asked if she could hold on to them for as long as she could, which downplayed the six-page letter she had sent us essentially begging for help because she had to sell her house and couldn't keep her horses for much longer. Then, she sent a list of demands for when her horses came to the ranch: what they could and could not eat, what medicines they would receive, how they were to be treated, how often they were to be groomed, etc. etc.

Here's the deal about surrendering your horses to a horse rescue or sanctuary that this woman didn't and wouldn't understand: upon surrender, you lose all ownership over your horses.

You don't get to tell another ranch-that will be footing the bill for your horses' food, medical care, farrier work, tack, and clean stall-what to do.

Every barn has different procedures for feeding and grooming and exercising and dolling out medicines. For another thing, many of the horses Tierra Madre took in over the years had incorrectly diagnosed medical conditions. Very well meaning owners often self-diagnosed problems, or treated a temporary medical concern for years without any follow up work. Our veterinarian clinic-one of the best in the southwest-did a full examination on every horse we took in and often found untreated issues or that current medicines were unnecessary. Coming to Tierra Madre was a clean slate for horses, a new opportunity to be thoroughly checked out. We didn't just take an owner's word for it that a horse needed to be on a medicine or had a navicular problem or had a bad back or whatever. We had a professional medical team properly examine, confirm, and diagnose.

Well, this particular situation evolved to pure insanity when this owner got wind that she would not be able to dictate every aspect of her horses' care upon surrender. This quickly escalated to hysterical accusations that we were hiding things from her, such as how supposedly we were going to lock her horses in an isolated pen away from the other horses, and how we were covering up horse deaths (I'd told her-in an honest answer to one of her many questions-that we had had an equine coronavirus outbreak in the past but we'd gotten through it). She furiously told me she would never allow her babies to come to such a terrible place.

Seeing how upset I was, Jim called her to give her a piece of his mind. There was literally no other place for the horses to land. Tierra Madre was it. And we were a damned good place for them.

Not long after he'd dialed her number, he hung up, came and found me and just shook his head.

"What did she say?" I asked, fighting back tears.

"Nothing even worth repeating. She's batshit crazy, sweet thing. That's all there is to it."

I still think of those horses to this day. I'll never forget their names. And I still hope with every fiber of my being they landed somewhere safe.

Another crazier one was a woman who constantly dropped her three kids off at the ranch and took off for the morning, leaving us to essentially babysit. Sometimes we'd be waiting for them to be picked up-or else one of us would drive them up the road to their house-because the mom couldn't be bothered to come get them. The oldest wasn't more than fourteen, and she and one of our hired hands at the time, who was eighteen and whom we'll call Kid, started making googly eyes at each other behind all our backs.

It was a nightmare. One day the girl's mother called me, screaming, demanding that we fire Kid immediately, because she'd got wind of increasingly flirtatious communication between the two of them and how on earth could we have not known about it??

Because your child isn't our responsibility? I wanted to say, but didn't.

We tried to figure out a solution that didn't involve losing Kid, who deeply loved the horses and the ranch and who busted ass for us. We told Kid under no circumstances was he permitted to set foot on Tierra Madre if he was in communication with this fourteen-year-old. He assured us that he would cut off all contact with her, and Jim and I offered a deal to the mother for the girl to come on different days than Kid. Maybe she figured out then that she shouldn't let her kids wander around unsupervised at a ranch, because she refused, and that was the last we saw of her and the kids.

But not the last we heard of them. One night, about a month after this fiasco, Jim called me and, without ceremony, told me he'd just received a phone call from Kid who was sitting in a jail cell.

"What the fuck?!" I screeched into the phone.

Apparently, more had been going on than we'd realized. Kid had lied to us, and had been going over to this girl's house to visit her in secret. The mom caught them watching movies in his car, called the cops, and that was the end of that.

Needless to say, we barred Kid from the ranch for life. It took us weeks to recover. Jim stayed behind from his meeting the day after Kid's phone call since I was the only one at the ranch, and the two of us scrubbed buckets and mucked stalls and fed the kids while bitching the whole time about the stupidity of Kid, who had been a hard worker and whom we had been so excited to have on board for the summer.

I updated the minor waiver after that and made parents specifically check a box that said, "I acknowledge that Tierra Madre Horse & Human Sanctuary personnel are not responsible for supervising my child." Good God.

My personal favorite crazier story, however, was an exchange of which I was never actually a part.

In the later years, I had a donor development assistant, L, who forwarded me an email some time after one of our fundraisers from someone who had come to the ranch for the event. This person was requesting permission from us to do, and I quote, an adult photoshoot on the ranch with our horses.

Uh…

I quickly replied, asking L to get some clarification. A few minutes later, I got this response:

"Apparently it's a fetish BDSM western theme. Crops and whips and leather stuff. Here, they sent me a picture."

Somewhere in between my screaming, crying, and laughing all at once, I managed to text L back.

"Um, no. HELL no."

By that time, Tierra Madre was serving families with small children.

Individuals with disabilities. Young adults on the autism spectrum. We were well known in our community as a nonprofit that welcomed families through our gates. What would they say if we allowed an Equine Fifty Shades of Grey photoshoot on the property? If they saw their favorite horse posing with a half-naked, leather-clad model?

I called one of my ranch managers afterward and told her about it.

"Just in case anyone ever asks about doing a fetish adult photo shoot at the ranch with the horses," I said, rubbing my eyes, "the answer is no."

CHAPTER EIGHTEEN
ALL IS WELL

On Christmas Day, 2015, Spencer got his face kicked in when one of our neighbors shot off a BB gun. In the panic that followed, a stampede exploded and Suze threw up her hind legs and nailed him square in the skull.

The entire left side of his face was fractured. The muscles that held his eye were so damaged that the orb rotated sideways, so that his pupil, which normally was horizontal, was vertical. His sinuses were damaged and he had nosebleeds for a while. To this day, he bears deep indentations in his handsome face.

But we saved his eye, barely. It was a miracle that the eyeball didn't rupture. In the weeks that followed the horrific freak accident, we must have put nearly a thousand separate eye medicines into his eye and had him on all kinds of pain killers and antibiotics. And Spencer never complained. Not once. The vet we used at the time was so impressed with his recovery but more so impressed with his calm, accepting nature of his accidental cosmetic surgery, as were we all.

"A bull," Jim said of Spencer. "He's a friggen bull."

Spencer had been surrendered by an owner who planned to ship him to a zoo to be used as lion meat if no one else would take him in. Horrified, we got him to Tierra Madre as fast as we could. A stoic and beautiful bay gelding in his early twenties, Spencer was beloved by everyone on the ranch and his terrible accident was a shock to us all.

"It can't get much worse than this," I remember grumbling to myself, looking out at poor Spencer's face from the breezeway one morning during the start of the New Year.

I'd eat every single word mere weeks later. Choke on them. And never say them again.

Because in the first few days of January 2016, on the heels Spencer's accident, we were shaken to our core by the most terrifying experience at the ranch.

Equine coronavirus.

Obviously, this was before the 2020 pandemic. Nobody we knew had ever heard of this before. Not even the vet we were using at the time knew what the hell was happening to our kids at first.

We certainly didn't know what it was when it first presented itself. Everything simply crashed around us as the horses started getting sick one after another.

It started with Sunny. One morning, Sunny acted colicky. She didn't eat, had diarrhea, and came down with a fever of 105. She was only six months old at the time and, panicking, we called the vet who ran bloodwork and helped us do everything it took to get her fever down.

Next, almost within 24 hours, her mom, Rain, colicked terribly. She too had a fever, and diarrhea so severe her cramps pained her.

Colic is a medical emergency in horses that can refer to any number of problems within the gastrointestinal tract. Specifically, it refers to abdominal pain, and at Tierra Madre, if a horse colicked, nine times out of ten we pulled them through it. Nine times out of ten, it was gas, or dehydration, or sand, or discomfort due to bloating or cramping. All serious problems, but problems that had solutions our vet could successfully administer at the ranch. The vet would administer necessary medicines and usually we tubed horses, which meant pumping water, minerals, and oil through their gastrointestinal tract to clean them out, or lube them up, if you will, to make for easier passing of manure.

But sometimes, there was displacement. Or an obstruction. Or a rupture. Or strangulation of the intestines from a tumor. Some of those problems had no solutions.

When a horse displays signs of colic-pawing at the dirt, rolling, thrashing-you never knew exactly what was going on until a vet could make the best educated guess based on an exam or procedure called an abdominocentesis, where a small incision is made in the abdomen to test bodily fluids.

That was the terrifying part, not knowing.

Not knowing what was wrong with your kids.

Not knowing if they were going to make it through.

We thought it was bad enough that Rain and Sunny both got sick within a day of each other. We managed both sicknesses, but it was still terrible.

But then Sonora-who lived next to them both -got sick too. One day, she didn't want to eat anything that was offered to her. Her personality was to show discomfort and pain by getting angry, and she spent the day with her ears pinned to her skull, kicking at Bentley through the fence.

Then, Hollywood went off his feed and showed signs of colic.

Then, the Min.

And Heighten.

And Sweet Boy.

And Nibzie.

And Rain again. And again.

And Hudson.

And Sweet Boy again.

We called the vet whenever someone displayed some kind of colicking symptoms or had a fever or else just didn't look right. Some of the kids got so sick we had to have them tubed. For others, some banamine got them straightened out. Again, we had no idea.

Our then-vet ran bloodwork and fecal samples on everybody and tried to figure out what the hell was going on. Jim and Bill and I frantically watched the world crumble around us and tried to figure out what to do. Clearly, this thing was spreading, whatever it was, though it seemed to jump over some stalls but not others. But we had to stop it. We had to do something.

So, we came up with the only option we had.

We locked the place down.

No one went into the stalls, except to muck. And even then, those who were permitted to muck had to wear gloves and sanitize their shoes, carts, and rakes after coming out of each one. We had special carts and rakes for the healthy stalls and special carts and rakes for the sick stalls.

During the worst of it, all the horses stayed inside their stalls for four days.

We didn't touch them. No one went out to the arena for turnout. Nobody was groomed. We fed everyone wearing gloves. Any mash pans or buckets that went into the stalls were sanitized coming out.

We had pans of bleach water scattered everywhere on the ranch. Any time anyone went remotely near one of the stalls, into the pans they stepped.

I sent out emails to the volunteers and posted a sign on our front gate barring visitors and telling anyone who hadn't heard of the new lockdown protocol to come directly to me or Jim prior to doing anything on the ranch. (I still had to chase people down who climbed into their favorite horses' stalls.)

I rallied all the volunteers together and together we scrubbed the absolute shit out of the ranch, literally. Because this was in the dead of winter, the turnout arena contained puddles from rain that we sprayed with bleach along with the sand and the toys. We scooped all the old poop that had been in there so long it had nearly composted, and we wiped down every inch of the bars.

We scrubbed feeders without going into the stalls. We cleaned every cart and rake and shovel on the property. It was war, us against the disease, and we were determined to win.

Before long the vet called us to pass along a suspicion that the disease was transferred via fecal matter, confirming we were doing the right thing by stepping our shoes in bleach and sanitizing anything that touched poop. But each day Jim and Bill and I walked around, terrified of seeing someone pawing at the ground, or refusing to eat, or standing next to a pile of diarrhea, or sweating, or looking sick.

The worst was simply not knowing what was going to happen next. Who was going to get sick next? To what degree? Would they colic? Would they make it?

When Chance went off his feed and stood dully with his head down in his stall, no one was quite sure what to do. At that point, no one had ever attempted to give him any kind of medicine, not that he'd ever needed it due to him always being so healthy. Trying to give him an oral dosage of banamine-or worse, take his temperature-would have been an impossible mission. He was still untrusting of most humans, and only allowed me and a few others to halter and walk him, but that was it.

Finally, I came up with a solution. For three or four days in a row, I sat by his stall and injected a few drops of banamine into pieces of apples and carrots and tossed them into his feeder. I had to do a little at a time, lest he refuse them because they were too bitter. I made warm bran mashes and injected a few of the cc's of banamine into them and gave him those, too. He happily inhaled the apples and carrots and bran mashes and after a day or two, the banamine took effect and he thankfully pulled out of it.

One day, Sweet Boy wasn't eating again and I watched him all afternoon so Jim, who'd slept only a few hours the night before, could take a nap. Jim came out of the house around 4pm and looked at me camped out in front of Sweet Boy's stall.

"How is he?"

I opened my mouth but before I could answer, I heard a thud. Almost on cue, Sweet Boy had just laid down. Groaning.

Jim cursed and pulled out his phone. I ran inside for the banamine. As the door slammed I heard him say, "Hi, Doc?"

Another night, Jim called me as I was starting dinner at home.

"It's Heighten," he said, and I ran to my car.

Heighten was incredibly sensitive to any discomfort or illness. Unlike Spencer, who took a hoof to the face almost without objection, Heighten was sometimes almost violently reactive to anything causing him pain. That night, he was pawing at the ground, trying to go down to roll.

This was sometime in late January, a few weeks into this nightmare, and when the sun went down, it was cold. As we stood there with Heighten, the emergency vet who'd answered Jim's call came out of the truck shaking a bit. Seeing this, Jim offered her a jacket.

"Oh no, thank you," she said, still shivering. "I have one in the truck. I'm just stripping down to do a rectal."

Silence.

Then-

We all burst out laughing. We couldn't stop for a good few minutes. Laughter. For the first time in weeks. The emergency vet then proceeded to do a rectal exam-which is very standard in a colic examination-where she checked for displacement or an impaction.

By February, we had a name for the disease: equine coronavirus, an illness that was gastrointestinal and characterized by three common symptoms, all of which we'd seen: refusal to eat, diarrhea, and sky-high fevers. And the vet had prescribed Bio-Sponge as a remedy. A supplement that supported gastrointestinal health in horses, Bio-Sponge worked miracles on every single horse that got seriously sick.

When a week went by in early February without anyone getting sick, we breathed again. We walked on pins and needles for a long time… but we breathed.

Because Jim and I were calling and texting at all hours, day and night, I panicked every time my phone rang and his name appeared on the screen. Usually his incoming call meant someone else was sick or something else was seriously wrong, and I would be speeding to the ranch a few minutes later.

But one time he called to ask me about printing a document at home to bring the next day. Another time it was regarding a meeting we had with a potential sponsor that week.

Then one time I was at the ranch while he was away on errands to let him know about a change in a delivery schedule. And he answered his phone sounding just as panicked as I did.

Finally, he called one evening to ask a quick question about a dinner mash and I lost it.

"I freaked out seeing your name on my phone!" I yelled. "Is everything okay? Is anyone sick??"

"What? No, everything's fine! We're all good here."

"I'm so used to hearing bad news every time you call now," I said, heart still racing. "It's like I expect the worst when I see your name come up."

"I feel the same way, kid. We need something that we can say when we call each other, so you or I know everything's fine, so we don't panic right away."

So we came up with our phone greeting, right then and there, that we would use when one of us called the other and no emergency was at hand.

All is well.

"All is well," we would say, before anything else. Before "Hi," or "How are you?"

All is well.

Those words became my life.

They defined the lens through which I saw my day. They told me if I could eat that night, or sleep peacefully, or if I would be laying in the dirt at two in the morning, in front of a horse stall, stomach churning in fear. They told me if I would be carrying on as per usual or if I would be dropping everything to rush to the ranch as fast as I could.

All is well.

Every horse who came down with equine coronavirus that winter recovered. Every single one of them pulled through.

Combined with Spencer's eye expenses, we spent something like three thousand dollars in medical bills in a single month. Dealing with the sick kids, the lockdown of the property, seeing poor Spencer's face crushed in, the constant fear and worry of the unknown…

It was a complete waking nightmare. One that haunts me to this day.

But as that year went on and the year after that and even now all these years later, Jim and I stick to our phone greeting whenever we call each other. The terror we'd lived through will never be forgotten. And the thing that can be said, right away, to alleviate some of the old fear… we say it.

And I'll never underestimate the power of those three little words as long as I live.

All is well.

CHAPTER NINETEEN
DANCING

Humans are predators. That is lesson number one in understanding horses.

In accepting this, we acknowledge that there are buried channels of instincts within us that are primal and threatening, that by our very biological nature, we are dangerous.

Horses know this. The instant they see us, they know this.

And to interact with them, we predators must learn their language, one that involves shedding our layer of predator instincts behind which we unknowingly hide.

When I first came to Tierra Madre in the summer of 2009, part of my daily routine was to muck the five stalls in the barn. I started with Sweet Boy's every day. And I noticed instantly that Sweet Boy moved around a lot when I was in his stall. His previous humans had shown him roughness and cruelty, so his reactions to whatever I did were increased tenfold.

Sometimes he stepped back uneasily if I pulled the cart forward and he had been standing directly in front of it. Sometimes a quick motion with the rake, with the pronged end flicked in the direction of his left side, made him shift quickly to his right. If I side stepped toward his chest with my arm outstretched, he moved back, but just half a step. He moved quietly, unthinkingly, mirroring my series of movements while I watched him, and adjusted my actions until his nervousness fell and he was content.

Over the years, Sweet Boy taught me one of the most important lessons I ever learned.

He taught me the language of prey animals.

He taught me the dance.

He taught me how to move gracefully around horses, without sharp or sudden movement as not to startle. How to turn just so, how to pivot away from hindquarters changing directions, how to slowly twist your chest and face parallel to a horse's body to appear less threatening.

How to relax your limbs, to give in to the ebb and flow of the moment, to raise and lower your arms and hands as necessary to reassure, to release pressure, to give in.

How sometimes closing your eyes and seeing with all your other senses accomplished so much more.

There were days I went to halter Sweet Boy, or put his flymask on, or put medicine on his left front bulb, where my predator instincts were still up, and he would move away before I could halter him. Both of us would stand and he would watch me carefully while I looked away, not facing him, arm outstretched in an arc, fingertips pointing down, halter on the ground.

I'd glance up and see unease in his eyes, achingly familiar.

He'd been abused. He didn't like being backed into corners.

I'd been abused. I didn't like being backed into corners either.

So we danced.

A beat and a turn, an extended arm, a dropped gaze.

One step forward, and one to the side. Hooves pivoting, turning quickly. A step back.

Flickering ears my way. A glance.

Another step forward, another to the side. The bow, to grasp the halter. Raising it slowly. Eyes on me.

The lead rope extended carefully, draped over his mane.

My hand on Sweet Boy's neck. A gentle pat. A turned shoulder.

Ease. Quiet.

Beats of stillness were still part of the dance.

Horses aren't ever in a hurry. They do things at their pace, on their time, at their comfort, and in their language. To earn the privilege of being with them, we predators have to keep up. We have to learn the complexity of their language and the poetry of movement that keeps them alive.

That first step in the dance is the hardest to learn.

But in the end, that first step is always the most important one to take.

CHAPTER TWENTY
MONEY

Other than dealing with disease or injury with one of the kids, getting money into the ranch was the biggest stressor in the universe.

Nothing happens at a nonprofit without donations. With individual contributions making up the majority of our income, Tierra Madre fed horses, provided medical care, kept up a clean facility, and paid its few employees because of donations.

Part of my job was watching the bank account.

I hated doing it. I hated seeing donations dwindle. I hated seeing big charges for the hardware store, or a squeeze of alfalfa, or a particularly nasty vet visit. But most of all, I hated seeing my paychecks come out of our account. I would have worked for nothing if I could. My salary was only what I needed to pay my bills, and there were many weeks I deliberately didn't deposit my checks until I knew the horses had the food they needed for the month or until a medical bill was paid. We had a reserve account for emergencies which we were to avoid using at all costs. But sometimes, when donations were low, we had to dip into it. And I hated that, too.

Somehow, we had to make sure money flowed in regularly. That was hard.

Before I went back to school to study nonprofit management, the extent of my knowledge in fundraising was what I Googled and what I knew how to do by instinct, which was-essentially-to just ask people to give. Only it wasn't entirely straightforward. We couldn't send someone a note that said:

"Hi, Person. We need money. Can you send some? Thanks. Sincerely, Tierra Madre."

Nope, that wouldn't work. Not that exact wording, anyway.

The act of asking for money is extremely sensitive and meticulous, and it must be done strategically, and with great care, while taking into account exactly what we're asking for, from whom.

We asked on our social media accounts all the time. We wrote posts about our work and outlined our monthly costs and told our existing donors how much their donations made a difference. Storytelling-one of the most powerful fundraising tools in existence-was our specialty. We raised the funds for vet bills many a time by telling the stories of our horses.

Sometimes, we did fundraisers in the form of open ranches.

Open ranch days were a lot of work. The chores still had to be completed. The medicines still had to be doled out. Dinner mashes still had to be made. And on open ranch days, someone had to clean the bathroom and Chance had to be roped off and a warning sign placed fifteen feet or so from his pen and "Do not feed the horses" signs had to be placed out and the merchandise table set up and the welcome table with waivers and pens and clipboards laid out…

But boy were those open ranch days a blast.

Visitors from all over the Valley came to meet the horses. The volunteers were in their element, giving tours and showing off the horses and talking about the ranch to new friends. We sold t-shirts and horse paintings and Jim's books and random knick-knacks that volunteers lovingly made and gave to us to sell. We'd ask for donations at the gate and have jars out for visitors to contribute. If the people got to see the horses in person, we reasoned, they would be more inclined to donate toward their care.

Sometimes, we had a theme for the open ranches. For a while, we did a holiday-themed open ranch the Saturday after every Thanksgiving, since Jim had a direct connection to Santa Claus and got him to come down to the ranch and give candy canes to kids. One year I came up with a Pumpkin Party theme around Halloween that went viral and yielded several hundred people. Back when we had a handful of older horses who were ridable and didn't mind ferrying small children, we offered horse rides, too.

During those open ranches, we made friends and wonderful memories. Usually, however, we netted a few hundred dollars to a thousand at best. Any money we made was nothing to sneeze at, for every penny was needed and appreciated. But even in those early days of being the director of Tierra Madre, I knew we needed more than those few hundred bucks every so often.

I started to think of better ways to get more donors, get more funds, and do more outreach. Tierra Madre, with over thirty horses, needed thousands of dollars to sustainably operate per month. There had to be better and more efficient ways to fundraise and ask for money.

And if multi-million dollar nonprofits could raise thousands of dollars with their fundraising events, I thought, *then why couldn't we?*

CHAPTER TWENTY-ONE
THE FIRST BENEFIT

In January of 2015, I sat down on the couch in Jim's house one afternoon and told him I had a crazy idea. Not the best way to start a conversation, but this was so par for the course with us that he just nodded and said, "Hit me."

"I want to put together a big event," I said. "Like, a Big Event. A fundraiser. Something that will raise thousands of dollars and bring everyone we know together. Something that will really establish us as a nonprofit. Something impressive. I want to do a dinner. A benefit, with an auction and presentation and fancy napkins and everything."

He mulled it over. "I like it. You know, years back, we did a dinner here at the ranch, for Kate Tweedy, Penny Chenery's daughter. We had someone cater it, and Kate gave a whole speech about Secretariat. We raised a few thousand if I remember. Though I don't think we had fancy napkins."

"I think we should do it off the ranch," I said. "Somewhere really nice, but not too crazy or anything. Somewhere where we can do a presentation and have people sit down at tables-"

We started brainstorming, Jim matching each crazy idea of mine with his own, until he was fully on board, and, though he would run it by his sister Jean, who was his fellow board member and shared ownership of Tierra Madre, I had permission to go ahead and start planning.

I hadn't attempted anything as big as a benefit dinner and silent auction before. By that point, I had a handful of open ranches under my belt and was somewhat prolific with arranging spaghetti dinners and outreach tables and hosting bake sales and posting social media asks. But this benefit was to be our first Big Event. And, as I told my new volunteers, I believed in trial by fire. The best way to learn anything is to leap off a cliff and figure it out on the way down.

So I leapt.

And immediately realized just how blissfully, stupidly ignorant I was about

Big Events on the way down.

First, I had to figure out how to put together a budget, so I could tell Jim and Jean how much money I needed, and in doing that I had to figure out for *what* the money was needed.

Then, I had to pick a venue.

At least that part was easy. There was really only one choice for a venue, as far as I was concerned: a beautiful western resort about twenty minutes north of the ranch in the outskirts of Cave Creek. Behind Black Mountain in Carefree and nestled among gorgeous Sonoran Desert scenery, its rustic vibe was everything I wanted for this Big Event.

I made an appointment sometime during the beginning of February and headed up there to talk business. When I sat down with E, the event planner who was working at the resort at the time, we were in their stunningly beautiful Opera House, which seated something like 500 people and had high ceilings, an enormous stage, pillars on the sides of the room, chandeliers, and an elegant atmosphere.

"For your very first event, I would start small," E gently told me as I looked around at the Opera House with stars in my eyes. "You'd rather have a few extra people crammed in a small room than an enormous room with not enough people to fill it."

She talked me into walking back through the main building into a smaller banquet room so we could look around. It seated about 80, but it had floor-to-ceiling pillars of wood that looked amazing and big windows that made the room seem even larger. Plus, there were pictures of running horses on the wall.

I agreed to the smaller room, and over the next week E worked out a deal with me so that we only had to pay a $100 deposit upfront, then pay the full balance on the night of the event. I picked out a date that had been approved by Jim and Jean-August 8th-and told everybody we'd saved a date.

It felt like I'd just announced I was planning a wedding. But for all the work that was put into this event, I honestly think I could have.

The rest of February and March and April and May and June brought everything, most of which I did on the fly, in the spur of the same moment I realized something specific needed to be done. Creating flyers. Drafting social media hype. Contacting donors. Creating an Eventbrite account and signing up for ticket sales. Promoting ticket sales. Passing out flyers. Getting a committee of volunteers together. Calling and emailing for basket donations. Sending donation receipts and thank-yous and follow up phone calls and emails. Room setup. Deciding on the menu. Figuring out if we'd have a band or not. Working with a volunteer film crew to get a clip up and running for a brief showcasing during the presentation. Planning the presentation. Finding decorations. Getting clipboards and pens and name tags and a new cashbox and new marketing collateral to put on an "about" table.

By the end of June, we were gathering silent auction basket items. By July, we were putting baskets together with themes like Date Night, Family Fun, Spa Day, etc. Gathering more items. Printing out certificates. Creating more hype over social media. Spreading more flyers. Meeting at the resort every few weeks to go over room plans. Selling more tickets. Figuring out music. Figuring out AV equipment. Going back to the dollar store for ribbon and plastic wrap and cheap picture frames more times than I care to admit.

Sometime in July, knowing I was basically walking into this blindfolded, I decided to look up "How to run a silent auction." Thank god for Google. I read all about bidding sheets and fair market values and reserve amounts and bid increment minimums and minimum bid amounts and bidding registration and bidding waivers and check out processes. As a result of this research, I spent many frustrating nights creating spreadsheets that organized all the items into a comprehensible inventory and calculating start bids and making bidding sheets and trying to seem as though I knew what I was doing.

I couldn't have done it without my committee. Composed of a handful of volunteers who frequented the ranch, my committee was phenomenal. They helped get donations, put baskets together, promoted the benefit online, helped with the room layout, and kept baskets at their houses when I couldn't cram any more in my apartment. The four or five people who were there every step of the way were simply amazing. They would have done more too if I had been better at delegating tasks, which I wasn't.

August came. I literally didn't know where the time went. All of the sudden, the Big Event I'd masterminded nearly eight months before was a week away.

The weekend before the benefit, I spoke on the phone with a wonderful lady who was a friend of a staff member at the resort. She was an event planner and graphic designer, and she wanted to offer her assistance for the evening as a donation. Um, YES.

Three days out, the designer met me and my friend A-my partner-in-crime for the entire event planning process-at the resort. She had some amazing props to show us: Western baskets, pails, signs, and burlap *everything*. She offered to decorate the basket tables and make the programs and the table numbers. I was amazed. These were the little details I'd been too busy to think about, and here this lovely person was offering to swoop in on a 72-hour notice to tackle them for us.

Then, we met with our new event coordinator, J, to go over our final room setup plan and confirm a final headcount. On our contract and during all of our discussions with both planners, I had arranged to have between 50 and 75 guests, though more would be great if we could get them. Ticket sales from these attendees would cover the entirety of what we'd paid for the venue, food, etc., and then some. The majority of the fundraising would take place in the silent auction and donations.

The designer and A and I were chatting in the lobby that day, waiting for J to join us, when the receptionist called me over saying J was on the phone. I stood up-trailing dirt and hay all over the glistening lobby floor as I walked to the desk-and took the call.

"Sorry I'm running a bit late, I'm just headed down there now," she said. "But tell me what our headcount is so I can get your bill and bring that down with me."

"I just realized I never told you this morning," I said, inwardly cringing as I realized about ten million other things I hadn't done at that point. "Right now we're up to a hundred and five."

Silence on the other end of the phone. Then…

"*What?!*"

We had expected around fifty. Seventy-five at the very, very most.

But a hundred and five?

We were thrilled. Astonished. A hundred and five people may not seem like many to a large nonprofit organization, but for a small horse ranch's very first Big Event, a fancy fundraiser where tickets were eighty bucks each… it was incredible.

The big day came. Jean flew in from New York for the event. At the ranch that morning, everyone was excited.

I was nervous. After running the ranch in the morning, I got to the resort at noon to check into the room I'd reserved for the night so I wouldn't have to drive an hour home after the event and so I could store all the auction baskets safely before bringing them into the event room. My friend A met me at the resort around and the two of us went over the game plan a final time.

At 2pm the designer arrived and started to set up her gorgeous decor. She had flowers to go with her burlap along with pails and cute signs including one she set up in the lobby that pointed attendees in the direction of the banquet room. She spruced up the tables too, on which the resort had put beautiful lanterns as centerpieces along with bandana styled tablecloths. And fancy napkins.

At 3pm, the rest of my setup crew-volunteers at the ranch-arrived on the scene. I'd written out a plan for the volunteers and directed them as best as I could with my heart beating like a drum. While the volunteers laid out the auction baskets with their matching bidding sheets and set up the check-in paperwork and put together the Tierra Madre marketing table, our AV equipment guy and I worked with the equipment for 30 minutes to try to get our video clip up and running, eventually getting success.

At 5pm, everything was mostly ready to go. The resort staff stood by to get us anything we needed and started to make the food and I got my volunteers into position and made sure everyone knew what to do and then all of the sudden it was an hour later and where had the time gone? It was go time, and the guests started to arrive, and I had enough volunteers to run the registration table, and my plan for check-in somehow went smoothly, and suddenly the bar was hopping, and the room was filled with guests and laughter and waving and excited talking and hugs and craziness and movement and awe-struck faces, and a hundred and five people looked around at the gorgeous setup of the room and the beautiful baskets and the stunning tables all perfectly decorated and said, "*Wow!*"

It was perfect.

The silent auction bidding went smoothly. The food, according to everyone, was fabulous (I couldn't eat. I was too full of adrenaline). After dinner, we had our program and the AV equipment worked and the film clip of baby Sunny running in the arena went off without a hitch.

I started off the presentation with welcoming everyone and thanking those who had made the evening possible. I'd put together a list of names so I wouldn't forget anyone. After talking briefly about the ranch, I passed off the mic to C, a volunteer who was working with us to develop an equine coaching experience program at the ranch, and she spoke beautifully about the connection between humans and horses and how important our work was.

Then, I passed the mic to Jim.

He told everyone about the mission of Tierra Madre Horse Sanctuary and the story of how it came to be. Jim was a very eloquent public speaker, and he drew both laughter and I'm sure a few tears from the attendees with his words. I watched the crowd with a full heart as he spoke. Everyone I loved was in the same room: the volunteers and the friends of the ranch and some of our big donors and lots of acquaintances who came to visit from time to time and some new faces too. And everyone was there in support of the horses.

Jim finished talking about the ranch, but rather than giving me back the mic as was the plan, he turned to me, grinned, and then turned back to the crowd.

"Alexis doesn't know about this part in the presentation," he said. "But I have watched her plan this event for the past-what, how long has it been now? Six months? She's planned this event for a long time. This would never have taken place without her-"

Everyone applauded. Then-

"-and Jean and I have a little surprise for her."

Jim told everyone how my dream was to go back to London someday. I had visited once before, during a week-long study abroad trip several years back. Jean had donated two round-trip first class tickets to New York City as an item for the silent auction, and I had joked with them earlier that morning about how if they were tickets to London instead I would bid on them.

And Jim proceeded to announce that as thanks for my hard work in putting together the benefit dinner while simultaneously running their ranch, he and Jean would personally be buying my airfare back to London. All I had to do was pick the dates for a trip.

I don't even know what my reaction was, I was so numb with shock to register what had been said. But as the room burst into applause again and Jim and Jean broke into huge smiles as they saw my face, I'm pretty sure I cried.

It was all too much.

I thought I was all cried out at the end of the night, when most everyone had gone home after telling me what a wonderful night it had been, and A and I and a few others were left to clean up. I was sitting down for the first time in hours, relieved that the event was finally over even though I wanted it to go on longer, reliving every moment, savoring the success it had been, all while calculating our donations.

But when I finally closed our cashbox, and added the cash donations with what had come through online as payment for the baskets and came up with a final number, another lump rose in my throat.

I had hoped for five thousand, which would have been five times as much as the high end of the spectrum we'd received during open ranches.

That night we had raised nearly nine.

As the years went on, I put together more fundraisers than I could count for the ranch. We had three more benefits after that first one. Silent auctions, festivals, art fairs, raffles, more open ranches, car washes, bake sales, root beer float nights, online campaigns, mail campaigns, and more.

Not one of them beats that first benefit dinner and silent auction.

It was an event that managed to occur despite my extreme ignorance and utter lack of experience. One that we managed to pull off despite the fact that I didn't have the slightest idea what I was doing. One, for some reason, that Jim had trusted me to figure out.

But we did it. The teamwork that occurred, the number of people who jumped in with both feet to help… it still humbles me to this day.

As a side project for the benefit, I worked with a photographer who had frequented the ranch a few times and whose shots of the horses stopped my heart with their beauty. She took pictures of each herd member for me and I created a black and white collage that contained a picture of each horse. And Lee. We displayed it on a huge poster board at the event.

I remember walking up in front of all the tables at the start of the program and turning to see the horses' faces, so breathtakingly beautiful in black and white, looking out at me as I spoke to the crowd. Like they were there. Listening.

We're all here for you, I found myself thinking, as I looked over the heads of a hundred and five people at the pictures of the horses I loved more than anything in the world. *All of this is for you.*

CHAPTER TWENTY-TWO
THE AWAKENING

Running a horse ranch-especially a nonprofit horse ranch-is a bottleneck in the sense that the more you learn, the more you realize you don't know.

By the time we had that first benefit dinner and silent auction, I had been running the ranch for close to a year. The beginning of a skeleton structure had begun to emerge.

We had volunteers and a way of contacting them. I had written down a handful of rules that became policies that were followed consistently. We had updated waivers, receipts were organized by date into folders, and I was watching numbers in our bank account with regularity.

Every day I wrote on a whiteboard in the breezeway about our projects for the day and general reminders. We had begun volunteer orientations once a month. People knew what to expect. We had places for things, detailed lists for feeding and schedules for turnout which I wrote down in the volunteer handbook. Jim was easing into the idea of changes around the ranch being good.

And the benefit? It put a stake in the ground. It put our best foot forward as a nonprofit organization that had a bit of structure behind its name. We weren't just some tiny little ranch in the outskirts Cave Creek. People were beginning to notice us. We had gained more donors, and more volunteers.

But looking at our finances, our nonexistent board of directors, our average way of thanking people for their donations, and about a thousand other things…

I realized that I was somewhat okay at running a ranch: the day to day work of mucking and scrubbing and feeding and caring for the herd and giving volunteers a general idea of what to do, with a dollop of fundraising thrown in.

But I knew nothing-nothing-about managing a nonprofit organization.

This almighty ignorance was thrown into even sharper relief in September 2015, a month after the first benefit, when I attended my first ever Homes for Horses Coalition Conference in Dallas. The Homes for Horses Coalition is a coalition made up of members dedicated to ending horse slaughter. The Coalition increases collaboration and shares resources, knowledge, news, advocacy work, and networking channels to horse rescues and sanctuaries all over the country.

With Jim and Jean's blessing, I flew to Dallas and attended the conference. I proudly wore my Tierra Madre shirt and walked into the assigned conference room we had at the Hilton, taking in everything in utter awe.

People from dozens of dozens of rescues were there. Some had been in business for decades and had saved thousands of horses from slaughter. Or they had founded rescues that were famous for their high-profile seizures of horses from severe abuse and neglect. Or they were instrumental in passing legislature that protected horses from falling into the slaughter pipeline.

It was a two-day event, with an introductory networking session during a Friday late afternoon and a nine hour conference the next day. On Friday, I exchanged business cards with people more important than myself then proceeded to keep my mouth shut so I could listen to what everyone around me had to say. I listened to many conversations about fundraising and sponsorships and volunteer training and liability and marketing and barn upkeep.

The actual conference took place the next day. We all sat in the big conference room at the Hilton Hotel and listened to seminars. Community outreach and engagement. Courting major donors. Working with law enforcement. Increasing adoptions. Innovative marketing. All presented by big, big names like the ASPCA, Best Friends Animal Society, and the Humane Society of the United States, who had affiliates all over the country.

I was enthralled. I must have taken something like twenty pages of notes, scribbling as fast as I could in my notebook, not wanting to miss a thing. I couldn't get over that everyone in the same room as me was doing the same thing as Tierra Madre. We were all part of a bigger plan. We all had the same problems with raising enough funds. We all wanted more knowledge, more experience, and more wisdom. We were all there to save horses.

I flew back to Arizona the day after on a high, took all of my knowledge back to the ranch, typed up my notes and distributed them to Jim and Jean and my Solids. The research began. The brainstorming. The dreaming.

There was never a moment where it hit me like a flash, more like a gradual realization that deep down, I knew what I had to do next.

In looking at my notes, I knew I needed to know more. We all did. If the ranch was going to continue to grow and thrive, we needed to have even more insight not just into the equine rescue world, but the broader, deeper nonprofit world. If the horses were going to continue to call the ranch their forever home, we needed an active board of directors. We needed more donations and more donors. We needed more connections in the community. We needed to know more about how to get grants. We needed stronger fundraising campaigns. We needed highly trained staff who could plan events and manage volunteers and lead outreach efforts and build relationships.

I searched master's degrees sometime that fall and applied for a nonprofit management program at Arizona State University's School of Community Resources and Development. As part of the application, we each had to write a personal statement that explained why we wanted to complete the coursework, and what we hoped to gain from the degree.

I began mine very differently than most: "Thirty-odd horses inspired my interest in Arizona State University's Master of Nonprofit Leadership and Management program."

I was sitting in front of the barn when I read my acceptance letter.

And a few short months later, a new cycle of work began.

CHAPTER TWENTY-THREE
RESOURCES

Every year, an organization called Giving USA releases a report that breaks down charitable giving in the United States: how much was given to what kinds of charities, and by whom. In 2019, for example, total charitable giving amounted to $449.64 billion dollars, and this money was given to ten categorized destinations: education, health, international affairs, and so on. And the money came from four categories of contributors: bequests (which are when people leave money to charity in their wills), foundations, corporations, and individual donors. For the past five years, the biggest source of money has consistently been individual donors, who make up 70% of all charitable giving, according to the Giving USA reports.

I analyzed these reports a lot when I was in school. If there were hundreds of billions of dollars being given to charity every year in the United States, where did all the money go? Why did Tierra Madre always seem to struggle financially? Why did the entire equine rescue community always seem to struggle financially? People told us all the time that we should apply for grants. Well, what grants were available to us? How did we find them? And further, how did nonprofits get money from individuals, if they were the top contributor year after year? How did nonprofits sustainably bring in enough money to lead solutions to the problems they were founded to solve?

Well, as it turns out, as big a number as $449.64 billion dollars is, the vast majority of it doesn't trickle down to horses.

The top receiving category, taking in just under one third of all charitable giving year after year, is always religion. For the past five years, religion has taken home between 29% and 32% of all donations.

Then (again, consistently for the past five years), education has received 14% to 15% of charitable contributions. Then, human services at 12%. Gifts to foundations came in next, getting between 10% to 12%. Health was after that, at 8% to 10%, then public-society benefits at 7% to 8%, then arts, cultures, and humanities at 5%. Then, international affairs took in between 4% and 6% of the charitable pie. Individuals took home 2%.

At the very bottom of the list of recipients is a lump sum category called environment/animals. This category has consistently received 3% of all charitable giving since 1987, when data was first collected for this category. For context, 3% of $449.64 billion dollars amounts to just under $13.49 billion dollars, given by individuals and corporations and foundations and bequests.

Now, here's the thing about that environment/animals category: it includes *everything* that has to do with both the environment and animals: conservation and protection; environmental education; environmental beautification; pollution control; botanic/horticulture activities; zoos and aquariums; wildlife preservation and protection; humane societies; nonprofit veterinary services; and many more functions. When completely broken down, we're looking at three different kinds of recipients of charitable giving within this category: environment, wildlife, and domestic animals. All of these different causes get some chunk of that 3%.

But it gets even more complicated than that. The environment and animal rescue sectors have their layers, too. The line between wildlife protection and environmental conservation is blurred, and so is the line between helping domesticated animals and wild animals. For example, look at the two huge cornerstone organizations of animal rescue and welfare: the Humane Society of the United States and the ASPCA (the American Society for the Prevention of Cruelty to Animals). Their fights for animals include ending pet homelessness, stopping dog fighting, spaying and neutering, rescues and seizures from hoarding or abuse situations, public outreach and education, putting an end to puppy mills, improving conditions for farm animals, ending horse slaughter, lobbying, protecting wildlife, ending cruel wildlife captivity practices....

The list of extremely important and noble causes goes on and on. Three percent of almost $450 billion dollars is a lot of money, but looking at everything that money has to fund made me realize that the amount of money that goes to horse rescues and sanctuaries–while impossible to determine–is likely a miniscule amount.

I dug deeper. I looked up random horse rescues and sanctuaries across the country–mostly organizations I had interacted with at the Homes for

Horses Coalition Conference-and looked at both their sources of funding and their annual budgets. 501(c)(3) nonprofit charities are required to make their annual 990 tax forms available to the public, and for all legitimate nonprofits, that information can be found on a site called Guidestar.

The organizations I researched on Guidestar operated on shoestring budgets, with annual expenditures that ranged from $5,000 to a few hundred thousand at most. Some equine rescues did manage to take in a reasonable amount of funding and those rescues were not only able to save hundreds of horses every year, they provided programs to the community such as basic equine education; equine-assisted therapy programs, and riding/training seminars. They had revenue in the form of payment for these programs as well as their adoption fees that enabled them to continue their cycle of rehabilitation. And some of the larger rescues had been fortunate enough to receive grants, which typically came from either the ASPCA, or a family or community foundation, in the amount of anywhere from a few hundred to a few thousand dollars.

And oh, looking at those grants made my head spin.

Researching the organizations who gave those grants away, I found out that many of them liked to see the rescued horses be useful to humans in some way and only offered grant applications that were specifically for equine-assisted therapy programs or some other form of human-related activities.

Some grantors only gave money for euthanasia or gelding.

Some grantors only offered funding for urgent emergencies such as natural disaster damages, emergency hay for a rescue or sanctuary closing its doors due to severe financial hardship, or for a massive seizure case.

Some grantors didn't publish requests for proposals but rather invited organizations they thought were worthy to apply and simply did not accept any others.

Some grantors only accepted applications from rescues or sanctuaries who were accredited through the Global Federation of Animal Sanctuaries or the American Sanctuary Association or the Thoroughbred Aftercare Alliance.

And those applications? The process of writing those grants involved hours and hours of articulating careful and detailed answers to questions as well as uploading budgets and bylaws and the board of directors' information and program descriptions and pictures of the facility and more.

How did small, barely-functioning equine rescues and sanctuaries that didn't have the structure, staff, expertise, or time go after grants and get them?

But I discovered something else that struck me more than the work required to obtain grants and how difficult it was to get one. It didn't shock me, but it fascinated me.

Individual donors still made up at least 90% of all financial contributions in every rescue and sanctuary that I researched, Tierra Madre included. Individual donors made up the vast majority of an annual operating budget for an average horse rescue or sanctuary.

A large percentage of individual donors meant that a large population of people existed who gave what they could afford to a rescue or sanctuary that meant something to them. And their dollars added up. Many streams made a huge, powerful river.

That moved me. Deeply. The power of one individual was a singular action and a team effort all in one.

With far less than 3% of all charitable giving going to equine rescues and sanctuaries in the first place, sustainably bringing in money was going to be a challenging and daunting task no matter where the money came from.

And it had to be done. Just like stalls had to be mucked and waters cleaned when no volunteers showed up, resources had to be found amongst a pool from which thousands of others were taking. Hell, Tierra Madre had done it for years and scraped by.

But if there were people out there who were willing to donate what they had, and lots of them, then maybe there was hope that someday we could do more than just scrape by. Maybe we could find out how to better reach donors, speak to donors, connect with donors, and thank donors. Those were the resources that would help us thrive.

CHAPTER TWENTY-FOUR
STORYTELLING

One evening, during my fundraising and resource management class, my professor asked us to name the number one reason people donated to a nonprofit organization.

My peers and I threw out answers like a donor had a personal connection to a cause, or a donor wanted a tax break, or a donor trusted the organization to make an impact.

The answer?

The number one reason donors gave?

Donors gave because they were asked.

How they are asked would yield different results for different donors. Different generations preferred to be reached in different ways, and different personalities sought different acknowledgements. There were a lot of differences. There was no one-size-fits-all when it came to asking for money.

Professional, for-profit businesses quite often employ marketing teams to advertise their products and promote their services. Nonprofits will occasionally attempt this strategy as well in the form of fundraising, but only if they have the funds to obtain a decent return on investment. Social media. In-person mail. Emails. Newsletters. Crowdfunding. Events. Each solicitation required careful investment of time and manpower and resources. And money. It cost money to make money, after all.

Another time in that same class, my professor had us do an exercise. Each of us in the room already represented a different recipient of charitable giving with our individual studies. For example, one classmate worked for a health-based nonprofit; another for a nonprofit educational institution; and so on. Surprise, surprise, I represented the animal rescue sector.

Given what part of the nonprofit community we represented, my professor said, we would each have two minutes to give a fundraising pitch to the entire class for our respective organizations. Everyone would get a certain amount of play money, and we would all "donate" toward the pitches we liked best, essentially voting for whomever had been most effective.

She gave us a minute or two to think, then said, "Who wants to go first?"

One by one, everyone spoke for two minutes to fundraise for their nonprofits. My classmates were fiercely intelligent, and spoke eloquently. Most of them worked at professional organizations that had million dollar budgets, in offices with more than one full time employee and whose clients didn't head-butt them into fences if they wanted their faces scratched.

I panicked. I was no match for my incredibly gifted peers. My brain was scrambling as I listened to my classmates, trying to think of what I could say, until my iPad mini lit up with a text message and illuminated the picture on my lock screen.

I was one of the last to go. When one classmate sat down and my professor looked around for the next volunteer, I stood up, picked up my iPad-hands shaking-and walked to the front of the class.

I flipped my iPad around and held it up so everyone could see.

"This is Sunny," I said. "She's a mustang living at Tierra Madre Horse Sanctuary, and she just turned a year old in May. Only she wasn't supposed to reach her first birthday. She was very close to being one of the thousands of horses that go across the border every year to slaughter."

In two minutes, I told my class about Sunny's mom Rain, how we had saved the pregnant mare from a kill buyer the day before she was to ship to slaughter. I said that a donation would go toward the feeding and medical care of Sunny, her mom, and nearly thirty other horses who had nowhere else to go. Then, feeling a little defeated, I quickly sat down.

When all my classmates had given their fundraising pitches, everyone was given a set amount to "spend" and voted by donating to the categories they thought were most effective. My professor collected our papers, tallied the numbers, and wrote them on the board. To my shock, "Animals"-my category-received the most of the money votes.

"As you can see," my professor said, smiling when she saw what must have been my stunned face, "there's a tool that is very powerful when it comes to fundraising, and it was very effective this evening."

"Imagery?" I asked, referencing the picture of Sunny I had shown the class.

"That too," my professor said. "But that's not what I meant. You, Alexis, told a great story."

CHAPTER TWENTY-FIVE
MIRACLE

Sunny wasn't supposed to reach her first birthday. In fact, it was a miracle she was even born at all.

Sunny arrived at Tierra Madre in Rain's belly, in February of 2015, after we saved Rain from a kill buyer.

Precisely three months to the day she walked through our gates, a sad little pregnant mare, after months of guessing and waiting and preparing and anticipating, Rain started dripping milk in the late morning on May 13th. The entire Tierra Madre family-volunteers and supporters and Facebook friends and donors and neighbors-went insane with excitement. This foal was like nothing Tierra Madre had ever experienced. As a sanctuary, we were the last stop before horses joined the Great Herd. Never before had we witnessed a beginning.

I left the ranch in the morning at 11:30. I lived an hour away at the time, and I raced home so I could grab a bag of extra clothes and some snacks and make sure all my electronics were charged before speeding back to the ranch to set up camp outside Rain's stall. The vet we had then told us that horses usually gave birth at night, but I wasn't taking any chances. I wasn't going to miss that foal being born for the world.

By evening, Bill had come back to feed the kids their dinners and he set up a hauling trailer that was parked on the property in the breezeway for me-right outside Rain's stall-so I'd have a place off the ground to lay down. Jim put his couch cushions in there too so I had a nice setup. Around 6 o'clock I went out to get a pizza for Jim and I but every other moment, I was there in that trailer, waiting.

Around 8 or 8:15, when the ranch was dark and all the other horses still, I heard Rain pawing and groaning in her stall. Every five minutes I'd get out of my little makeshift bed to try to check on her. We had a baby cam which connected to an app on our phones, but about half the time it didn't work and wouldn't connect, and that night was no exception. But every time Rain saw me she'd stop.

So rather than having her see me and get scared during the early stages of labor, I changed tactics and went into the house where Jim was watching her on the one monitor we had that was hooked up to the camera and actually worked. By then it was just before 9 o'clock, and Rain had been pawing and groaning for almost an hour.

"She's really restless," I said as I walked in. Then I looked at the monitor. "She just went down!"

"Yeah, she's been doing that for a while. Getting up and down and up again. Let's stay in the house a while; now is the time she needs to be alone."

We pulled up chairs and watched the monitor. I called our ranch manager and told her to book it down to the ranch if she wanted to be there for the birth. My mom called and asked how everything was going, and right as I started to answer that Rain was down and seemingly groaning, Jim jumped and pointed. A hoof. A foal hoof.

We both ran out to the stall-Jim flipping on the dim barn lights-slowing when we got to Rain's stall, creeping around the corner to see Rain on the ground, sides heaving. She stood up once and flopped the other way, groaning quietly. The hoof we'd seen on the monitor was still peeking out.

There I was thinking we were in the early stages of labor, that it would be another few hours before any real action happened. We backed away as not to scare her and thought to wait for another few minutes then-

Then.

There came the head.

There it *was.*

I gasped when I saw it; it absolutely knocked the wind out of me. Jim grabbed my hand as we watched it slowly, steadily slide out, wrapped delicately in its milky sac. We stood there watching Rain in complete and total awe as she pushed and pushed and pushed until that tiny, perfect little head was followed by its tiny, perfect little body. Then that body met the Earth and Rain groaned again and lay her head down and rested and that little body lay quivering in the straw.

Out of nowhere.

Out of nothing.

There that baby was.

There *she* was.

Mere minutes after we'd run out of the house to make sure everything was okay.

After so much waiting. After so much excitement and anticipation.

There *she* was.

She peeked her little head out from the sac, nose twitching, lips nibbling at the air, and we laughed and cried as Rain turned her head back toward her foal and gently nickered in greeting, seeing her baby for the first time after nearly a year of carrying her.

And that baby blinked and looked around with the vastness of the world reflected in two liquid brown eyes.

Months and years later, when Jim told the story of the night Sunny was born he would sum it up with: "God was in the house that night."

Up until that point, I never understood why everyone called it "the miracle of life". To me, being born was the most ordinary thing in the world.

But that night I saw the wonder of life for what it was: a delicate little body held up on thin, shaky legs that grew steadily stronger by the minute and eventually jumped and kicked and bucked with the pure joy of being alive.

A balance of fierceness and gentleness.

A push to try to stand again and again and again.

A breathing, beating miracle.

CHAPTER TWENTY-SIX
SIMPLE JOYS

When everybody in the shed row whinnied as the feed cart came around.

When the Bermuda bales flaked off seamlessly and each flake was the perfect weight for each horse.

When it was 70 degrees outside and blue skies were above.

When the chores were done by 9am, the dinners were made, the carts were loaded, and we got to play with the horses.

When we got a new alfalfa squeeze that was beautifully green in the summertime.

When we danced in the sprinklers in the arena.

When we received a sizable donation when our medical bills were overwhelming.

When the kids raced back in forth in their stalls with excitement when they saw me coming with a halter.

When an open ranch brought several hundred smiling people out to the property to meet the horses.

When a new load of grindings or clean dirt was dumped onto the property.

When the tack room was swept and the grain buckets were wiped down and all the medical buckets were organized and put away.

When we got a new cart or rake.

When somebody dived into a bran mash and slopped bran and grain and sweet feed everywhere.

When we sat in the breezeway and talked and laughed and ate donuts or cake brought in for someone's birthday.

When a volunteer orientation group was eager to be there and asked a ton of questions and laughed at the horses' antics and was so excited they even applauded when I had wrapped things up.

When everyone else had gone home, and I got to wander around and whisper to the kids while they dozed or bring Sonora out to the arena to play.

When somebody happily kicked up their heels in the arena and bucked just for the sake of kicking and bucking.

When my emails were answered and the latest receipts had been sent out on my last work day of the week.

When Chance followed me around the arena and put his nose on my shoulder.

When I left for the day and all the gates were latched, and all the waters were filled, and everything was put away.

When I closed and locked the gate, secure in the knowledge that all of the kids were happily munching away at their lunches.

When I drove away knowing that everything in my home was at peace.

CHAPTER TWENTY-SEVEN
RECORDS AND MINDSETS

I kept medical records for each horse on the ranch in a giant plastic tub at my apartment. Annual exams, dental work, shot records, farrier trims, illness or injury... everything was there for each horse. We couldn't afford fancy barn management software so things were handwritten or printed out and stuck in a physical folder. One year, I even put lined paper in each horse's folder, brought them to the ranch each day, and cheerfully encouraged volunteers to write in the horses' journals whenever they could. (Imagine coming to a ranch to muck poop and be brightly told by the executive director that you could write essays if you wanted, too.)

I tried to go through each of the kids' folders every month or so, to organize the new receipts I'd throw on top of the tub each week and double check numbers. Before we had a singular vet who knew and took care of all the kids, it was helpful to know what antibiotic worked for what horse when they had an infection or who had received GastroGard in the last month or whatever.

Sometimes I had to take records out and put them in a binder titled "The Great Herd". That was always a knife in my heart.

The folders were all different sizes. Heighten's was an inch thick. Danny's was nonexistent, just a sheet tracking his farrier trims. Sedona's held a few pages, as did Rusty's. Studley's could be used as a paperweight, and Tater's had next to nothing.

In between the numbers and medical lingo on the records were the untold stories: the ones of pain and terror as well as relief and strength. Chiquita's record told the story of her slow, graduate decline due to laminitis. Jazz's told of his survival of the same disease. Buddy's shared the small quirk in his sinuses: we'd radiographed his entire head to find a tiny, insignificant tumor pressing on a sinus which explained why he sometimes had discharge from his left nostril. River's few pages told how she got her dimple in the middle of the face-when Suze nailed her in the nose and broke it one winter.

One of the more heartbreaking folders was Marvel's. An older paint gelding with laminitis taken from a neglectful situation, he was with us for five days one blazing hot August. By day two, it was apparent he had an impaction when he hadn't pooped once in over 24 hours. By day five-after three straight days of IV fluids and tubing and staying up with him all night to change out bags and hoping and pleading and praying-we ended his battle before he began to suffer.

Colic episodes. Radiographs. Blood panels. Questions. Answers. Nightmares. And triumphs.

And something else, too. Something else was reflected in those records and the numbers they carried:

Our commitment to the horses.

But not just our commitment to the horses to ensure that they received medical care. Tierra Madre ensured that they received *good* medical care.

On several occasions, Jim and I-and Tierra Madre as a whole-were questioned or even criticized publically for using the exemplary and simply magnificent veterinary office the ranch had used for over fifteen years and uses to this day. We were ripped apart time and time again for not trying to find a vet's office that would cut us cheaper deals for services. Someone even once suggested using medical students in lieu of veterinarians, since, "they would do it for free, for the experience."

Because we were a nonprofit, some people reasoned, we should be trying to skimp on medical care as much as humanly possible. We should be content with secondhand care that may or may not have been the best choice for the majority of our horses who had significant health issues. Because we were a nonprofit relying on public funds, we didn't have the right to spend a lot of money on medical care.

Honestly, that whole notion deeply offended me. It still offends me.

And my offense ran deeper than simply wanting the best medical care for horses who had survived enough already, for not wanting to risk the horses' health for the sake of saving a few bucks. No, it harkened to the mindset that many people have when it comes to funding nonprofit organizations in general: that nonprofits should only survive by scraping by on next to nothing.

Think about it. When Thanksgiving food drives occur, people clean out their pantries and throw out the expired food they don't want, but which is clearly fine for the less fortunate to eat. If people are going through their closets, sometimes they toss their old, stained, ripped clothing in bags and dump them at homeless shelters. And when some people hear of a nonprofit serving previously abused, neglected, injured, or surrendered horses, they show up unannounced with a truck bed full of junk they cleaned from their barns including broken halters, cracked buckets, and medication from the 1990s (yes, that happened at Tierra Madre on numerous occasions).

Nutritious, fresh foods that nourish those who are hungry. Brand new clothing that honors a person's dignity and keeps them warm. Needed supplies for a ranch that are new or at the very least gently worn and functional. Those things cost money. Those things are an investment. And god forbid if a nonprofit organization actually obtains them by spending money for them.

We didn't cut corners when it came to our horses' health. We cut corners wherever else we could. We scrimped and saved on just about everything. But we spent money where it mattered, where it best benefited the health of our kids.

Just as food banks need good food and homeless shelters need good clothing, our horses were no less deserving of good medical care, just because they happened to live at a nonprofit horse ranch. In fact, they were more deserving of it because there was more of a need for it.

And the reality is, if society continues to harbor the expectation that nonprofits should be content with the scraps, then real social change will never happen. Nonprofits exist to combat a problem. And without the resources they need to move forward from just tackling the symptoms, the root of each problem will never be addressed.

In fact, the same questions that we asked whenever one of our horses had a medical condition and we had to figure out our way forward are the same ones that nonprofits should continuously ask too:

Are we managing a problem?

Or are we leading a solution?

CHAPTER TWENTY-EIGHT
TEAMWORK

In the fall of 2016, Rain was diagnosed with acute laminitis.

She'd been moving stiffly for a few days. Her neck was thick, and-though she'd given birth to Sunny the previous year, she still looked pregnant. All bad signs, and which all pointed to endocrinopathic laminitis, which is a fancy way of describing laminitis that stems from a hormonal condition such as Cushing's Disease or metabolic syndrome.

Behind colic, laminitis is the number one killer of domesticated horses. It is a hoof disease that affects several parts of a horse's foot, most commonly in the front hooves. In laminitis, the laminae-strong, interconnected tissues that hold the coffin bone in place within the hoof capsule-break apart. This trauma to such sensitive membranes and blood vessels in the hoof causes the laminae to release the coffin bone, and this causes the loose coffin bone to rotate or sink within the hoof capsule. Not that anyone should ever let it get to this point, but the bone could potentially sink so far that it would push through the bottom of the hoof.

The disease is intensely painful for the horse and can mean a slow, excruciating end if not treated correctly and swiftly. And sometimes, even with the best possible treatment, by the time a diagnosis is made it's still too late. A lot of medical mysteries still shroud the nightmare that is laminitis.

Laminitis is a horror.

We were scared. Hearing that 'l' word was-far too often-a death sentence. So many others at Tierra Madre had joined the Great Herd at the mercilessness of laminitis, and for any chance of making it through, Rain needed help fast. She needed hoof support, a changed diet, medication, cushy footing, stall rest, and intensive, regular hoof trims. In this last regard, a partnership between a veterinarian and a farrier who knew how to treat and trim laminitic hooves would be critical.

Our vet, who had been Tierra Madre's official veterinarian for a few months at that point, very kindly told us she wanted to bring out a therapeutic farrier she knew to work with her on Rain's feet, instead of using our usual farriers. This therapeutic farrier would construct a special shoe for Rain based on the radiographs, she told us. He had expertise in working with laminitic horses and would be our best shot of helping Rain make a full recovery.

We trusted our vet completely. Jim and I agreed.

And a few days later, our vet showed up bringing the new therapeutic farrier with her. Just as it had been with her, I liked our therapeutic farrier right away. He was cheerful and took enormous care to explain everything he was doing for Rain, with great enthusiasm.

The first step in treating a horse with laminitis-once you catch your breath- is to do radiographs.

Lateral (outer side view) and dorsal (front view) x-rays showed how much the coffin bone had rotated and how much sole depth the horse had to worth with. The sole depth was the amount of space between the bottom of the hoof and bottom of the coffin bone, space that held essential sensitive tissue called corium. The more sole depth, the better. The less there was, the more perilous the situation.

We did Rain's radiographs at the ranch, in the breezeway, with a portable x-ray machine brought by our vet and her assistant. With the radiographs in front of her, and after completing a physical exam of Rain (which included watching her walk in a figure eight to see her shift weight in all directions) our vet could determine exactly how much of the toe or heel had to be trimmed, and what kind of support the hooves needed. A horse with longer hooves, with lots of toe, meant the laminae were stretched and strained. The point of a trim would be to ease that stress, so the laminae had a better shot of recovering, but it had to be done exactly right. Our therapeutic farrier studied the radiographs with her, and his intelligence and experience was such that he too knew exactly what needed to be done, at a glance.

That first time I watched our vet and therapeutic farrier work together was certainly not the last. Over the next several years, we would be hit with several laminitis diagnoses, some more serious than others. And the pair of them were called every time to do everything they could to help save our kids.

They were our call to action, our only shot of saving our horses from laminitis. And they delivered.

They would intently study radiographs together and discuss the best way forward. Depending on the horse's confirmation, and the degree to which the coffin bone had rotated, and how much sole depth there was to work with, and the condition of the hoof wall, and the existence of a laminar wedge, and a thousand other details that went over my head… they would make a game plan.

When they worked on Rain, she got a special clog handcrafted from plywood with a fiberglass tape product cast that provided extra cushioning for her feet and which rocked forward to provide breakover support. Our vet also pulled blood on her to test insulin levels, and prescribed Thyro-L as well as pentoxifylline and bute. She was to be on stall rest for a minimum of six weeks.

But not every horse they worked on received the same treatment as Rain. There were banana shoes. Heart bar shoes. Special booties. Clogs. Impression material. Treatments were often combined with Manuka honey or thrush buster or special topical hoof ointment, as needed. The trim would be specialized to each horse, and some of the time, we did part of a trim one day then wait a week to finish it as not to cause too much of a drastic change to the horse's already uncomfortable movement.

They treated kids with other severe hoof problems too, not just laminitis. Hudson, who struggled with his feet on and off, got a shoe fitted perfectly to his club foot, with extra support in the heel. Buddy, who once had a deep abscess for over a month, received a hospital plate that protected the sole while it surfaced and drained. Sometimes in treating somebody, one front hoof would get one treatment while the other front hoof got something else entirely. There were so many options, so many moving parts and pieces to the hoof that it seemed like so much could go wrong… and yet they got it right every time. They had to try. Our therapeutic farrier once said, "No hoof, no horse."

There was always laughter, chatter, joking and storytelling in the breezeway. Some of the best days-despite the circumstances under which they were there-were the days I saw our vet's truck and our therapeutic farrier's trailer pull in through our gates. To simply be in the presence of experts who loved horses and wanted to help us help them was incredible.

And each and every time their work was finished, and we led their patient who had limped to the breezeway back to his or her stall, that horse walked with more ease. More comfort. Sometimes, with even a spring in their step and with brighter eyes.

Six weeks after Rain received her initial diagnosis, her laminitis was declared no longer active.

And months later, she ran in the arena again.

To me, what our vet and therapeutic farrier were able to do for our horses was nothing short of miraculous.

To me, their teamwork was magic. And to the horses, their teamwork was very often the difference between life and death.

CHAPTER TWENTY-NINE
DEAR RANDOM VISITOR

Dear Random Visitor,

Hello, and thank you for coming to Tierra Madre! We are so glad you are here-without warning, and in full expectation of entertainment-and we can't wait to get started making your visit as memorable as possible.

To make things easier for you, we've compiled a ten-step guide to touring our nonprofit horse sanctuary that will instruct you on the proper way to go about this whole visit thing.

Enjoy!

Step 1: Walk in without an appointment. Rest assured, there are always dozens of people scattered around the ranch at any time, and every single one of them will be glad to drop everything to show you around and answer your questions. None of the volunteers have assignments or chores to be completed, we have no programs to run or groups to oversee, and because we have no timeframe for completing any tasks, you are the only thing that matters. Please, don't be shy. And if that gate is locked? Just stand outside of it and honk your horn or yell. We'll come running. Don't mind that sign that says, "Tours by appointment only."

Step 2: Go directly up to the horses and start petting them. Instead of finding the human in charge to speak with first, be sure to go right up to the horses you've never met and immediately begin petting their faces. All horses are great with strangers mauling them, and we don't have any herd members with behavioral/aggressive issues. And your kids want to pet the pretty ponies? All at once? Go for it! The more, the merrier.

Step 3: Let your kids run wild. Speaking of your kids, children should be encouraged to let loose at a horse ranch. After all, it's outdoors! All horse ranches strongly encourage small children to run, scream, jump up and down, and make quick movements, particularly around the horses. After all, horses are completely placid around loud, energetic, fast-moving humans, so your kids will never be in any danger around these prey animals with strong survival instincts. Don't worry about supervising those kids, either. We have babysitters scattered all over the property with nothing to do besides care for your children, just for you.

Step 4: Interrupt horsemanship lessons. Is a manager giving a brief lesson to a volunteer about the correct way to lead a horse? Is she showing a group how to clean hooves? Be sure to walk right up to her and begin talking as though she's not there by describing what you see wrong with the horse you met five seconds ago. Everybody will appreciate the concern, and applaud you for your boldness in speaking your mind. It's important for us to know that you, a complete stranger, know far more about our herd than we do.

Step 5: Feed the horses anything you see on the ground. Don't worry, none of our horses are on vet-approved, restrictive diets and all hay is exactly the same. Go ahead and scrape up whatever bits of hay you find on the ground and offer it to the horse directly in front of you. Furthermore, feel free to bring whatever kind of fruit you have at home-bananas, pears, apricots, etc.- to feed to the horses without asking. Horses can eat apples so they should be able to have unlimited quantities of other fruits, right?

Step 6: Give us lots of advice. The words, "You know what you should do?" are music to our ears! You're wearing cowboy boots and rode a horse on a trail ride once so you've got this whole horsemanship thing down. Be sure to describe to the humans in charge everything we're doing wrong, in detail. Don't leave anything out about horses or our nonprofit structure itself because rest assured we have no idea what would make our nonprofit better ourselves. After all, we have all the time, manpower, energy, and money in the world to make anything we want happen. We are just waiting for you to tell us what to do.

Step 7: Discipline our horses. Do you see a horse doing something you don't like or find weird? Did you watch a YouTube video once about training horses? Walk right into that horse's stall and start correcting their behavior! Ranch management will appreciate you keeping tabs on our herd. None of our horses have quirks, medical problems, behavioral issues rooted in years of abuse, dislikes, or fears of which you need to be aware, so go right ahead. Again, *you*, visitor, know more than we do.

Step 8: Wear heels and expensive clothes. Close-toed flats are so old-fashioned, and horse ranches are the perfect place to bust out that $2,000 vest that can't be dry-cleaned or thrown in the wash. When you visit a horse ranch, take the time to dress up. The ground is very flat and clean around a horse ranch, and there is no chance at all you might ruin your shoes walking around. While you're at it, don't wear a hat or sunscreen and don't even think about bringing your own water.

Step 9: Ask to ride. What else are horses good for, right? Whenever you stop by, be sure to ask the humans to saddle up the nearest horse so you can leisurely stroll around the property. Because all of riding is just sitting on a horse, it's the easiest thing in the world and all horses absolutely adore being ridden. Know what you're doing in the saddle and don't need an instructor? Don't hesitate to ask us if you can stop by at your convenience, at any time of the day, and saddle up one of our horses on your own, whether or not we're there. *Of course* we'll say yes.

Step 10: Last but not least, don't offer a donation. Talk about insulting! Horse ranches are made of money, nonprofit horse ranches even more so. As you leave, don't even think about giving a few bucks to the humans as a tax-deductible donation as a way of saying thank you for our time for making your experience worthwhile. After all, horses aren't that expensive.

Thank you so much for stopping by, and we absolutely cannot wait to see you again soon.

Warm regards,

Tierra Madre Management

CHAPTER THIRTY
CHANCE

A few years in to my role as director of Tierra Madre, I was still really the only one handling Chance.

Two or three others were able to halter him and walk him if I wasn't there. Bill-who knew the horses more than anyone-Jim, and our ranch manager could get close to him too. But other than them, nobody else was permitted to walk him or even get near him. He still lunged at people over the fence. He was domineering, sensitive to nervousness, and trusted next to no one.

And he had every reason for it. Being abused for the first four years of his life had left permanent scars, and not just the bumps on his nose from a stud chain.

He had been abused through the fences of his stall. Because he had been confined to such a small space, he'd been unable to run from the danger that presented itself in the form of beatings and loud noises and angry voices and god knows what else. So, he did the only thing left for him to do: he fought back. Years after landing safely at Tierra Madre, he was still triggered when approached through a fence, and he lashed out at anyone who got too close.

For five years, I talked to him from outside his stall.

From that first summer at Tierra Madre up until the day it was decided I would take over for the woman who ran Tierra Madre in Jim's absence five summers later, we got to know each other through a fence.

And as I saw him through his barricades, he saw me through mine.

And the day Jim gave me the job of running his ranch, I thought, *the director needs to handle every horse.*

So I fetched a halter, went into the tack room, made a mash, placed it on the ground a little away from the barn, marched up the field hallway, threw my apprehension to the winds, and walked into his stall.

Chance didn't react with surprise or fear or anger or anything. He just stood and studied me.

"Come on, brother," I said, and I shook the halter a bit so he could see it. "Let's go get a mash."

He walked up to me at once and put his head in my halter.

I love mashes, was his response, and away we walked together for the first time, and we never looked back.

Chance needed to know what to expect every time he interacted with me, so I kept things very simple. Walk into his stall. Halter him. Walk him to the arena for turn out. Unhalter him. Repeat in reverse. We went to the treat can on the way home from the arena, which he loved. Walk back to his stall. Unhalter him. A swift move to quietly leave his stall once he'd been unhaltered. An occasional pet on his face. But nothing more. He'd put people in the hospital for much less than a pet on his nose. If he was happy with our arrangement, I reasoned, then I wasn't going to change anything.

And I was happy with our arrangement, too. Just being near him, close enough to him to feel the warmth of his skin or his breath on my arms when he nibbled at me filled my heart with joy.

"Hi, baby boy," I'd call up the hallway when I was walking his way with a halter, and he'd immediately start banging on the fence with a hoof, eager to get out. "Are you ready?"

He'd respond with a nicker or an impatient neigh. He couldn't get his halter on fast enough. He wanted to charge down the hallway in excitement to get to the arena to play. It was my greatest pride, walking him down the hallway and unhaltering him in the arena and watching him trot off, knowing that he was comfortable with me.

He was happy. Over the years, I watched his fear melt away to reveal contentment that we hadn't seen at for his first four or five years at Tierra Madre. He looked at people-from a distance-with interest.

Over the years that followed our first walk together, we slowly tested each other's boundaries and pushed at trepidations ever so slightly. If he tried to drag me somewhere, I made him stop before letting him go to wherever it was he wanted to go, but on my terms. He knew exactly what he wanted, and wasn't afraid to go for it. And whether it was pinning his ears at a stranger or throwing his head up suddenly to do battle if something startled him, he knew exactly what he needed to do to feel safe.

Just be who you need to be, I told him, over and over again. *And that is enough.*

Then, one January on a cold morning, Chance started limping horribly.

He could barely walk on his hind right and all signs pointed to an abscess, which was problematic in that we didn't have a tranquilizer gun or somebody willing to lose a couple of limbs in order to touch his hind feet, which had never been attempted in all his years of living at Tierra Madre. He had never had a serious problem with his hooves before, and because his stall was so big and he got so much exercise there and in the arena, we never had to trim them; like horses in the wild, the terrain wore his feet down for us.

But I couldn't just sit and do nothing. I gave him bute in a mash to ease his discomfort but watching him try to power through the pain was too much. I texted a video of him limping to our vet and she texted back and said she would be out that day to see him.

Because Jim was in New York that week, I was at the ranch alone when our vet drove through the gates in the late afternoon. She got out of the truck and started unpacking her hoof care kit and drawing a sedative like it was any other horse while her technician started firing up the x-ray machine.

I was nervous.

"I've never asked him to stand still in his stall before," I said anxiously as she put the cap on her needle. "We have a routine and he gets upset if we stray from it."

"Well, why don't you go in and halter him first, like he's used to, and we'll just go from there. I'd like to do it in his stall, I don't think he'll be able to walk out here."

"But, like, it's Chance," I said, incredulous. "He's bitten people before for getting too close to him outside his stall, let alone for trying to put a needle in his neck."

"Let's just try."

"I'm just worried he's not going to cooperate, and I don't want to do anything that's going to scare him...he doesn't know you all that well-"

"Listen," our vet said gently, picking up her hoofcare kit and facing me. "I've worked with horses my whole life. I founded a rescue where I dealt with horses that no one else could get near. I hear you, I hear what you're saying. I'm going to be careful. I'm going to work slowly and I'll stop if things get out of hand. But I'm not going to *not* try. I want to at least give him a chance. Okay?"

She was so calm and confident that my next argument died on my tongue. I walked up the hallway, went in to Chance's stall and haltered him.

Expectantly, he started to move forward, limping terribly on his hind right, and I tugged the lead rope back a bit to make him stop.

"We're going to stay here," I said to him quietly, as our vet and her assistant started walking up the hallway.

"Can you see if he'll back up and stand still over there?" our vet asked, pointing to the back of his pen as she slipped through the gate.

"I-I can try. I haven't asked him to do that before."

With her not far from him, Chance pinned his ears at her and made a move as though to bite her. Our vet reached out her hand. "Can I try him for a sec?"

I gave her the lead rope and she calmly put her hand on the cheek piece of the halter, to keep him from lunging at her, and walked him around in his stall.

He fought her. He didn't want to stay still and he wasn't sure about the new human who had taken over his lead and a few times, he lunged at her in warning. Our vet calmly moved around him in a dance, deescalating, deflecting, asking him to move this way and that then to back up and then to stop.

Around and around they went until it became clear that Chance wasn't afraid; he just simply wasn't used to not getting his way. But he was no match for our vet, who quickly and smoothly got a needle into him with the sedative, and she stood patting him gently as he got sleepy.

And before I could process what had happened, her assistant had come in and they had begun taking radiographs.

"He almost seemed like he was throwing a tantrum," I said in astonishment as our vet worked.

"He is a very pushy horse," our vet answered, smiling a little. "You have to challenge him. You have to push back a little so he learns manners. And learns to interact with other people. And that things that happen in his stall aren't bad."

When the radiographs yielded no significant findings, our vet got to work digging in his foot, where, sure enough, she popped the mother of all abscesses. She dressed it and bandaged it and suggested she come out the next day with our therapeutic farrier-who had taken up all our farrier work at that point-to drug him again so he could get his feet properly trimmed.

The sedative our vet had given Chance was fast acting, and as the technician finished getting the last of their things out of his stall he was starting to shake his head and stir. Our vet took his lead rope, rubbed his face lightly, and said, "That feels better now, doesn't it?"

Chance blinked and studied her, then flicked his ears back slightly. She responded by scratching his neck.

"See, look, come here," she said to me. "He likes this, right here." She kept scratching him and to my surprise, Chance's lips quivered and he stared straight ahead, stretching his neck out just enough to make me realize he was enjoying being patted. Our vet moved her hand and let me scratch him too.

"We left him to himself for so many years because that's what he needed," I said, more to myself than to our vet. "But maybe it's time to do more."

"He definitely has his challenges, don't get me wrong," our vet said. "But he'll never learn differently if he doesn't have the opportunity to learn."

I decided two things, right then and there as the sun was setting and our vet and her technician packed up their materials and a newly abscess-free Chance-once deemed fully awake-tore into his dinner.

First: I decided that I was going to challenge Chance, like our vet had said. I was going to push him, bit by bit. Take him step by step out of his comfort zone. Show him an entirely new world of interaction and opportunity.

Gently, lovingly, I would do this.

I knew I had to be the one to do it. When given the right person, Chance wouldn't react to new things with fear. He would react with curiosity, and perhaps a bit of a tantrum. But the thought scared me as much as it exhilarated me. Getting Chance comfortable with human touch? Showing him how to lunge, to pick up his feet, to stand still to be brushed? Letting him learn how rewarding it was to listen?

It was going to happen. I had just learned how to make it happen.

I decided on a second thing that day.

I decided that come what may, I was never going to doubt our vet again.

We started slowly.

We drifted from the routine bit by bit, slowly extending our walks to and from the arena to up the driveway, to the round pen, down the shed row.

When he stood at the treat can, I got a brush and groomed him for a minute or so at a time. I started touching his legs, knees, going down to his hooves and squeezing his fetlocks. A few weeks later, I was lifting up his front feet. A few weeks after that, I was cleaning them out with a hoof pick.

He didn't fight so much as he reacted with curiosity, just like I suspected. He didn't know what I was asking him to do when one day, in the round pen, I turned him to the left, faced his hindquarters, and raised my right hand to encourage him to move forward in a circle around me. Or he didn't know what I wanted when I stopped him then moved to his side to put a hand on his withers to groom him.

Sometimes he did know what I was asking, and didn't want to listen because he knew what he wanted, damn it, and he was going to get it. He was pushy, after all. My heart always melted a bit when he glared at me with impatience but listened to me anyway. He was opinionated, but he wanted so badly to try. He was fiercely intelligent, and he wanted me to know it.

"You're so good with him," one of my Solids told me one morning as I came back from walking him back to his stall.

"He's good for me," I said, and I meant it.

Because working with Chance wasn't quite like working with any other horse on the ranch.

When he threw up his head in apprehension, I saw my own walls I'd built during the months I was stalked and molested by a classmate at my high school in Florida when I was fifteen.

When his eyes moved warily to glare at a new person who approached him, I saw my mistrust of people that had been embedded in me as a teenager, when I'd endured five years of emotional abuse at the hands of my stepdad.

When his eyes flickered with confusion and fear, I heard the screaming from across my house at how worthless I was, how nobody would ever love me, yelled at me enough times over the years to make me believe it.

I understood the unlearning that had to be done after being taken away from abuse.

And every time Chance pawed at the ground with unease, every time he pinned his ears, every time I felt his nervousness radiating from deep within... I told him it was okay.

It was okay to do what he needed to do to feel safe.

It was okay to be afraid.

It was okay to not want to let the world in.

The world is a scary and uncertain place.

And sometimes it is very dark, and it doesn't seem that light will ever shine through.

And there were times I couldn't differentiate between the words of comfort that I would tell Chance, and words I would tell myself.

The world went on around us on those mornings when we walked around the ranch, just the two of us, taking in everything. Some days were harder for us than others. And some days he walked beautifully, carefully backing up or turning or stopping when I asked, joy in his eyes when I praised him.

Most of the time during our walks, he liked to stop halfway to the front gate and just stand in the wood chipped driveway, looking around. I always stopped with him and waited until he was ready to keep going. At first, I often thought he paused because he was fearful of the volunteers' cars that were parked up front, or because he heard a sound on the dirt road beyond the gates. But he never seemed afraid. He just wanted to stand still for a while.

"What are you looking at, baby boy?" I murmured to him one day, as he stood for a long time, blinking in the golden light.

The morning, he answered. *It's great, isn't it?*

That day, like most Arizona days, the sky was blue overhead. The birds were singing. M'Stor and Hudson were in the arena kicking up dust as they ran around.

I looked at Chance. Unlike most of the other horses' eyes, his eyes are a golden, lighter brown.

"Yes," I answered him softly. "It's really great."

He nudged me and allowed me to pat his neck, and we continued our walk up the driveway.

Every now and then during our walks, I would think back to the day we first met, when he pinned his ears and banged the lower bar of his stall gate over and over with his hoof, telling me to stay away.

I found that I never dwelled on that memory for too long.

Because when I was with Chance, the past didn't matter. His, or mine.

We were together, and it was morning.

CHAPTER THIRTY-ONE
FAIR

Sometimes, at the end of a morning, it felt like I had failed spectacularly at running the ranch that day.

Sometimes it was because I'd pissed someone off by not taking extra care to be nice and sensitive to their feelings when I asked them to do something. Or because I had only a few seconds to ask them to do a project but I requested it done a certain way, without explaining why. Or because I had to explain why their advice wasn't helpful or appropriate for our situation.

Sometimes it was because Jim was in a bad mood because our bank account was low, or because the manure dumpster pickup was running late, or because one of the kids had an unexpected abscess or an infection.

Sometimes, at the end of a morning, it felt like I was holding the ranch together by a thread. Those were the days, far more often than I care to admit, I'd stay behind when everyone had gone home and Jim had gone to the store, and I'd go over to a secluded corner of the ranch-usually by Chance's stall-to sulk.

And I would think:

"It's not fair."

Sometimes, the volunteer schedule I would painstakingly put together would fall apart one day when one volunteer called in sick, and one more just didn't show up, and another had an appointment she'd forgotten about, and another decided she'd come the next day instead, and I would be on my own to scrub all the water tubs and do all the turn out and do all the feeding and make all the dinner mashes and administer all the medicines and load all the carts and I would think:

"It's not fair."

Sometimes, the end of an open ranch fundraising event would only yield a hundred dollars and only a handful of people after I had busted my ass for months to make it happen and my volunteers had worked so hard for such an awful payoff. And I would think:

"It's not fair."

Sometimes, I said it out loud.

And one time, Jim told me the story of a man he'd once known in New York, who had children who often said the same thing, and this man had responded to them in this fashion:

"Fair?" he would say to his kids in outrage. "*Fair*? Fair is where you go to see the pigs."

CHAPTER THIRTY-TWO
SURVIVAL MODE

In summer, when the temperature was 100 degrees before the sun was even up, we entered what I called survival mode.

The volunteers got to the ranch at the crack of dawn. I was lucky if I had two or three of them with me during those heat waves. Having four or five was incredible. Six or more? We were all in heaven, because the work would get done that much faster. Stalls were mucked as fast as humanly possible and water tubs were scrubbed at the speed of light and hay was pulled down to load the carts for lunch before we were wiped of energy.

We were in tanks, shorts, hats.

We had bandanas tied around our necks to keep the dust out of mouths and to wipe our sweaty faces.

I passed out sunscreen and made sure the fridge was stocked with water bottles and Gatorades. Heat exhaustion warnings were posted on the huge whiteboard in the breezeway.

I walked around with a spray bottle, telling the volunteers with pink faces to sit down and drink water.

The misters and the fans ran 24/7. The waters were topped off every hour. The sprinkler was turned on in the arena. After 9am, the horses stayed in their stalls.

We did medical care, made the dinner mashes, fly sprayed the horses, and washed salty backs. And that was it. I forbade any kind of labor intensive projects.

I wrote "SURVIVE" on the small white board where I put each day's to-do list.

The sun beat down as we fed lunch early then took shelter, drained. It could as hot as 108 degrees by 10:30am. In the afternoons, the horses stood still as statues under their shade structures and misters, with only their tails swishing the flies from their backs and legs and their heads shaking occasionally. The misters cooled them, but they conserved as much energy as they could by not moving.

The next day, we did it all again. And again. And again. Arizona summers are brutal, but the heat waves were the worst. Some days, it was all we could do to keep moving forward.

To put one foot in front of the other. To survive.

CHAPTER THIRTY-THREE
WE WIN THESE

In the early years of Tierra Madre, our veterinarian at the time coined a phrase that we would come to use each and every time we fought tooth and nail for a horse's life.

We win these.

Even when the battle looked helpless, even when the odds were stacked against us, we didn't give in. We didn't give up. We fought with everything we had, with the belief and the hope and the prayer that we were going to win.

We win these.

Sometimes this phrase-this conviction-was all we had.

And I never clung to it as much as we did one late afternoon in the spring of 2017, the day after our Help A Horse Day fundraiser, when I was home working on receipts and Jim called me to tell me Heighten was going crazy.

Kicking at the fence. Pawing at the ground. Pacing in his stall like a maniac. Refusing food.

Colic.

Banamine had been given. The vet had been called. Someone was on the way.

I got in my car and rushed to the ranch. Bill and I got there within minutes of each other and helped Jim hose Heighten down and walk him in circles around the arena while we waited for the emergency vet. At one point, because he kept trying to go down no matter what we did, we turned him loose in the arena and let him roll. He rolled then got himself up, but he resumed his pacing and pawing.

He was nervous and agitated, but the banamine started to kick in and he began to act more calmly. He even took a small treat from Jim, which was the ultimate test of seeing if horses were feeling better after they'd been unwell.

The emergency vet pulled up around feeding time. Despite a relatively normal rectal exam and the fact that he was somewhat more like himself, we decided to have the emergency vet tube him anyway since she was there.

"We're not taking a chance with Heighten," Jim said stoutly, to general agreement. Heighten had had severe problems with colic in the past. Not tubing him could mean disaster.

We were all feeling more at ease as the emergency vet tubed him, which took next to no time under sedation. Then, with a tube of Gastrogard in him and a freshly cleaned out feeder (it's dangerous for horses to eat when they're not fully awake), we put him back in his stall and hypothesized that perhaps he had an ulcer that had flared up and caused sudden pain in his gut. And Heighten, being the sensitive horse he was, reacted to the discomfort with anger and bewilderment.

"Keep an eye on him," said the emergency vet as she got all of her supplies together and prepared to leave. "I'm on call all night, so give me a ring if anything goes wrong."

We nodded and thanked her and she left.

With Heighten on the mend, Bill went to feed all the kids their dinners and Jim and I talked about getting Heighten back on a daily preventative dosage of Gastrogard. Then I left for the night.

Or so I thought.

I was in Target, grabbing some things for dinner, when my phone rang again. My heart dropped when I saw Jim's name.

"It's Heighten," he said as soon as I answered. "He's bad again. The same as he was before he was tubed."

Shit.

I sped back to the ranch. The sun was setting as I trotted up the wash to the driveway between the barn and the arena, where Bill was walking a visibly distressed Heighten.

Pawing. Refusing to eat. Looking around anxiously. Pawing again on the dirt. And again. And again.

That damn pawing.

I hope I go the rest of my life without hearing that awful sound.

I could see it in Heighten's eyes as he looked around: *Something is wrong. Please, help me.*

Jim had gotten the vet back on the phone. She was at another colic emergency, of all things, but said she'd be there as soon as she could.

I texted our ranch managers and let them know what was going on before taking Heighten to the arena so he could walk around on his terms. As it was getting dark, right before the vet came gain, he lay down and looked somewhat comfortable (head up, looking around), so we let him stay down.

But just as the emergency vet pulled up, he put his head down and started twitching. Whether the pain was that bad or he was trying to get back up, I don't know, but it almost looked like his body was seizing.

"Doc!" I yelled and she came hurtling out of her truck. The words, "Let's try to get him up," weren't even out of her mouth before Heighten had-in one astonishingly powerful movement-pushed himself off the ground and stood before us. He was shaking, and he started to paw again.

Bewildered, I grabbed his halter and put the lead rope back on him. The vet examined him again. Listened for gut sounds. Heart rate. Rectal exam. Something was wrong.

"It's like we never even tubed him," Jim said to her. "I'm thinking-"

"Yep," said the emergency vet, and I felt my heart drop again.

I'd heard of intravenous bagging before. I'd never actually seen it happen.

Over a decade ago, Heighten had colicked and had been bagged all night long in an effort to save his life. Jim stayed up with him all night and said it wasn't until dawn that he knew Heighten was going to live.

We were about to go through the same thing. And we had no idea of the outcome.

We brought Heighten to the front half of Chiquita's stall, which was located at the western end of the barn closest to the shed row and above which hangs a lead rope from the rafters that Jim said he hated with a burning passion. I walked an increasingly frantic Heighten in circles outside of it while Jim and the vet got a ladder and hung two bags of fluids from the lead rope. Then, after a good amount of sedation, Heighten calmed down and we brought him inside so the vet could insert a catheter in his neck, with a port for more sedatives and which hooked up to the bagged fluids above him. He would receive fluids, intravenously, all night long.

And, god love them, at that time our two ranch managers showed up right as we were attaching hoses to ports and the vet was sewing in the catheter, around 8pm. They were both nurses and while Jim and I gave each other a look of confusion as the emergency vet explained how to change the bag and clamp the fluids on and off, those two nodded and assured us when the time came to change everything they'd be on it.

With the first two bags of bolus fluids set, the vet left the ranch for the second time and Jim, our managers, and I settled down in chairs outside Chiquita's stall (Chiquita herself shut safely in the "outer" portion of her stall) to watch our boy.

Under sedation, Heighten was very calm and while he walked around a bit in the unfamiliar stall, he seemed worlds better than he'd been just a few hours before. He watched us while the four of us sat just beyond the stall door and talked and drank some leftover soda from the event the day before. I stole a few pieces of turkey from Jim's fridge and shared them with Lee, who curled up at my feet.

It was dark then and the weather couldn't have been more than 75 degrees. The stars were out and the crickets were chirping and the night was warm and perfect and as I sat there, watching Heighten improve steadily, all of us talking comfortably, I thought that we were out of the woods.

We won, I thought happily. *He's going to be okay.*

At 10pm, I assured our managers, who ran the place on Mondays during my office days, that all was well and that they should go rest up before they had to be back in the morning. Their hearts were so big that I know they would have stayed all night, but with some assurance, they decided with Heighten acting more himself, it would be okay to leave. They changed the IV bags before they did, showed us how to change them ourselves again, and with two full bags of fluid in Heighten and another two at a slower drip on their way into his system, we all hoped for the best.

Jim and I sat watching Heighten for a few minutes longer after they left and I kept thinking I'd rise eventually and get in my car and go home too.

I don't know what possessed me to keep sitting in that chair. Instinct, maybe.

Because around 10:30 or so, Heighten started pacing again. Pawing. He lay down once-the spiraled tube connecting the IV bags to his catheter stretching as he did-then got up again and resumed his anxious pacing.

We caught him with some difficulty and gave him some domosedan. He calmed down and I took the opportunity to untangle the IV tube. Still pawing. Still hurting, somewhere, somehow. Sometime between 11 and 11:30 we went in to give him another sedative-xylazine-in the port in his catheter. The emergency vet had left us a few needles and warned us, "If you stab yourself with the xylazine, call 911."

I kept Heighten as still as I could while Jim carefully gave him the xylazine then we got out of the small stall to give Heighten his space. He lay down again, this time comfortably.

At 11:45 we got the vet back on the phone to give her an update. At midnight, I left the ranch for the vet's office to get some more sedatives in case we needed them.

I pulled up to the back of the clinic where the emergency vet was replenishing her truck.

"How is he?" she asked as she gave me the bag of drawn sedatives. I sighed.

"He's still pawing," I said. My voice shook. "Still hooked up to the bags though. He keeps pacing."

The emergency vet look at me anxiously. "You're doing everything possible for him," she said. "Call me with any updates, okay?"

When I got back around a half hour later, Heighten was on his feet and calm again. Despite having the new sedatives, we agreed that we wouldn't sedate him again in the hopes that if he had another attack of pain he would work through it. We couldn't walk him or let him roll when he was hooked up to the IV fluids. We couldn't do anything but keep him as calm as possible while the IV fluids went into his system.

Around one in the morning, everything became a haze, like something out of a living nightmare.

Heighten started to wake up and as he did, his pawing returned. His anxiety. He paced and paced and paced around and around and around that stall in distress, stopping every now and then like he was going to roll, twisting the IV tube.

Jim and I watched in silence, helplessness.

"Should we sedate him again?" I asked half-heartedly at one point and Jim shook his head.

"Let's see if he can power through it," he said. "And we can maybe see whether it's getting better or worse."

At one point, I got a blanket from the house and laid it in the dirt outside the stall to lay down, trying to sleep for a few minutes. Lee, who refused point-blank to go in the house, put his wet nose on my face until I assured him I was fine. When I closed my eyes I could still hear the pawing and the pacing. If I close my eyes now I can still hear it.

Around 2am, Jim got up from his chair and turned the barn lights off. Heighten, fully out of sedation now, continued to pace as though still in pain. But with the lights off, his eyes could adjust to the dark and he could check on everything around him. So he'd go peek in one corner at one end of the shed row of stalls then walk to the other corner to look at the other end. Back and forth, back and forth, around and around, like a merry-go-round straight out of hell.

His constant circling and pacing kept twisting the IV tube and we rushed in at one point to untangle them, exhaustion and anxiety taking over as we barked orders at each other while Heighten stood, trembling, and we tried to straighten the tube as best we could while trying to keep him from pacing.

After we had done what we could we got out of there and Heighten lay down again. And he'd shortened that damn tube so much that when he lay down, he pulled open one of the bags of fluid. And it started dripping on him.

The rush to turn on the lights. Grabbing the halter. Fumbling with the ladder. Jim reaching to grab the bag to try and release it. Me trying to get Heighten up. Heighten on his side, eyes scared, sides heaving, that bag dripping steadily on his side.

The image is burned in my memory. One of the worst. One of the worst things I've ever seen.

But not as bad as what we realized as we stood gazing at him.

Heighten didn't want to get up.

Jim and I looked at each other. And we called it.

We got the emergency vet on the phone. We asked her to come back out as quickly as she could.

We stood on the edge of that abyss and looked into Heighten's eyes as he lay in the stall, defeated, and we thought for sure he was telling us it was over. And we weren't going to draw it out any longer.

And as we waited for the vet to come I sat in numb disbelief, Heighten raising his head every now and then to look at Jim. Jim gently reassured him to lay back down, because everything was alright, it was all going to be alright. All will be well again, he said. Lay your head back down, my brother. I've got your back. All is well.

Heighten lay quietly, breathing deeply, but I knew with all my heart and all my soul he was listening to Jim talking to him and hanging on to his every word.

Because as we sat there waiting for the emergency vet-me trying to comprehend the horror of what was happening-something changed.

Heighten stayed down, but as the minutes passed he seemed to slowly, slowly begin to calm down. He stopped shaking. His breathing evened out. His sides stopped heaving. When he raised his head to look at Jim, there was a different look in his eyes.

It was quiet. The stars were the only light as we all sat, Jim occasionally murmuring to Heighten.

The emergency vet pulled in at 3am. She looked at Heighten laying quietly and said, "Let's get him up and get him back to his stall first. Let's see what happens."

What about the IV? I thought stupidly, but the vet unhooked him, despite the one unbroken bag not being empty yet, and out of nowhere, out of nothing… Heighten was standing again.

I dazedly grabbed the lead rope and lead him back to his stall.

The three of us watched him for a few minutes. His attitude shifted when he realized he was home. Despite not having any kind of sedation for several hours, he relaxed.

After watching him a while, Jim said, "I'm starting to think the pacing was an emotional thing. He woke up and realized he wasn't home. He got stressed out."

The emergency vet nodded. "That's definitely an option," she said. "And the stress could contribute to the initial cause of what pained him to begin with."

We haltered him up again and she listened to his heart rate, then for gut sounds, then did another rectal exam. Heighten stood still, eyes alert, and she eventually declared, "Everything feels normal. Gut sounds are normal. No displacement. In fact, this exam is better than the exam I did last night after he was tubed."

I let out a breath, astonished, and Jim put his arms around Heighten's neck.

"What caused him to go crazy?" we all wondered. "What could have caused this?"

We pieced together a hypothesis. He colicked for a time, then the bagging with IV fluids helped, but he was stressed out upon being in a new stall. Maybe his ulcers had acted up throughout the night too, suddenly and randomly. We couldn't be totally sure.

But we did know one thing.

Heighten, who looked like he was on his last leg an hour before, stood in his stall with authority and not without unease to be sure, but without pain. No pawing. No pacing.

It was a miracle.

We talked about getting him tested for ulcers in the next few weeks, but we were pretty sure that ulcers were a very likely culprit. We gave him another tube of GastroGard and left his stall so he could resume exploring his stall like he'd never seen it before.

"He's just been through some trauma," the emergency vet told us. "It'll probably take some time for him to settle back down."

We agreed, and she left around a quarter to four. Heighten paced a bit in his stall, but without the same amount of urgency, and without pawing or fear or pain.

At 4am with Heighten on the mend, I left. I was terrified of getting another call telling me he was bad again, but at that point I was going off adrenaline and about 15 minutes of Lee-interrupted sleep.

I slept for a few hours then called Jim at 7:30 for an update.

And he said Heighten was calmer, happier, better. Our usual vet would be out again later that day to check him again and take out his catheter. But by all accounts, he seemed almost totally back to normal.

I went back to the ranch an hour later to see for myself.

The sun was burningly bright to my sleep deprived eyes. It seared my vision as I walked through the wash and past the round pen and down the shed row to Heighten's stall.

And there, in the blinding light, in contrast to the image of my head of his silhouette against the starry sky hours before, he stood.

Impossibly.

Bravely.

Surely.

Jim came over. He looked exhausted, but beside himself with happiness.

"The same thing happened over a decade ago. I didn't know if he was going to make it until dawn," he said, watching Heighten who was nibbling slowly on a small handful of Bermuda. "And today, just before dawn broke, we won again."

And as I stood there in the sunlight looking at that beautiful liver chestnut Thoroughbred standing in his stall, miraculously alive after a hellish night, three words kept ringing in my head.

We.

Win.

These.

CHAPTER THIRTY-FOUR
THE TALE OF THE DONKEYS

During the middle of the summer in 2017, Tierra Madre got an email that preceded one of the wildest, most convoluted experiences in my entire ranch career.

As a sanctuary, Tierra Madre didn't do horse rescue missions. Nearly all of the time, people brought their horses to our gates and surrendered them to us on our property. Only on rare occasions would we go somewhere with a borrowed trailer to get horses out of their homes.

But this time, we got ourselves into a rescue mission. Or rather, I did.

The woman who emailed Tierra Madre worked for a company (which we'll call Company) that managed systems and structures primarily outdoors. Company housed employees on rather obscure land so they could watch over certain components of the organization's work. And over ten years ago, an employee brought his four donkeys to live with him at one particular site.

The property, for a bit of scene-setting, was in the middle of private land only accessible by employees of Company, deep into the heart of wild desert along the Central Arizona Project canal east of Phoenix. Next to the home within this Company-owned land was an enclosed 12-acre lot upon which the employee let his donkeys roam. And after a year, this Company employee moved off the land and abandoned his donkeys on the lot.

There was more to the story. The next Company employee to live at the house seemingly cared for the donkeys after their owner left them. Over time, she trained them to walk from wherever they were hiding on the huge plot of land to the front of the gates, by the employee house, whenever she rang a bell that she'd placed over their automatic waterer. While these four donkeys were left to themselves most of the time, this employee would occasionally feed them carrots. But some time later, that employee left too. And the donkeys were left to survive on their own for many years. And they lived there still, miraculously still alive.

I must have re-read that email four or five times. Bewildered, I picked up my phone and called the woman who'd sent the email, who we'll call Angel.

Angel had worked for Company for years. Her boss informed Angel and the other employees that the donkeys kept to themselves and didn't need to be bothered. "They eat whatever's out there in the desert," he apparently told Angel, referring to the mesquite seed pods and leaves that hung on the mesquite trees. "They've lived on their own for years. They're fine."

But despite her boss's insistence that the donkeys were fine and the nonchalant attitude of her fellow employees, Angel looked up horse sanctuaries and rescues, found us, and wanted to know if someone could come look at the donkeys and confirm that they were really okay, as the Company boss said. After seeing one with what looked like curled up feet, she was concerned about them.

"But I don't want to make a big deal about this, because I'll lose my job," Angel told me on the phone that day, as I sat in my car outside my apartment talking to her. "My boss was very clear about not wanting anything done about them. He doesn't want the bother. He really thinks they're okay...."

There wasn't ever a point where I considered telling Angel Tierra Madre just didn't do rescues. Four donkeys, out in the wilderness with no reliable food, for so many years....

"We're going to have to be very discreet about this," I told Angel, "but I do want to go look at the donkeys myself, if I can. Is there any way I can get on that property to see them without your boss finding out?"

She was quiet, but only for a moment. "Here's what we'll do," she said. "Can you meet me at my house? I have to unlock the gates on the property to get us in. They know my car, they'll know it's just me. If you were to drive behind-"

"It'd look suspicious," I said. "Totally get it."

"But if you were in my car with me, I could say I have a friend with me and we're just going to give carrots to the donkeys."

We made a plan to do just this the next day, a Friday. And so, just over twelve hours later, I found myself being driven on a rickety dirt road to the middle of nowhere by a complete stranger with nothing around us but wild desert. In hindsight, probably not the wisest decision I ever made. But after Angel had welcomed me into her home and spent a few minutes introducing me to the ten or so cats who lived there (all of which were extremely well cared for), I decided the chances of her being a serial killer were probably next to none.

After driving 25 minutes off road, Angel and I pulled up to the house for Company employees, which was being renovated or something for the next employee to live there. By the time we got to the property, it was around 11am, humid, and hotter than hell.

"So there's the entrance to the lot," Angel said as she parked the car. We got out, grabbed the carrots we'd bought, and as we started walking, she pointed past the small, enclosed area that made up what was essentially the house's back yard to wild land that disappeared into the thick mesquite trees in the distance. "They're never up by the gate, they're usually hiding…"

The fenced 12-acre lot consisted not only of mesquite trees that created several acres of shade but palo verdes, desert brush, an occasional cactus, and-on the very edge of the property closest to the house, by the fence-a concrete tub that looked like it was hooked up to an automatic watering system.

"Is that their water?" I asked Angel. She nodded.

"And that's the bell that's on top, there. We'll ring that first… it usually takes them about ten or fifteen minutes to walk up…."

We reached the fence. I looked down at the water tub and recoiled.

It was green, with slimy sides and thick layers of algae floating on top along with dirt, dead bugs, and god knew what else. If I'd put my hand an inch under the slime it would have vanished. The Roman Baths were cleaner.

I turned to Angel, who looked disgusted.

"This is unacceptable," I said. "This is their only water?"

"I think so," she replied. "And it actually looks cleaner than it did the last time I saw it. They must have put bleach in it or something."

I bit back a furious stream of swearing and instead took my phone out to take some pictures while Angel rung the bell. "I'm glad to hear you say it's bad," she told me. "My boss told all of us the donkeys were fine. I just didn't think they were."

"You definitely did the right thing, contacting us," I said, and I meant it. "Can we hop the fence?"

We hopped the fence, then we waited. Angel had said it could take up to ten or fifteen minutes for the donkeys to get to the front of the lot after hearing the bell, but I was too impatient to find them and started climbing through the trees after a few minutes. Angel, bless her, walked with me.

We only had to walk for ten minutes. While in a patch of trees that were spread far enough apart for me to stand up straight (other areas of the land involved walking hunched over as to not scrape our heads), I spotted two of them.

The first one I saw was a shaggy brown jenny. Even from a distance I could tell she was extremely overweight, but incredibly sweet. She approached us softly, big fluffy ears swiveling around her to catch all sounds, while her companion, a gray jenny, crept up slowly behind her.

After a few more minutes, a third jenny, a darker brown, almost black, approached us too. She was their leader, clearly, and was more used to humans as she was more forthright in her asking for carrots. This darkest one was so overweight that her fat patches were actually distorting the crest of her neck. Later, when I studied their poop, I saw the mesquite pods in the manure and concluded that the donkeys ate the sugary pods all they wanted, every day, without being stopped, and had become grossly overweight as a result.

I pointed out the fat patches to Angel and explained a little bit about basic equine care-dentals, annual vaccinations, proper exercise and diet-and told her that the donkeys needed medical attention. At the time, I was worried that the darkest donkey had a tumor on her neck, but later I learned that donkeys grew fat patches there and despite the lumps looking like tumors, they were really just lumps of fat.

Which is why I felt guilty giving them a few carrots as we studied the three of them. Their hooves for the most part actually looked decent, as they'd worn down naturally over time as the donkeys walked around on the hard terrain. After another ten minutes or so, however, it became apparent there was another problem.

"There are only three donkeys here," I said to Angel, who was cautiously patting the shaggy brown jenny. "Isn't there a fourth?"

Angel nodded, eyes wide. "There were four just last week. I saw them from a distance, and that was the one whose feet looked bad, really bad…"

We searched for an hour. We waded through thick mesquite trees, blinking sweat out of our eyes, cooing lightly in the hopes that we could coax the fourth out from hiding. The darkest jenny, who I nicknamed S'more, followed us, hoping for more carrots.

Finally, unable to climb any more through the thicket of sharp branches, we decided to end the search. We were nearly out of water, it was past noon, it was over 100 degrees, and it was only going to get hotter.

"We need to get them out of here," I panted to Angel as we finally stumbled out of the mesquite trees towards the entrance of the lot some time later. "They've survived on their own this far, but their health's only going to get worse. And we don't even know the condition of the fourth."

Angel nodded. "I had a feeling you'd say that."

We started talking about the logistics of getting her boss to agree to sign them over as we got to the edge of the property, where the well of slime and algae awaited. I threw the empty bags of carrots over the fence and our now empty water bottles and made to jump out while Angel (wisely) walked around to open up the gate. Before I hopped the fence again, I looked over and saw S'more, our little follower, standing nearby and blinking at me.

I walked over and gave her a few pats. The other two hung back, looking at us.

"We're coming back for you," I whispered to S'more and her companions. Her ears twitched as she listened. "Hang in there. We're coming back."

One week later, Angel met me at the entrance to the Company's property in the late morning.

I had reached out to the absolutely amazing equine network to which Tierra Madre belonged. One of the most prominent local rescues in our area had arranged to drive two trailers out to the entrance to meet us there. They would drive the donkeys to a secondary rescue, who had agreed to take all of them and find them homes. Originally, the plan was to drive them out of state to a donkey rescue in Texas, but that plan was scraped after only a few days when it became apparent that the recue in-state would be a good fit for them.

I drafted a surrender form and sent it to Angel to obtain a signature from her boss. If he didn't consent to surrendering them, I told her, then we'd have to go through the Arizona Department of Agriculture to get them to safety. By law, any animal classified as feral had to be sent to a livestock auction, where we would have to fight kill buyers to claim them. So I'd told her exactly what to say, how to phrase our rescue mission in a way that released the boss from responsibility in exchange for handing over the donkeys. The plan worked, he agreed, and he signed.

Angel and I were to go to the property a half hour or so before the trailers arrived so we could ring the bell and get the donkeys up into the smaller, enclosed 'backyard' pen by the house so they'd be easier to round up. I'd brought Bermuda, treats, and halters for this. Then, Angel would drive back to the gate to unlock it for the trailer then bring them to the donkeys, who would be haltered and ready to go.

Oh, if only I'd known then about the stubbornness of donkeys. The first part of the plan worked out great. The second, not so much.

Angel and I got to the lot and rang the bell right on schedule. The three young donkeys that we'd seen the first time walked right up. S'more came first. The bonded pair walked up next. To stick with my food theme, I was calling the shaggy brown jenny Snickers and the gray CC, short for Cookies-n-Cream.

I put the Bermuda I'd brought on the ground in the smaller, enclosed pen. Angel had opened up the gate to the big backyard to the 12-acre lot, and they waltzed right in.

Just as I was about to open my mouth and lament the absence of the fourth and voice my fear that something had happened, suddenly, from the shadows of the mesquite trees and the brush, came the fourth little girl.

She crept quietly, walking gingerly, looking around her with a softness and a sad acceptance that blew me away.

She was old. She was little, smaller than the other three by far. The others were fat; she was skinny. And her feet were in absolutely horrendous shape, curled up at least seven inches out in front of her.

I stood in shock for a minute, just looking at her. She looked back at me, blinking.

"She came!" squealed Angel, coming up behind me. "I was so worried, too!"

"She came," I repeated. I pointed to her feet. "Angel, I am so, so glad you did what you did."

Angel gasped, seeing the donkey's hooves. "I thought they looked bad, but up close they look even worse."

I nodded. I was too angry to speak. I approached the donkey quietly and showed her the halter in my hand. She stood there, motionless, and let me put the halter on her face without objection.

Two or three maintenance workers of some sort were off in the distance, doing work to the house some fifty feet away. I barked at them to fill a bowl with water and bring it out. And while Angel went to help them find water that wasn't swimming in a million species of bacteria, I put my arms around the sweet donkey's neck and put my face in her mane. "I'm sorry," I told her. "I'm so sorry, little girl. We're going to make you better."

Angel came running with a bucket of water and held it out to the older jenny. That little girl gulped down every last drop so Angel went back for more. And during this process of getting her water as well as putting some down for the other three donkeys in the smaller pen, we got the older girl into the smaller pen too and shut the gate, trapping them all inside.

Eventually two volunteers from the local rescue-T and B-brought their trailers and we began the process of rounding up the donkeys. Only we never finished it.

Four hours.

We herded those donkeys for four hours.

The littlest, oldest donkey was haltered already, and we were also able to halter S'more with relative ease. We tied them to the fence with a quick-release knot so they'd be ready to go once we got the other two.

Snickers and CC, on the other hand, were not interested in going into a big metal box on wheels after living for ten years out in the open wilderness, and they expressed this disdain by treating us to a long, fun game of donkey tag.

At first the mission was just to halter them. We herded the two of them from one end of the yard to the other as they moved away from us at every turn, turning their butts then charging past us, creeping slowly to get the treats out of our hands one moment then turning on a dime to get away the next.

We tried to use a human shield to keep them in a corner long enough to halter at least one of them, but they broke through it each time. We tried putting the halters down at one point and just leaving them alone for a while, but the moment we picked the halters back up all hell broke loose again.

We tried everything.

Finally, something like two and a half hours in, we managed to get a halter onto Snickers after T, Angel, and I got her in a corner and B managed to keep up with her flailing while haltering her at the same time. One of the maintenance workers joined the fun for twenty minutes or so and-while trying to halter CC-demonstrated what could only be described as a donkey rodeo as CC spun and bucked and kicked and he bounced up and down with her. It ended with him finally getting knocked down and the halter flying across the yard and all of us running after the donkey yet again, Snickers and S'more screeching, "EEE-HAAAAW" and the oldest jenny just standing off to the side looking bored.

Eventually, as we all stood in 110-degree weather, sweat pouring down our faces and backs, the mission became just to chase the stubborn asses onto the trailer, halters be damned.

We thought that maybe if we managed to load Snickers and keep CC in the same area as her, CC would follow her friend or at least be somewhat easier to capture.

B backed the trailer up to the outer gate of the yard. And we pulled, we pushed, we tugged, we pleaded, we bribed with treats and pats and even got a bang stick to smack on the ground behind Snickers' feet but she. Did. Not. Budge. We might as well have asked the house to grow legs and walk into the trailer.

Finally, around 4pm, as we stood red-faced in the heat, we called defeat.

We'd have to come back another day and bring panels to create a corral around the trailer. Once herded into the corral, we could make the pen smaller and smaller until they had nowhere else to go but in.

We all agreed that we would try one last thing, which was to attempt to move the oldest jenny with the awful feet. Bailey, I was calling her.

We were hopeful, as she seemed way calmer than the rest. If we could at least get *her* into the trailer, our efforts would all be worth it.

After we'd all stood around catching our breaths, chugging water and wiping sweat out of our eyes, I went over, took Bailey's lead rope, and walked her in the trailer with absolutely no incident.

All of us breathed a sigh of relief.

And so, Angel went to let the other three donkeys back into their 12-acre lot, and we all headed to our cars, the trailer headed to the rescue with Bailey safely and calmly inside the trailer. The others would have to wait.

Yet another week passed. Angel, the rescue with the trailer, and I arranged for another attempt. This time, the rescue's executive director, S, came too.

Angel and I got there first again. Rang the bell. The three donkeys came walking up. By the time the trailers were pulling in they were trapped again in the smaller yard.

S calmly looked around at the three donkeys, started settling up the panels with T and another of her volunteers, and then told us exactly what we'd need to do to get them in the trailer.

We constructed the panels to make a corral leading to the trailer into which we drove the donkeys. Once they were herded inside, we snapped it shut and-through S's instruction-gradually made it smaller and smaller, using carefully placed noise and movement to encourage the donkeys to step into the trailer.

Finally, after CC and S'more walked inside, it was down to Snickers, who we'd managed to halter again. S and T held her lead rope, her other volunteer and I had opposite ends of a strap which went around Snickers' butt, and Angel stood by ready to push. On "GO!" S pulled the rope with T helping, her other volunteer and I pulled on the strap, and Angel pushed

Snickers' hind end until-with extreme effort-we had pushed one stubborn, irritated donkey onto the trailer and shut her inside.

We cheered when the trailer doors were safely latched. The donkeys protested, not knowing they were safe, not knowing they were on their way to good food and clean water and medical attention and more love than they could imagine. But boy were we glad. All in all, with the panels, it had taken less than an hour to get them in the trailer.

Looking back, I know there was no way it could have been done without S and her team. I was in awe of their expertise in rescuing feral equines and their willingness to drive to the middle of nowhere and haul them an hour away.

There was no way it could have been done without the other rescue that housed the donkeys, either. Bailey had been with the executive director, C, and his team for a week before we got the other three to them, and in that week Bailey had gained weight, gotten her feet done, been put on necessary pain meds and joint supplements, and soaked up more human attention and devotion than she'd probably seen in her life.

And there was no way it could have been done without Angel.

Here was a woman who might not have known a great deal about horses or donkeys but she had followed her instinct and reached out to get them help. Had she listened to the people at her work who told her to look the other way, had she listened to her boss who insisted that the donkeys were fine, who knows what could have happened to them out there, especially Bailey.

C told me outright he was worried about her on that first day she came to his rescue.

"I'll be honest with you, I don't think she's going to pass a Coggins test," he said as we stood watching her quietly eat her soaked alfalfa pellets. "And I hate to try to rehome her."

I nodded. Bailey was old. Her teeth were bad. She'd probably be walking a little stiffly for the rest of her life, after having to adjust to such horrendous hooves. The market for older, vulnerable donkeys and horses was slim. So I didn't hesitate to say:

"If you can't find a home for her, we'll take her."

Which was why, a month later, C drove a much healthier, much happier little old donkey through Tierra Madre's gates. Jim was beside himself. I'd kept him in the donkey rescue loop from the start and initially he'd wanted all four to come to Tierra Madre. When he realized we didn't have the room for all of them, he'd backed my offer to C to take the oldest at some point and anxiously waited to hear that she was coming home.

My choice of the name Bailey wasn't entirely popular with the Tierra Madre team, and Jim came up with the idea to call her Abuela, which is Spanish for grandmother.

And so, Abuela she became.

The other three donkeys lost weight. They got the medical attention they needed as well as plenty of gentle human interaction and training. And they each went to a loving home by the end of the summer.

Thanks to our careful plan and the casual manner in which we approached the subject of rehoming the donkeys to the boss at Company, Angel kept her job.

And the littlest donkey-despite the deplorable state in which she was found-lived for another year, probably the happiest of her life. Despite the hell she had lived through, she was a sweetheart above anything. For someone who had gone through so much, she was still as gentle and soft and kind as the grandmothers we all know and love dearly.

She was another life spared from a cruel fate and given love and peace and dignity, all because of one woman who listened not to authority, but to her heart.

CHAPTER THIRTY-FIVE
HOW BAD AND HOW OFTEN?

Jim often said that when you work with horses, you're going to get hurt. There are only two questions: how bad, and how often?

I used to believe this was a paranoid way of thinking. But then I started working with horses on a daily basis.

Over the years, I've been given sweet little nips that left bruises and bitten hard enough for teeth to break my skin. I've gotten scrapes and gashes from horses lovingly rubbing their faces against me and knocking me into a wall. I've been stepped on more often than I could count, though I've never had any toes crushed thanks to my Ariats.

I've been kicked by accident and kicked on purpose. I've been given bruises the size of my head and had my muscles strained to the point I couldn't move without pain. I've been lunged at, charged at, and I've perfected the summersault roll out of a stall. I was constantly thankful that I fit between stall bars.

I've been pinned against fences and thrown into them. I've been dragged on the ground before I learned how stupid it was to hang onto ropes attached to horses that want to run. I've had my hands ripped open by lead ropes being torn out of them and been given rope burn so bad it was agony to touch anything for days. When Sunny was a baby, she kicked in the air as we were flipping her over (she'd cast herself) and took the skin off my middle finger by my nail.

I've sprained wrists holding onto feet that were slammed down in irritation at my keeping them up, and gone home with mysterious bruises, cuts, and scrapes. I've had horses rear up and buck for all it was worth when I was walking them. One time, Danny got spooked while I was leading him out of his stall and his back hoof caught me in the butt, shattering my phone in my back pocket but which took brunt of the kick. Another time, while walking Studley home from the arena, Danny launched himself over the bars at him and Studley slammed his body into mine in haste to get away. I hit the lead-pipe bars with such force I got the wind knocked out of me, and I staggered everywhere for a week.

I've almost had my nose broken by Rusty swinging his head upward when I least expected it. Sonora once kicked at my head with both hind legs and I felt the wind from each hoof on my cheek as she missed me by inches. Later that same year, she knocked me down and nearly trampled me on Christmas when I was walking her to the arena and the same BB shot that started the field stampede that ended with Spencer almost losing his eye scared her, too.

After a while, I knew what to expect.

When their heads went up and their eyes got wide, I made sure I was at their shoulder should they lurch forward, or kick out.

When Hudson went up on his hind legs and boxed, I knew where to side step so that I was out of harm's way and knew how to act until he calmed down.

Eventually, I saw accidents before they happened with the volunteers. When I saw someone snuggled up close to a horse laying down, or not listening to warning signs of a horse telling them they were scared, or crawling between bars into the stall of a horse running back and forth, I saw impeding disaster and corrected them as fast as I could.

The physical pain could sometimes be avoided. Sometimes.

But there were other pains—worse pains—that couldn't be escaped.

CHAPTER THIRTY-SIX
RINGING SILENCE

Sometimes, during a duo visit from our vet and therapeutic farrier, it wasn't all laughter and chatter as we worked in the breezeway.

Sometimes, the horse we'd given our blood, sweat, and tears to for the past few weeks or months or even years stood shakily.

Sometimes, our vet or therapeutic farrier had a hard time keeping a hoof in the air as the horse struggled to stand, and it was all Jim and I could do to help them get the x-rays that needed to be taken.

And something happened during those particular visits that shifted the time we all spent together as a happy, hopeful endeavor to another kind of appointment entirely. Something would occur, without fail, each and every time, that drove the final nail in the coffin.

Ringing silence.

When the exam had been made and the facts stated.

When the casting had come off to reveal solar corium coming through the underside of the hoof.

When the radiographs had been taken.

When our vet stared at the radiographs and our therapeutic farrier stared at the radiographs and Jim stared at the radiographs and I stared at the radiographs and the rotation of the coffin bone was so stark and significant and terrible.

Ringing silence.

Around us, the volunteers worked and talked. The rest of the horses ran in the arena or ate in their stalls or were groomed or were walked around the ranch. Birds chirped. Clouds rolled by.

And in the breezeway, there was ringing silence.

Sometimes, we all talked about it for a long time.

Sometimes, we didn't need to talk about it for more than a few minutes.

Sometimes, we set a time and day, right then and there.

Sometimes, Jim and I talked and decided later, alone.

Always, we cried afterward.

Because louder than the deafening stillness on each decision day was always the acceptance in our horse's eyes.

And one time, after seeing my tears I had been unable to hide when the ringing silence came for Abuela, our therapeutic farrier told me something I never forgot:

"Better a month too soon than a day too late."

CHAPTER THIRTY-SEVEN
HOW?

How does one life that seemed well lived suddenly feel so short in a matter of days?

How do you fight the rising terror in your throat, your stomach, your veins, when your horse seems to be fighting a losing battle?

How do you keep composure when you ask your vet to confirm that your horse doesn't have long left on this earth, and she does?

How do you look your volunteers in the eye and tell them one of their members of the family isn't going to live much longer?

How do you explain that surviving is not the same as living?

How do you come back from knowing your horse is in pain, and will soon suffer if you allow it to happen, which of course you can never do?

How do you find the line between managing and suffering?

How do you answer questions-like which bucket goes where and can so-and-so can have a carrot and would you look at a scratch on so-and-so's face and when are we going to feed-when your horse is stumbling in pain?

How do you drag yourself through the rest of your work day when all you want to do is curl into a ball next to your horse and feel his warm skin against yours for as long as you can?

How do you answer phone calls and emails about the next fundraiser when your heart is shattering on the floor?

How do you hold it together for your volunteers who need to see strength and hear reassuring words when you are falling apart?

How do you go on when the world is ending?

How do you live when an extension of yourself is dying?

CHAPTER THIRTY-EIGHT
SONORA

Jim came up to me on a cold December morning in 2014.

"There's this woman down the road," he said, and immediately I knew where the conversation was headed, "and she has this horse she wants to put down. Apparently, the mare is dangerous and this woman's afraid of her. She wants to get rid of her as soon as humanly possible."

We were full, as we always were. But the situation had grown perilous as this mare was frightening her owner with her erratic and aggressive behavior, which was supposedly bad enough for euthanasia to be considered. Without even knowing or seeing this horse, something in my spirit stirred upon hearing these words. In my heart of hearts, I knew we had to get the mare to safety. We all did.

So Jim called her owner back and said, "We'll take her."

I called the owner the next day to go over logistics and scheduled the mare's arrival for December 16th. I think she was supposed to be at the ranch around 9:30am.

The 16th arrived and 9:30am came and went. An hour went by. Then, the horse's owner called me when we were almost at closing time.

"She won't go in the trailer," she said. She sounded hysterical. "She knows something's different, she can sense it! She's gone crazy. She's scared…. I feel like I need to get my vet out right now-"

I didn't think.

"Where are you located?"

Fifteen minutes later, I was pulling up to her property. I got out of my car and was greeted by the horse's owner and her sister, who was helping with the situation. "We've tried everything," they said. "She just won't go in the trailer…"

"I'll help as much as I can," I said, fully aware that I had never loaded a horse in my life and both of these women were far more experienced than I was. "Are you okay?"

The owner was near tears as she and her sister answered me, and as the three of us stood and talked, I looked just beyond them and saw her.

A beautiful red mare, with a white blaze and deep, expressive eyes. Standing in a tiny pen. Gazing at me.

My heart skipped a beat as our eyes met.

"It's the alfalfa," her owner was saying nervously. After spending so long attempting to get the mare into the trailer, the poor woman looked completely distraught. "I can't believe I didn't have her tested for PSSM. That's it. I know it is."

I was listening but not able to absorb her words. I was mesmerized by the mare. She was gazing at me unblinkingly.

"It's like she knows she's going away for good. She's different," the woman continued as we stood watching the mare shake her head and pin her ears a little. "She's been different for two years. I've never been afraid of her before. But she's just out of control. I just-"

"Can I go in with her?" I asked her, and she sucked in her breath and looked at me with fearful eyes.

"Oh, yes, yes, whatever you want. As far as I'm concerned, she's your horse now. Go meet your new horse."

I took a brief second to explore all my options as I walked over to the mare's pen. I could avoid any potential accident by *not* going in with her. Of course, after working with Chance, anything this horse had to offer might be a walk in the park. And this woman had said she was ready to put her down if she couldn't get her to another home.

And all the while that mare kept watching me with uneasy eyes. I couldn't decipher them.

There was no other option. I threw caution to the winds, slung the halter over my shoulder, opened her stall door and went in.

She immediately came over to sniff me, more curious than aggressive. As her owner and her sister continued talking about the horse's current behavior, things they had noticed, tests she'd undergone, that horse and I just looked and looked and looked at each other as the world moved on around us. She was nervous. She was in perfect physical condition and her mane was nicely combed, but she couldn't keep still and her eyes kept wandering. Every now and then she pinned her ears back and tossed her head a little, as though she was having an anxiety attack. But as I stood calmly in her small pen, her amber eyes kept settling on mine.

I haltered her and walked her out of that tiny pen and around the property a bit. Or rather, she tried to walk me as she pushed me around in what I would soon come to realize was her typical pushy fashion. I worked with her for an hour while the trailer sat ahead of us. And all the while, I talked to her.

I told her about Tierra Madre.

I told her that at our ranch, she could just be a horse and not have to worry about pleasing others. She could run around to her heart's desire by herself or with as many friends as she wanted. She could be nobody but herself, and no one would prevent her from being anything else.

Again and again I brought her to the trailer and let her explore it.

But she wouldn't walk in. She didn't want to get in that trailer.

After an hour of us walking around in circles, nearly all of my hope was lost. We were all exhausted and while the mare had put a tentative hoof in the trailer once or twice, she still didn't want that much to do with it. Her owner mentioned calling her vet again for euthanasia. How dangerous the horse was. My anxiety started to buzz. We were running out of time.

Finally, as we stood at the base of the trailer and the mare hemmed and hawed and twitched and laid her ears back and looked around nervously, I played my last, craziest, desperate card.

I put my head against hers, closed my eyes, soaked in every ounce of her wild energy, and whispered in her ear.

"You have no reason to trust me on this," I said, hoping against hope she would listen, "but I need you to trust me now."

She looked at me, looked at the trailer, and looked at me again.

And then…

Okay.

I pulled on the lead rope one last time.

And in she went.

We drove her down the road to Tierra Madre and in through the gates and when I opened the trailer door, she charged out like a bat out of hell, taking in her surroundings with a fierceness I've never seen before or since. And the first thing I did was turn her out into the arena. Around and around she flew, mane flying, tail streaking out behind her, a blaze of red as she galloped with joy in her heart for a good twenty or thirty minutes. Her owner and sister were near tears of happiness as they watched her. They loved her, I could tell. Ultimately, they had wanted to do the best thing for her.

Eventually they left and Jim came back from his meeting. He went over to say hi to her in the arena. "There ain't nothing wrong with this horse," he said as she sniffed him, blowing air out of her nose.

"Isn't she beautiful?" I exclaimed. "She just took my breath away. She's perfect. She's perfect."

I haltered her and brought her over to the round pen, where she would live in quarantine for a week or so. As I took her halter off, she rubbed her face all up and down my legs. She looked at me and I looked at her and thought, *I've known you for a long, long time.*

Same, I heard her say. *Same.*

Jim watched the two of us together, he pointed at her, pointed at me, and said, "She's yours, sweet thing. That is your horse. You saved her. That is your little girl."

Later, we stood watching her in the round pen. And I took in the craziness of that day, not knowing that my next few days and weeks and months would be spent working with the mare and letting her ease out of her nervous habits, not knowing that she would be more than a handful, not knowing she had no intention of ever tolerating a saddle again, not knowing that by the end of that week she would be following me around in her pen and putting her head against mine in something damn near devotion.

I did know one thing. The mare I was now to call my own was as wild and as utterly, breathtakingly beautiful as the desert around us. And it made naming her that much easier.

"Sonora," I said, as we watched the mare eat contentedly and look around at her new home, safe at last. "Her name is Sonora."

In the two and a half years she spent at Tierra Madre, Sonora-or Nora, as I nicknamed her-blossomed into one of the most unique and strong-willed and loving horses I've ever known.

A month or so after she'd been with us, our farriers at the time tried to trim her. She fought them tooth and nail, going so far as to rear up on them and make an effort to charge.

I didn't know it then, but that was the earliest sign of her hoof problems. And boy, did she *constantly* have problems with her feet.

For as long as we had her, Nora always struggled with abscesses no matter what we did to her stall. We tried her with shoes, then without, then with again, then without again as we tried to figure out what worked and what didn't. Within a year, I learned she'd suffered an acute case of laminitis with her previous owner, and the owner before that one.

Isoxsuprine. Ichthammol and bandages. Hoof supplements. Bute, then Previcox. Diet changes. Special booties. We all spent hours and hours on her feet. Whatever she needed during a sore phase, we did. Sometimes, she would be sore for weeks. Sometimes, whatever we did one day would bring her completely back to normal the next.

And when she was feeling her best, she was a force to be reckoned with.

She charged out of her stall when it was her turn to go out in the arena. She hopped and jumped and leapt and ran and kicked with fearlessness, with reckless abandon. Twice at the ranch I've been in life-or-death situations that would have ended in disaster had it not been for a few inches of space. Twice, she was the cause of those incidents: one in which she accidently kicked at my head and another in which she turned, knocked me down, and nearly ran me over after getting spooked.

But within the untamed wildness of her heart lay kindness, and trust, and an intuition that was always right on target.

Everyone who walked within our gates loved her. And she humbled us all by loving us back.

In the spring of 2016, I was absolutely terrified for her when it became clear that abscesses were not the problem behind another round of soreness but rather a flare up of laminitis. After several months of visits from our vet at the time, corrective trims, booties, supplements, a cushy stall, and more prayers than I can count, she flew around that arena again by the end of the summer.

But in March of 2017, the soreness came back. Worse. A thousand times worse.

Our new vet and new therapeutic farrier came out and diagnosed her with severe, acute laminitis on the spot.

Going through the downfall hurts even now and blurs together.

The little sole depth she had that kept decreasing. The day the solar corium began to rupture through the sole. The brief twenty-four-hour period where we thought she had improved and her attitude was good and we really, really thought we were going to make it. The day she sunk to the ground in pain rather than stand on one foot while we checked the other. The weight she lost. The way her legs shook. The look in her eyes, determined and strong but fighting pain every instant of every day.

That awful, awful day we all looked at the radiographs. The coffin bone nearly coming through.

The ringing silence.

Jim and I sat in the house for a long time after our vet and therapeutic farrier had left that day. Silent.

Finally, Jim took a drag of his cigarette, exhaled, and said quietly, "I don't think we're going to win this one, sweetheart."

We always wait for them to tell us they're ready.

But this time, our vet said to general agreement that Nora was the type of horse that would keep fighting even when she was walking on bone.

This time, we had to be the ones to decide for her.

And I hated that.

We called our vet. Scheduled it for noon the next day, on May 4th. I told all the volunteers. And that morning, Nora was surrounded by so many people who loved her and wanted to send her off with love.

We gave her everything she wanted: alfalfa, watermelon, carrots, apples, peppermints… hugs and kisses and pats and scratches. In the haze I was under that morning, I remember getting a bucket of anti-fungal shampoo and water and washing her legs one last time, because I couldn't bear the thought of her leaving without perfectly clean legs.

After feeding at 11, everyone left one by one, leaving me alone with her in her stall.

And just as I'd talked to her on our first day together, I talked to her on our last.

I told her about the Great Herd.

How the horses in it didn't live in fear. How they could walk perfectly and jump and buck and run across fields of grass as fast as they could for as long as they wanted. How they lived forever in happiness, with no fences or terrible heat or restricting booties or awful pain.

I told her that in the Great Herd, she could be nobody but herself, and no one would prevent her from being anything else.

Far too soon, our vet and her technician pulled through the gate. Nora was quiet, accepting. I was aware of every breath entering and leaving my body. The two of us would only be breathing together for just a little while longer.

Our vet looked at me with complete sympathy and compassion when I walked over with a halter.

"You don't have to watch," she said. "You don't have to be there."

Breathe in. Breathe out.

"Yes, I do."

She nodded. I walked. Walked to Nora's stall. Opened the gate. Haltered her. For the last time. The very last time.

I looked at my little girl, so different from the anxious mare I'd walked into the trailer that first day. I put my head on hers. I took a breath, one that took all my strength.

And I repeated the words.

"You have no reason to trust me on this," I whispered in her ear, and it was then I felt my heart break, truly break. "But I need you to trust me now."

She looked back at me. Her body was weak and her legs were quivering, but her eyes were strong and confident and impossibly beautiful.

Okay.

Our vet was worried Sonora wouldn't be able to walk up the lane all the way to the spot where we always sent horses to the Great Herd. "She will," I said.

And Nora walked, sore and in terrible pain but never wanting to stop, never hesitating, never turning back. Inch by inch she limped. I couldn't have stopped her if I tried. Even with her last few steps, she knew.

We started up the lane up which we'd walked together a thousand times, exploring the ranch, learning to trust one another. We moved slowly, with purpose, as we had during all the days I'd spent showing her the trees, and the cacti, and the desert around us for which she'd been named, and all the days she'd spent showing me what it meant to be living.

We walked away from the barn where she had spent her first year with us before we moved her to the field side, where she lived when Sunny was born. I remembered how we switched her and Bentley so she could be the one living next to Rain and the new baby, how she and Sunny used to groom each other over the fence when Rain wasn't looking.

We walked past the nearly-gone sand pile she'd play in and over the woodchips she'd occasionally attempt to eat. The day I rushed off the ranch to save her, my volunteers were spreading eucalyptus wood chips on the driveway. To this day, whenever I smell that tree, I think of the day we first met.

We walked past the side gate to the arena that she'd broken with a spirited kick to the handle so that it only ever opened outwards. It was the arena into which I had turned her the moment she came off the trailer, the arena she tore to bits time and time again in her eagerness to run and kick and buck and leap in happiness. It was the arena I'd lunged her in frequently, where she listened to my thoughts rather than my commands. It was the arena where we'd played together, time after time, after everyone else had gone home, where we could run and dance and chase each other and she would follow me, trustingly, every which way.

We walked up the lane and I saw the round pen in the distance, where she'd lived for her first few weeks and where we often returned to goof around. Someone once took a video of us playing together, with me skipping and her trotting happily at my heels.

We walked to the place where she had stepped off the trailer and that is where she stopped. Took in the world around her.

We stood still, waiting. Breathing.

Jim followed us, as did our vet and her assistant, who was armed with the two pink syringes.

As was protocol, Nora was sedated first, so she wouldn't feel a thing. And after a few minutes that lasted hours, as the sedation began to take effect, our vet looked to me. I nodded.

The injections went in. The first, fast. Her knees buckled. Then, the second.

I put my face on Nora's for the last time. Breath in, breath out.

And when she went down, I went down with her.

Her eyes reflected such a state of peace and contentment that I gazed into them as she left me. Knowing I couldn't speak, Jim murmured, "Love you, angel," over and over again so it would be the last thing she heard.

It was quiet for those few, peaceful moments-or minutes or hours or days for all I knew-as our vet listened for the final beats, the final breaths.

Then she said, "She's gone."

And every fiber of my being cracked and involuntary sobs burst out of me and just like I had done so many times during my hard days, I buried my face in Nora's mane and held her to me and cried. Only this time, the final time, she wasn't there.

Fourteen years old, in the prime of her life, gone to the horrors of laminitis.

Gone from the ranch, gone from all of us who had ever loved her… gone from me.

Gone.

CHAPTER THIRTY-NINE
OUT

Exactly one week after Sonora died, I walked across the stage at Arizona State University's Wells Fargo Arena and received my master's degree in nonprofit management and leadership.

I did the coursework in fifteen months while running Tierra Madre full time. It was a feat that I look back on even now and don't know how I accomplished. I did it for each of the horses.

And ironically, as I stood smiling for pictures with my degree, heart ripped open, I thought, *this is my way out.*

This degree.

I could find another job with this degree.

My world crashed and burned after I lost Sonora.

I was done with horses. With rescue. With the ranch.

I wanted out.

I wanted to up and leave, leave behind every possibility of torment and never again have to feel like my heart was torn out of my chest and scraped against every rough edge on the planet.

I wanted to find a job where I could be numb to pain, numb to unfathomable grief, numb to the unimaginable suffering of innocent, beautiful spirits with their lives ahead of them.

Sonora hadn't been the first horse we lost at Tierra Madre by far. But her death was the one that put me over the edge.

Who does this? I thought to myself that day, for many days.

Who *does* this?

Who keeps pouring every ounce of love they have into such amazing horses over and over and over again only to have them taken away so unfairly?

Why would *anyone* go through agony such as this? Why would anyone in their right mind do horse rescue?

I spent weeks drowning in grief. I was caught off guard at the ranch constantly, particularly at the end of the mornings when everyone else had gone home. When I walked around checking waters and gates, watching the herd happily eat their lunches or slip into their afternoon naps, I glanced over to look at her.

I glanced over to see her pin her ears at Nibzie or stomp her foot at M'Stor.

I glanced over to see her sniffing the ground around her feeder, hoping to find just one more scrap of Timothy hay leftover from lunch.

I glanced over to see her beautiful face, looking contentedly back at me.

But she wasn't there.

And some days it hit harder than others.

The day Bill finally took down the gate panels that had made her stall smaller in her final days, to protect her from moving around too much, I locked myself in my office and cried until I couldn't breathe.

But then, a week later, for the first time I remembered not to put another flake of Timothy on the field side feeding cart for her at lunchtime. And I looked at the other hungry horses whinnying at me to hurry up and get moving.

And somewhere within the ache deep in my heart, raw with loss, something flickered.

Horses live in the here and the now.

On my first day at Tierra Madre, a seventeen-year-old with next to no knowledge whatsoever about horses, Jim asked me which I thought a horse would prefer: a large field of grass a hundred feet away from them, or a tiny scrap of grass right at their feet.

I had laughed and said, "Well, they're going to go over to the giant field of grass because there's more!"

Wrong. They'll eat the few blades of grass directly in front of them before they move on.

There is no past for horses, nor is there a future. Only this breath, this bite of food, this itch that needs to be scratched, this urge to run and kick, this desire to roll, this love from a human, this precious, unstoppable, irreplaceable moment in time.

Now.

Only now.

You could leave, that nasty little voice in my head said that day, as I stood looking at the loaded lunch cart. *Just go. You have a master's degree now. You have a way out.*

A whinny, somewhere on the ranch. A swish of a tail. A stomp of a hoof.

Nora's empty stall.

You have a way out.

Nickers from the herd, yelling at me to hurry up and feed them.

And I lifted the feed cart, adjusted the few buckets of grain on top, and started to push it forward.

"Okay, okay, guys-I'm coming!"

No, another smaller, weaker voice in my head whispered. *I don't have a way out.*

I have a way through.

CHAPTER FORTY
SEASONS

Every ranch has its seasons. At Tierra Madre, our seasons lined up with those of Mother Earth's, though being in Arizona meant those seasons weren't four equally divided parts of the year with varying color swatches and weather patterns. Arizona seasons revolved around heat. They were Pre-Summer, Summer, Fading Summer, and Not Summer. Tierra Madre seasons waxed and waned alongside them.

Baby Season came in the Pre-Summer, when we were prepping for the inevitable high temperatures by fixing the mister system, testing all the fans in the barn, ordering fly predators, and stocking up on fly spray and SWAT and masks and Studley's summer sore medicines. Quail eggs were discovered in the hay bales. Pink and hairless mice were found in the corners of the tack room in nests of old torn paper and towels and gauze pads. And we had to be careful not to rake the hay around some of the stalls because bunnies had made their lairs there, and they were full of babies.

Baby Season went hand-in-hand with Hair Season, during which most of the horses on the ranch lost their winter coats and horse hair flew around the ranch on the breeze like dandelion seeds. We found horse hair on our clothes, the hay, the grindings, the poop, and spat it out of our mouths. Sometimes birds would take hair for their nests, which were all over the place: the trees, the rafters of the barn, and the inner corners of shade structures. The horses with Cushing's disease didn't lose their hair easily, and we had to shave them or else spend hours brushing them. One spring, Solo had matts of hair hanging from his belly that were so bad that I finally took a pair of medical grade scissors to them and gave his coat the equivalent of a bad at-home bowl haircut. As was the case when I snuck pain meds into a carrot for him years back, he didn't speak to me for a while.

Some of the ex-racers-Suze and Heighten and M'Stor-didn't grow thick winter coats. Jim said that animals didn't grow winter coats due to the change of weather, but rather due to the change in light. The coats started to grow when the sun rose later in the morning and set earlier in the evening during fall. And racehorses were often kept in barns with the lights on all the time for the purpose of preventing thick winter coats from growing. It stuck with their body chemistries long after they had each retired from the track.

For six months out of the year, we were in Survival Season. Summer. For six months out of the year, especially during heat waves, we were in survival mode.

Ant Season happened for a few weeks during the summer, and it was always kicked off when someone would go to pick up a flake of hay then yelp in agony as fire ants engulfed their arms. Ants-suddenly-would be crawling everywhere: in the breezeway, on the railings of stalls, surrounding any scrap of food on the ground, engulfing crusty mash buckets or feeders. We'd spend days going around the ranch with food grade diatomaceous earth, which killed anything with an exoskeleton and which wasn't toxic to the horses. We sprinkled it so much everywhere that it looked like snowfall. When they wandered the ranch in the mornings, Bentley and Solo would often sniff at it, and Jim made fun of them for having questionable white powder on their noses.

Monsoon Season came on the tail end of Survival Season, though we were lucky enough that most monsoon thunderstorms missed us by inches. When they hit, they didn't last a long time, but they were intense with their strong winds and heavy rains. Even a ten-minute monsoon storm at the ranch meant we would spend days bailing water out of stalls and draining the arena by digging trenches.

The storms' subsequent haboobs-apocalyptic with their walls of dust that were thousands of feet tall-tended to disburse by the time they reached Cave Creek. We almost never got those. But one of the worst ones I ever saw struck the ranch head-on one morning in mid-September when Jim was at his meeting and I had three Solids with me. Though we had been watching the sky all morning in anticipation, the sky still turned grayish tan at the speed of light, and faster than we could think the wall of dust was nearly upon us, and we all looked back at the huge, uncovered squeeze of alfalfa and thought… *shit*.

The storm struck just as we were scrambling to tarp the hay. The rain came first, and the wind was so strong that the raindrops hit us sideways like bullets, and we pulled on the tarp against the wind with all we had to try to save the alfalfa. One of the Solids ran for the full lunch carts and dragged them under the barn roof over the breezeway.

Somehow, with lots of shouting directions at each other over the wind, we managed to tarp the hay right as the dust hit the ranch. The horses all turned in their stalls, backs to the wind, heads lowered against the dust, buddied up with their neighbors over the rails to weather the storm. With the hay tarped, we all ran for shelter. The wind was so strong that it was blowing Lee sideways and he was clawing his way across the concrete in the breezeway. I grabbed his collar and yelled, "Everyone get in the tack room!"

The Solids piled inside, me on their heels. Buckets were flying across the driveway. Papers I'd taped to the whiteboard were breaking free and gone to the winds in an instant. I pulled Lee over the threshold into the tack room and made to shut the door.

Then I heard whinnying.

And realized-

"Bourbon and Nibzie are in the arena," I said out loud.

With the exception of the five in-and-out stalls in the barn, the horses didn't have walled shelter, but they had shade structures that sheltered them from the sun. The structures wouldn't help against dust and wind, but the horses could weather the storm from the familiar safety of their pens. I heard Bourbon and Nibzie galloping around, screaming. In the open arena, they were scared.

"Stay here," I told the volunteers as I ran out the tack room door. Before I could close it, one of my Solids, L, ran out with me.

"You're not going out there alone," she said flatly.

It was our shining moment of glory. As the wind roared and the dust billowed so we could only see past maybe thirty feet in any direction, we grabbed halters, pulled our bandanas up over our mouths and noses and ran into the arena. Bourbon and Nibzie tore across the dirt to us, wild-eyed, and came to a screeching halt in front of us long enough for me to wrangle Bourbon and for L to halter Nibzie. We ran them back to their stalls as quickly and calmly as we could and cheered as we latched their gates. Back in their pens, they quieted at once, and we high-tailed it back to the barn, where we got the others and raced to wait out the rest of the storm in the house.

Haboobs sucked. Most times they missed the ranch, but when they hit, they *hit*.

Mush Season came a few months after Monsoon Season, in December and January. We tended to get rain in the late winter, and though it wasn't as intense as monsoon rains, the stalls still flooded and because the hard desert ground didn't know how to handle large quantities of rain, the arena turned into a swimming pool.

We bailed out stalls. We dug trenches in and around the arena to redirect standing pools of water to the wash. We adjusted storm gutters and put buckets under dripping roof corners. We tried desperately to keep the horses' stalls free of manure, though it was hard when the mud and poop mixed together in the parts of their stalls not covered by shelter. During Mush Season, I drove home with mud splattered on my jeans up to my knees. Some of the volunteers wore rain boots, but I never did since they didn't have the same footing as my Ariats, and it was easy to slip while trudging around in what Jim called "boot-sucking mud."

Sometimes, on cold, rainy days, the volunteers and I took turns bringing hot coffee or donuts or bagels. During rainstorms, the horses stayed in their stalls and we'd get through the chores as fast as we could, huddle around the breezeway to get warm, then see how fast we could feed everybody lunch. My record for feeding thirty-one horses solo is eight minutes flat, but only if the Bermuda flaked off its bales perfectly.

I liked most parts of all of our seasons. Not the rain so much. But even during Mush Season there was a feeling of contentment that came with looking out at the herd in their stalls, dry under their shelters, eating away at their lunches while the rain fell around them.

But my favorite season was one that occurred as we left the brutal summer months. Usually it happened in late October. Or early November. The timing was a little different every year.

Changing Season.

The air changed. The hot, stale air of summer fell away to crispness in the morning.

The energy of the horses changed. They rejoiced in the cooler weather and wanted nothing more than to be out in the arena, running and bucking and playing.

The pace of all the people changed. Rather than run for shelter from the sun after feeding lunch, sometimes we all stood leisurely in the breezeway and talked for twenty, thirty minutes at the end of the morning, basking in the 70-degree weather that was typical for an Arizona fall day.

During this season, the fly masks came off for the winter. I went around happily taking them off, washed each one, and then tucked them away in one of the gray sheds until March.

We closed every day at 11 year-round. But during fall time, sometimes we did activities in the afternoons. Every so often we would do a riding lesson for somebody, using Buddy or Akira or Jazz. Or we would have an equine experiential coaching group spend time in the arena with some of our gentlest horses and one of our volunteers who walked them through exercises. For a while, Jim taught I Hear You, Horse horsemanship sessions which were based on his book, and small classes learned how to approach, halter, and lead some of the herd.

Sometimes, I would stay at the ranch in the afternoons just for the sake of sitting in one of the chairs by the breezeway to savor the silence after a morning of chaos.

Sometimes, I would work outside in the breezeway just so I could get up and walk around to see the kids whenever I wanted.

Sometimes, I would go sit in the house and talk with Jim for hours about the horses, fundraising ideas, new policies, the volunteers, or just dreams we had for the ranch.

And it was during these days of my favorite season, after surviving six months of summer, that I began to notice the biggest change of all.

The sun.

The sun's path shifts in the sky as the seasons change and the Earth moves. In the summertime, the sun rises high and its light is stark, unforgiving. But in the fall and all through winter, its arc is lower in the sky and it seems to cast softer rays. In direct contrast to the weather it brings, the hues of light are warm. Gentle. Golden.

The sun's purpose never wavers, but its path sure does.

It rises and falls every day like always, but the road it takes to get from horizon to horizon is gradually different every day, changing with the fading of one season, and the beginning of the new.

CHAPTER FORTY-ONE
ON BEING A LEADER

"Being a strong woman leader means being respectful of everyone. It does not mean being tolerant of every behavior." ~ Unknown

I discovered this quote when I needed it most, in October of 2018 after I dealt with an awful situation that floors me to this day. It occurred three days before our fourth annual benefit fundraiser, the one where we officially shifted from Tierra Madre Horse Sanctuary to Tierra Madre Horse & Human Sanctuary, when I was already losing my mind with last minute event details.

I'd spent all summer overseeing the creation of our new logo. The Tierra Madre logo was over a decade old at that point, and it wasn't as crisp and clear as we would have liked for new t-shirts, marketing collateral, our website, etc. The new logo was to be unveiled at this fourth annual Big Event. We showed it to the volunteers beforehand and we were all incredibly proud of it.

But the situation I dealt with three days before this event involved a single volunteer who-against my direct orders, which were straight from Jim and the rest of the board of directors-went behind my back to complete a project with the brand spanking new logo that turned out disastrously wrong. She had the logo printed onto a sign that distorted it, and had elements missing, and which didn't represent the new brand that we had spent months building. Through the grapevine, I heard this volunteer was also planning on "surprising" us by interrupting our thirty-minute program at the fundraiser to present this sign with our distorted logo, despite the fact that every second had been planned with speakers and video presentations.

Jim was very clear: no one was to do anything with our new logo without permission. And if permission was granted, the logo damn well better be correct.

I told the volunteer we couldn't use her project, and she would not be permitted to speak during the program because there was simply no time for her. I also reminded her of our policy regarding our logo and that I needed to approve anything before it was completed, let alone presented to an audience. When she protested and started disrespectfully pushing back, I snapped. I told her I was done, and the following Monday after the benefit was over, she would sit with me and Jim for a disciplinary meeting.

I'll spare all the details of what happened next. They aren't necessary here.

All that needs to be said is that this volunteer attempted to blackmail us, tried to turn a number of the volunteers against me, and sent something like six pages of flame about me to Jim. She was kind enough to send it to me directly as well. I didn't read it word for word but curiosity got the better of me and I skimmed it after the benefit was over. In this massive novel of a document, this volunteer called me names, said I had control issues, promised to ensure donors would never give us a dime again if she could help it, and spewed a dozen other nasty things that left me in disbelief over the immaturity of a woman twice my age who didn't get her way.

And the entire situation made me think a great deal about what it meant to be a young woman in a position of power, an executive director who had a board of directors to answer to and policies to uphold.

That particular volunteer, that particular situation, was not the first time I dealt with absolute bullshit.

Throughout the years, I was barked at on numerous occasions by people who didn't like me telling them how our systems worked and what they could and could not do with each of the horses.

I was bullied, bombarded, ridiculed, questioned, laughed at, and ignored by those who didn't believe I-a woman in my twenties-was capable or worthy of being a decision maker. A boss. A leader.

I was told, "Do it this way. Don't do that. You shouldn't do this. You should do that," more times than I can possibly count.

I was handed binders of capital campaign literature from other nonprofit organizations with the instruction to read over it and learn about how I and the ranch could be doing better.

I was informed on several occasions that, "You're too young to be the Executive Director." One time, I introduced myself to a visitor only to have them look around and say, "No, really. Who's in charge here?"

I came down firmly when I received pushback, in ways that might have earned men praise for being good managers, while I received backlash from those I supervised for being "bossy" or for "overreacting" or "fanning flames."

I watched person after person storm off the ranch in a huff because I wouldn't meekly step aside and let them push me around. Because I put my horses first. Because I refused to be disrespected as a boss and as a woman and as a human being.

I worked for the horses and I worked for Jim, who backed me every single solitary time someone challenged me. I did not work for people who didn't know me or the ranch or anything about our history, resources, and policies.

I made mistakes, to be sure. Oh, I have made many mistakes in the realm of leadership.

But over the years of listening to those who loved me enough to gently call me out on my actions that were wrong, I also learned to discern between someone who didn't like me respectfully asking them to do something differently, or not at all, and someone genuinely teaching me a lesson in communicating with people. Jim, and some of my Solids who were my dearest friends, guided me through many a time where I couldn't tell the difference.

And after so many years and many more to come of dealing with the types of situations like the one I dealt with before that benefit fundraiser, I find myself with something to say, and it's to every other woman or young leader out there who often find themselves expected to tolerate all behaviors:

Be kind. Be firm. And be strong.

Don't engage. Don't retort. And don't retreat.

Draw your lines in the sand and stick to them. Allow no one to redefine them for you.

Raise your standards, and hold them there.

Stand your ground. A brick house doesn't fear a storm.

Embrace the challenge. I am ever grateful for the lessons that allow me to grow and lean into the person I want to be.

Never tolerate disrespect or insubordination. Never.

And some people may not like the fact that you set boundaries or the fact that they can't get their way.

You know what? That's fine.

They can get on your team, or they can get out of your way.

The choice is theirs.

CHAPTER FORTY-TWO
HORSES AND HUMANS

Tierra Madre Horse Sanctuary became Tierra Madre Horse & Human Sanctuary on October 12, 2018, at our fourth benefit fundraiser.

Jim and I had talked about the name change for a long time. With agreement from Jean, our Solids, and our growing board of directors, we finally moved forward with it.

By that point, volunteers had been coming to us for years to share how our horses had impacted their lives for the better, how changed they were because of their experiences with the herd. On more than one occasion, we even heard the words: "Tierra Madre saved my life."

We had become a sanctuary not just for the horses, but for its humans, too. We had become a place for people to come and just be in the presence of honest animals who didn't care who people were so long as each person had the integrity to be honest back.

And the horses didn't just have that impact on volunteers. By the time we officially changed our name, Tierra Madre had been partnering with a number of organizations for several years, offering experiences to those who were in need of healing, understanding, confidence building, or some combination of the three.

Adolescents with autism. Individuals in half-way homes. People recovering from addiction. Students in high school with special needs.

The bruised and the broken. The weary and the misunderstood. The ones with unique gifts and the ones trying to find themselves again. We accepted everybody.

When we began partnering with local nonprofits, schools, and businesses, I spent many a morning teaching horsemanship lessons to groups of teens or adults. Because horses are prey animals, they are reactive to the energy of the humans surrounding them. If somebody trying to halter one of the horses was anxious, that horse knew and they too became afraid. If somebody trying to walk a horse didn't have confidence in themselves, that horse didn't have confidence in them either and stopped listening completely. Every action or non-action the horses made was a discussion, a learning moment, an opportunity to interpret and reflect. There was something to be learned in every aspect of horsemanship. How to be patient. How to be assertive. How to be gentle. How to relax. How to be self-assured. How to just be.

I worked with one of our amazing volunteers, C-who founded her equine experiential coaching program based out of Tierra Madre-to individualize programs for groups. We worked with different members of the herd depending on the confidence level of each group. Sometimes we would do arena time during which a handful of people created obstacle courses out of materials and drove horses through them without touching them. Sometimes the groups would observe horses interacting and interpret their behavior, which always revealed a different result for each person that was based on what that person was going through in their lives. Sometimes we had groups communicate with each other silently to accomplish a particular goal with a horse as team building exercises. And sometimes groups were there to learn a specific skill and to feel accomplished in giving their time; those groups mucked stalls; scrubbed feeders; fed horses; and filled pens with grindings.

C also co-hosted a number of workshops at the ranch during which she partnered with therapists, meditation specialists, writers, healers. Classes of a dozen people spent the day with the horses, taking breaks to eat lunch and write and reflect in the garden. I got to spend time with so many incredible people those days, walking each group through safety protocol before handing them over to C, watching them fall in love with the horses that served as mirrors, teachers, friends.

The effect the Tierra Madre horses had on people was nothing short of miraculous. I saw grown men and women terrified of approaching the herd at first introduction bury their heads in our horses' manes by the end of their time with us. I saw smiles stretch wide across faces that had been grim and withdrawn. I saw dull, empty eyes grow bright with conviction. The horses sensed confidence, thrived off of it, and they reacted to people simply believing in themselves again by giving their trust-utterly and completely-to people who needed it the most.

Sometime just before the official name change, I was talking with a man who often came with his young kids to volunteer on weekends. He had been in the military and had spent time oversees in Iraq. He dealt with depression and PTSD. By the second or third time he was there to volunteer, he was telling me about some of these struggles. I listened patiently. Many, many of the volunteers told me their stories.

"I don't know. I just got to a point in my life where, you know, I just-" He hesitated. His two children were just out of earshot, fawning over Rusty, and he watched them giggling with a faraway look in his eyes. "Where I just-"

"Where you haven't decided to make the play yet," I said quietly, "but all your cards are on the table."

He turned and stared at me.

"Yes. How did you know that?"

"Because I've been there too," I said. "It's hard."

He nodded, and was quiet. We were loading the hay carts and around us, the volunteers were topping off waters, making the dinner mashes, preparing to feed lunch. Over on the field side of the ranch, M'Stor was already pacing back and forth in his stall in anticipation of food and next to us, Sedona was boring holes into us with his hungry gaze.

"I like these horses," the volunteer finally said. "It's easy to think around them."

"They simplify things a bit, don't they? Make things easier to understand?"

"Yeah. People are hard to talk to. That's why I don't like therapists much. But you can just be around a horse and think about stuff. Just be. And they just stand there."

"They're amazing," I answered fervently. "They've been through hell too, you know. They get scared sometimes about things that remind them of abuse, or trauma, or whatever it was they went through. They have their moments. But they just needed time. They got the help they needed. And look at them now."

He smiled a little.

"Are you talking about the horses," he asked, "or yourself?"

CHAPTER FORTY-THREE
RAIN

Some dates are inscribed on my heart forever. February 13th, 2015 is one of them.

The day before, I was scrolling through Facebook at 8 o'clock at night when I saw a post that would change my life and the history of Tierra Madre forever.

It was a post in one of the local public groups dedicated to saving horses, and it was made by someone whose neighbor was a kill buyer.

"PLEASE HELP!" was the caption. "Pregnant mustang in hands of kill buyer. Must find home at once!!"

I could have kept scrolling. I saw those posts in horse networks online all the time. Kill pens are notorious for utilizing emotional blackmail in order to get money from people, which then is spent on more horses to fuel the slaughter pipeline. Either way, horses die.

But something about this little mustang mare caught me off guard. Something in her face moved me. Something about the way she stood with her head turned to face the camera but only so, as though she had very little will to do anything but stand in misery. Something just behind her eyes that was calling, pleading.

I shared the post. I got a hold of Jim and passed along the contact information to him. Waited. Hoping.

He called me back later. By that time, it was close to 10 o'clock at night.

"She'll be here tomorrow afternoon," he said. "She's due to ship across the border any day. And she's pregnant. I can't allow that."

The next day, February 13th, 2015, Jim and B, our ranch manager at that time, and I sat around in the house looking up names. We were excited beyond anything we'd ever experienced before. A new horse was coming and not only were we getting a new friend, she was bringing a baby with her, too.

Before long, Jim's phone rang and we saw the trailer begin to pull up outside our front gates. B and I practically ran up the driveway. The horses started whinnying in eagerness to see the inhabitant; they knew a horse trailer when they saw one. The kill buyer was driving the truck. The neighbor who had posted about the mare sat beside him. Apparently, the kill buyer only agreed to give us the mare with an upfront payment, which the neighbor had spotted for us. We would give half the money to the kill buyer and the other half to spot back the neighbor.

Sensing our hatred, Jim turned to B and I before the truck had come to a complete stop and warned us, in only a few words, to be nice. "He gives us the mare," he said, "we give him the money, he leaves. That's it."

We grit our teeth as the kill buyer and his neighbor got out of his trailer, and bit our tongues as they greeted us. I'm not sure what I expected a kill buyer to look like-something out of a mug shot, probably-but the kill buyer bringing the mare was very neat, with trimmed facial hair, even white teeth, and a clean, tucked in shirt. He greeted us, then walked into the trailer to get the mare. As he made to take hold of her halter, she cowered away from him.

Before I could stop myself, I walked up the ramp. "I'll take her," I said shortly, and grabbed the rope out of his hands. Without waiting for a response, I turned my back and led her away from him. As I walked I heard him say, "I need that halter back."

Silently B handed me the one we had brought from the breezeway and we quickly switched her, handing the kill buyer back his halter. Jim gave him his money, and the neighbor hers. And they left. And that was it.

I lead the mare through the gates and walked through the little wash area, toward the round pen where she would be living in quarantine for the next few weeks. She was a dun, with a black stripe down her back like the Kiger mustangs, and had an M7 brand on her right shoulder. Her face was scratched, her hooves were in need of a trim, and her winter coat-already coming off-was matted and hanging in clumps on her belly. She wasn't underweight, but for a horse that was supposedly pregnant, she didn't look it.

But it was her attitude that was the saddest of all. She walked with her head down, defeat etched in every inch of her face. She hardly seemed interested in the thirty-odd horses all running around in their stalls screaming at her in greeting. She didn't care about our hands that reached out to gently touch her and didn't seem to hear our quiet voices. She just followed me into the round pen as though each step forward cost her more energy than she had left. Like she wanted nothing more than to lay down and never get up again.

I turned her loose in the round pen, walked out, and closed the gate. Jim and B and I stood around watching her. She stood still for a few minutes, then crept over to the feeder and hesitantly began to eat the hay we'd placed there for her. She chewed her hay quietly as we still tried to think of what to call her.

And I threw out a name I thought summed her up perfectly.

It was a name I'd loved for many years, one that stands for that which is precious and life-bringing in the desert. Here this little mustang was, about to be the bearer of life, and whom we could already see was a rare, cherished little treasure, though she didn't know it yet.

Jim and B agreed with my name choice.

And so, the little dun mustang-carrying a baby and snatched from a kill buyer in the nick of time-became Rain.

It really was the nick of time. The next day, Jim talked to the neighbor to give her an update. And we learned the chilling news: a slaughter truck had stopped by the kill pen that day.

Had we not taken Rain, she and her unborn foal would have been on that truck.

The following Monday, the vet we had at the time came to examine her. All our new intakes got a vet examination, and we not only needed to make sure that Rain and the baby were healthy, we needed to learn what we had to do to prepare for a foal. But upon seeing Rain, the first words out of the vet's mouth were, "I hope she's not pregnant, because she's awfully skinny."

We jumped for joy when it was confirmed she was. And we promptly made plans to fatten her up.

We saved Rain in February of 2015. Up until then, Tierra Madre was really only known within the Phoenix Valley. Jim had several out-of-state contacts through an online forum that was dedicated to saving horses and whom had been our friends for many years. Other than them, most of the people who knew about us lived in Phoenix.

But when Rain entered our world, word about her traveled across the country. Stories were done in the local papers and shared online. Posts about her on our Facebook page went viral. Thousands of people heard of her story, the story of a little pregnant mare with sad eyes who was saved from horrific death.

We held a baby shower fundraiser for her in March. We had pink and blue themed games and food and decorations. Everyone suggested names for the foal and brought us bags of grain and buckets and halters and supplements, "for Rain and the baby and all their friends." Several news teams came out that day and interviewed Jim and I then proceeded to share her story.

And hundreds of new friends started following us after that baby shower. Our donors and supporters wanted to stay posted on her progress and throw out baby names and guess her due date. Our following and our donors increased exponentially. Everyone wanted to be a part of her story. Everyone fell head over heels in love with her.

And Rain soaked it up. She felt that love and it showed in the way she became the happiest little girl, how she became the soul of Tierra Madre and epitomized everything we stood for.

We nourished her mind, body, and spirit every second of every day… and she blossomed.

The scratch on her face healed. Her mane and coat shone brightly. And her happiness was infectious.

She whinnied with joy when Bill came through the gates to feed everyone, or when the door to Jim's house opened, because she knew hay or carrots were on the way. She scarfed down every bit of her food at mealtimes. She ran and bucked and kicked with reckless abandon in the arena. She tugged at her lead rope when we walked her around the ranch because she was so eager to see what the world had in store for her. And when she walked, she held her head high, her eyes shining.

She brought us new family members. She brought us hope. She brought us Sunny.

Every tour I gave, every story I wrote about the ranch … Rain was front and center. Our shining glory. One of our proudest saves. A tribute to the resilience of horses. A symbol of hope and goodness and courage and the power of a mother whose gift was that of bringing life. Strength and gentleness in one. Rain was the symbol of what Tierra Madre gave to horses and what we were given back in turn.

Rain was one of the greats.

She was maybe in her mid-teens.

One late afternoon in September 2018, Jim called me as I was driving home from running errands.

It didn't begin with, "All is well."

"It's Rain," he said, and my stomach flipped at the fear in his voice. "It's Rain. I walked out of the house and she was down in her stall. Doc just got here and did a rectal. Displacement. We're tubing her now. It's bad. It's really bad."

Panic rose inside me. I broke every traffic rule in the book as I turned around and sped to the ranch, heart beating, terror pumping through my veins.

When I got there and ran through the gate, Jim and our vet were in the arena with her and Bill was holding her halter. Everything in me crashed and fell down deep into despair when I saw her.

Her beautiful face was swollen and bloodied. She had been thrashing. Her sides were bloated. She had been sedated, but she was trying to go down desperately to roll.

The sight of her burned into my memory right then and there, a horrific sight that I will never unsee. Even though she was sedated, the pain in her eyes was there. It had come from nothing. Every second ticking by was precious time.

She'd been tubed, and our vet said she was going to do an abdominocentesis. By making a small cut in her abdomen and testing the fluids that came out, our vet would be able to determine if we were dealing with a torsion-a tear in her intestines-and if she was bleeding internally.

We didn't have time to think. Rain's sides were bloating more rapidly with every passing second. We got her to the barn. Jim and I exchanged a look of pure terror as the procedure was done. The fluid was collected in about two minutes flat. I knew from a past procedure on another that it should have been clear fluid that came out, but Rain's was dark red.

The tech sprinted to the truck to test it as our vet quickly, expertly tended to the wound then ran to join her. Time was ticking, ticking. Rain groaned and tried to go down again. Jim and I held her up with everything we had, talking to her, praying to everything we knew, clinging to hope, begging her to hold on, hold on, hold on.

Our vet ran up to us.

"So I've tested the peritoneal fluid. We measure lactose and glucose in numbers. A zero is normal. A three would warrant candidacy for surgery. But she is at a six. She is not a candidate for surgery. We can't. We're looking at a torsion, we're looking at internal bleeding, possible severe peritonitis. And the pain that would cause this kind of bruising and blood on her face from thrashing is catastrophic. We can't do surgery."

Ringing silence.

Ringing silence.

Ringing silence.

"Can't we bag her?" I choked out, faintly. Everything was fading from me. Rain was breathing, hard.

Our vet started to cry. In the two years we'd been together as a team, despite every hardship and emergency and heartache we'd endured, she was collected and calm. Not this time. This time was different. This time was about to break us all.

"I hate to say this, because I know how special she is," she cried. "But we can't. There is no other way."

Just one beat more of ringing silence. Then-

"Do it," Jim said.

Our vet turned and ran to the truck, her tech on her heels. Jim began talking soothingly, lovingly to the mustang who had changed all of our lives, who had changed Tierra Madre forever.

"We're going to make it better," he said to her softly, head against hers. "That's my word. We're going to make the pain stop. Right now."

We pulled her out of the barn and our vet was back and there were the two pink syringes, and our vet got the first one in her, and it was thrown aside, and the next was in shortly after, and before my mind could register what was happening, Rain was laying lifeless on the ground, out of pain, blood dripping down her neck from where the needle pierced, mane splayed on the woodchips, eyes peacefully staring, and three and a half years of joy and happiness and miracles were over.

Numb, broken, I crumbled at her head and sobbed.

Hardly any time had passed since I'd come running through the gate. Things had moved that fast. I simply couldn't take it in.

Rain was gone.

A horrific, inexplicable torsion and internal bleeding, the worst of colics.

We got three and a half years of her life. And we wouldn't get any more. Our Rain had gone to a place we couldn't follow.

I wanted to lay in the dirt with her and never get back up. Instead, in shock, I called two of the Solids who were deeply bonded to Rain. I didn't want them to find out on our volunteer page on Facebook. Both of them reacted the same way: came speeding to the ranch to see her, to see the nightmare for themselves. When they each arrived, I tried to head them off away from the barn and warn them that what they were about to see wasn't pretty. Both of them pushed past me to collapse at Rain's head and kiss her face and tell her they loved her.

The sun was setting when Trail's End came.

I hate Trail's End. I love them because they're such good people who haul away livestock with such kindness and dignity, but I hate them. I hate what they have to do.

They cut Rain's tail and gave it to me, then started the process of loading her into their trailer. I looked away as they did it. I went in the house and wrote them a check.

The sun had set by the time she was loaded. As the truck started, I walked toward the closed trailer, where Rain lay, and put my hand to its cold door, so close to her, but so far away. Slowly, the trailer began to move, pulling away from my hand, and began to drive toward the gate. Jazz, Rain's stall mate, cried out for her and anguish seared my heart. My volunteers and I held each other and cried.

Seeing the life leave their eyes is agony. Seeing them dragged into the trailers is somehow worse. But when the trailers take them away, part of my soul leaves with them.

And as the trailer pulled through the same gates Rain had entered three and a half years before, I remembered that day she first came to us. When she had walked in skinny and sad and scared. Head down. A big scratch across her nose. Eyes defeated. How she had changed for the better over the years. How happiness had finally found her.

Those three and a half years were part of our golden age. Those years represented change, all spearheaded by a mustang with a foal in her belly who had nowhere else to go, who thrived on love and returned it to our ranch tenfold. Those years were the happiest of her life, and some of my most cherished memories on this earth.

Rain in the desert is precious. A rarity and a blessing from above, it is the bringer of life and of thriving opportunity.

But as I watched that trailer take her away from me forever, tears streaming down my face, I realized there was one last thing I had to learn about rain in the desert.

Its impact goes on forever.

But it doesn't last nearly long enough.

CHAPTER FORTY-FOUR
MY FEAR

Some days, when the darkness comes creeping in and the heaviness settles more firmly in my chest, I live in fear.

But it's not a normal kind of fear, I don't think.

Because my fear isn't that someday, I won't be able to make the decision to let them go.

My fear isn't that I won't be able to watch them dragged into trailers and hauled away.

My fear isn't that I won't be able to watch the light go out in their eyes.

My fear is that someday, I will become too hard to feel. Too callused to care. Too numb to feel a twinge of anything but cold blankness when they leave me.

My fear isn't the pain. My fear is the lack of it.

My fear isn't ever saying goodbye.

My fear is that someday, I won't care if I say it.

CHAPTER FORTY-FIVE
THE MOOSE

The day I walked into Tierra Madre at seventeen years old, I had a plan.

It was a plan that had slowly materialized in the fog of depression that began years before. It was a plan that had crept forward, wrapping its tendrils through my mind until it was so deeply embedded in my subconscious that I forgot what it was like to live without it.

No one knew about it but me. No one could ever know about it but me.

I never carried it out.

But at that point in my life, the plan made the darkness bearable, if only because I believed it was a way to rid myself of it forever.

There have been times since those few awful years when glimpses of that overwhelming heaviness and emptiness have come billowing back. Times when whispers returned. Times that lasted days and sometimes weeks and sometimes months, when it seemed easier to lay face down in the dirt after being kicked down.

To let the world go on.

To let me stay behind.

It didn't need me.

And during each of those days and weeks and months, I thought of Moosie.

One of the Original Twenty-Nine was the Moose.

Jim called him the Medicine Man. Moose was a National Show Horse, which was some cross between an Arabian and a Saddlebred, with a rich coat containing every warm, beautiful shade of brown... but it was everything else about him that defined him.

Moose had deep, soulful eyes that held the wisdom of a thousand generations of horses. There was a greatness to him that dwelled from deep within, a greatness which went beyond the ability all horses possess to just be. He reflected things that others didn't. He reacted to disturbances within spirits as disturbances to the very universe.

He was the Moose.

Moose had Cushing's disease. He also had a chronic case of laminitis, the hoof disease that would claim my Sonora and several more of the Tierra Madre herd in later years. And in living with laminitis, Moose had good days and bad days. His feet hurt him often. He needed daily medicine to manage his pain and his ACTH levels and our vet at the time-our beloved Dr. R-visited frequently to look at his hooves and make sure he was as comfortable as possible.

There was a great deal of uncertainty around laminitis in those days, more so than there is now. In the late 2000s, laminitis wasn't as treatable as it is today. Our vet didn't have portable radiograph machines, treatment options were limited, and the outcome for most cases was bleak.

But Moosie never complained. Not one time. He patiently allowed the vet and the farrier to work on his feet. He allowed Jim to give him medicines several times a day without protest. No matter how uncomfortable he was, in the face of the unknown, he was content. He was steadfast and quiet in his existence, but the center of our ranch just the same. And like the elders who were called upon in their communities for their ancient knowledge of the world, Moose was a constant source of wisdom to many.

Not to me, at first.

The vines of my plan were wrapped so tightly around me that I didn't possess the ability to understand the Moose, at first. As the months passed at the ranch, however, they began to loosen. The person I was before them had begun to emerge, ever so slightly, bruised and scratched but somehow still there.

Then one day in late September, when I had been volunteering at Tierra Madre for four months, I was in Moose's stall, shaving his coat. Horses with Cushing's disease tended to grow thick coats which were uncomfortable in the hot Arizona sun, and I had been tasked with shaving Moosie's. He wasn't haltered and he could have gone anywhere in the stall away from me and the clippers, but he stood quietly and allowed me to trim him.

And as I stood there with him, letting my mind wander, Moosie turned and fixed me with a gaze that pierced me right through to my soul.

The language of horses is that of Equus. They communicate in imagery and feelings and body movement.

And I'll never forget the melody of thoughts that Moosie communicated to me in those moments as he stood looking at me: himself as a foal, young then but older and wiser now, which turned to the realization that I myself was still a child, though I had just turned eighteen and-though I didn't realize it then-was in desperate need of professional help.

Barricades. My heart, locked. Scared. Moosie's kind eyes, brown and honest. A world that was filled with things that made me both want to shrink in fear and throw my arms out to face them. And me struggling, struggling, and then reaching-

It would be many years before I came to fully understand what the Moose told me that day. In fact, I think many more years will pass and I will realize something else about what the Moose told me that day.

But I know with every fiber of my being that Moosie sensed my plan and objected to it. More importantly, he saw who I was without it. Everything I was, and everything I wanted to be, I saw in his eyes.

I turned the clippers off and set them down, just outside his stall. And I put my face in his mane as the tears welled up and he quietly stood and let me just breathe. Breathe in. Breathe out.

I felt tired. I was struggling. Reaching.

Do you think I could be brave like you? I finally asked him.

His answer was my own thought, reflected at me:

I think you have a great deal of courage in that barricaded heart of yours.

So in that moment, I promised him, with every bit of conviction I possessed, that going forward I would be brave, like he had shown me how to be. For all my life. For always.

And with that promise, on that day in Moosie's stall, I broke free. For the first time in years, the suffocating tendrils of my plan loosened forever.

I stood there with him for a long while, shaving his coat, thinking to myself over and over again: *I'll be brave, Moosie. I'll be brave.*

And when it was time for me to leave, I kissed his nose and he looked at me with his great eyes, love deep within them, and I left his stall lighter than I had felt in a long, long time. Though I would later benefit from years of professional therapy, as of that very day, the plan was no more.

Moosie died not two days later. He up and left. In his sleep. During a crisis during which Guess was horribly sick with colic that was so bad her chances of survival were next to none.

And Jim swears Moosie laid down in his stall and sent her all the healing energy he could to save her life before he joined the Great Herd peacefully, on his terms. There could not have been a more noble way to leave, no other death song a Medicine Man could have sung.

His death came from nowhere. It rocked me to my core.

And if my promise had meant something to me while Moosie lived, it meant something far greater when he was gone. Because what other tribute could I possibly offer to such a great spirit than to keep my promise?

There have been so many times since my last encounter with the Moose where I have been called upon to be brave and I didn't know how. That's how it is for a lot of people, I think. There's an expectation of greatness that comes with being brave, and it's easy to feel like unless you do something great to demonstrate courage, you fall short.

The Moose showed me that just *living* is brave.

And deciding that I wanted to live was the bravest thing I ever did.

To keep up with the world. To not fall behind. Because maybe-just maybe-it needed me.

And when those times come where I'm struggling to stand after being kicked down into the dirt, I hear the echo of my last words I whispered to a great horse all those years ago.

I'll be brave, Moosie.

I'll be brave.

And I rise.

I have a promise to keep.

CHAPTER FORTY-SIX
THANK YOUS

During the fifteen months I worked for my master's degree, I ran the ranch in the mornings then went home and did office work in the afternoons. Then-depending on the day-I either did my coursework or drove downtown for class that would start at 6pm and get out three hours later. Then I'd drive home, collapse in bed, wake up the next day, and do it all over again.

I ran on a bit of sleep, the love of thirty-odd horses, and coffee. But the knowledge I was gaining in my classes was beyond worth my exhaustion. I excitedly discussed ideas, statistics, and my fresh understandings of how other nonprofits were managed with Jim after attending enlightening classes or reading interesting articles. We bounced ideas off each other and off some of the volunteers. They were priceless in their love and dedication to the horses and additionally had connections to potential community partners, experience in facilitating corporate sponsorships, or otherwise just had incredible input for strategic fundraising and were willing to help with the legwork.

Slowly, the internal structure of Tierra Madre was emerging in the form of a management committee, an events committee, a volunteer coordinator, ambassadors and outreach volunteers, a donor relations manager, and, eventually, a formal board of directors, most of whom weren't ranch volunteers but who were connected to our mission and had a great deal of input and insight regarding the ranch's governance.

And within this multitude of amazing people rose one of the most important lessons I ever learned in all my years of study and work in the field of nonprofit management: the importance of relationship building.

To continue along the pathway of organizational sustainability, we needed strong, working friendships with our volunteers, with each member of our board of directors, with partners in our community, and-perhaps most importantly of all-with our donors.

Now, because Tierra Madre was a 501(c)(3) tax deductible nonprofit organization, all of our donors received tax receipts for every donation they sent us. A nonprofit's tax receipt should always include a statement about how no goods or services had been exchanged in return for the donation, and it needed to list the amount given plus the date the gift had been received. I wrote a generic letter to serve as a receipt which also included a heartfelt thank you message from me, telling the donor how much we appreciated their gift.

But in my classes, I learned about donor cultivation. How important it was to get both the ask and the thank you correct. How each point of contact couldn't always include a request for money lest donors get burnt out. How donors also needed to hear from us frequently in the form of newsletters, updates, and reports.

I started to think that maybe sending a receipt and acknowledgement letter wasn't cutting it. If our end goal was to establish *strong* relationships, then what could we do to show our appreciation for those who made our mission possible?

I started writing newsletters and sending them a few times a year. I wrote an end-of-year report and made a holiday card for that year's donors. We did social media shout outs and acknowledgements. For big gifts, I sent a painting done by one of the kids and a personal letter. And I decided that given the budget and resources we had available, Tierra Madre would start sending handwritten thank you postcards for every single donation we received.

I'd gleaned the idea from another rescue who did the same thing and thought it was brilliant. Who didn't love receiving a handwritten thank you card? We had to send the acknowledgement letters with tax receipts anyway, so why not just tuck a thank you into each envelope?

So that's exactly what we did. I spent hours writing thank yous every month-though in later years volunteers helped me-personalizing them as best I could by telling the donor where their donation had gone. We couldn't afford donor management software, so I made notes on my master Excel spreadsheet of who each donor was, and why they gave to Tierra Madre. That person loved Hudson. Another loved our Arabians. Another donated for Bella because her daughter had fallen in love with her during an open ranch years back. Another was an aspiring veterinarian and wanted to help with medical bills. One of the perks of being a small nonprofit with fewer than five hundred regular donors was that it was possible to get to know the donors and remember important, personal details about each individual.

The results were incredible. While there were certainly other factors at stake (such as our social media visibility and improved transparency over the years), the combined effort of contacting donors more frequently plus the thoughtful thank you cards tripled our donor retention rate in just two years. Better yet, we had a 47% increase in donors in that same amount of time. More people were donating per year, and more of them were giving more than once. We threw ourselves into relationship building, and we were rewarded with not only more funding, but with wonderful friendships with some of the best people I've ever known.

Sometimes after we sent that month's thank yous out, we got cards back. Little notes of appreciation. Letters that shared stories of horses that were loved and long gone. Our donors shared their lives with us, just like we shared our horses' lives with them. And during this transformation, our mindset of soliciting donations changed. We weren't begging for money to scrape by. We were offering people an experience, an opportunity to be a part of something bigger than themselves. We were thanking them for being on our journey with us.

I didn't stop the thank yous with the donors. Volunteers were donors, too- the only difference was that they gave their time, which was just as valuable. I loved putting together small tokens of appreciation for them: homemade applesauce in Mason jars ("You're the APPLE of our eye!"), peppermint hot cocoa mix ("Thank you for your commitMINT!"), miniature succulents ("You're the ROOT of our organization!"). Once a year we did a volunteer appreciation dinner either at a local restaurant or at the ranch itself. And though I didn't get around to it every time, I tried to write thank yous after big events, where the volunteers put a thousand percent into making the event a success.

Every so often, like the donors, a volunteer would bring a thank you card for Jim and me, completely out of the blue, to say thank you for what we did. Those touched my heart more than I could ever express.

And ironically, the most memorable thank you that stands out to me over the years wasn't one I sent to anybody or one I received from a donor or a volunteer. It was one we received a volunteer's mother.

We saw a number of younger volunteers at Tierra Madre. Teenagers, preteens, and small kids came with regularity. Each of them made an impact on our ranch. But one girl-Willow-I'll remember forever.

Willow was perhaps ten or eleven, and she came to the ranch often with both her grandfather and her best friend, who was the same age as her. The grandfather often sat in one of our chairs outside the breezeway and chatted pleasantly with us while the two girls helped with the chores then played with the horses. Like I always did with the young ones, I kept a close eye on the two girls, but I needn't had worried. Willow and her friend were extremely cautious around the herd, hardworking, respectful, and sweet as pie.

Willow was drawn to Iron Man and her friend to Slayer. They weren't experienced enough to walk them, but they were still eager to help wipe down stall bars or rake aisles or make mashes and deliver them, smiling and giggling all the while. One day, they came up to me, very concerned, because Iron Man had a small scratch on his face. The scratch was a few millimeters long, but I showed them the betadine and the triple antibiotic cream and the aerosol bandage we used for wound care and asked if they'd like to help me patch him up. You would have thought I'd offered them the sun and stars. They lit up and excitedly helped me administer first aid to their beloved patient, and Iron Man received perhaps the best wound care service in the world that day.

Then, suddenly, Willow's grandfather passed away. I didn't see either of the girls for a while.

In fact, it wasn't until several months later I learned about what was going on with this happy, joyful little girl who came to the ranch so fascinated with life and with a smile on her face. That she struggled with depression. That losing her grandfather had nearly put her over the edge. That she was recovering from an attempt on her life in a hospital.

One morning, the girl's mother came to the ranch without her. Her eyes were red. I invited her into the house where she gave Jim a card ("With a small donation," she said, wiping her eyes) and handed me a beautiful horse necklace which had belonged to her father, Willow's grandfather, which she wanted me to have.

Choking back tears, I asked about her daughter.

"She's doing a lot better," her mother answered. "I just wanted to come by and say thank you. I hope she'll be back here soon. I think she will be."

She left not long afterward. I sat on the couch while Jim opened the card and read it. He stared at it for a long time. Then, silently, he handed it to me.

It read:

Dear Jim and Alexis:

I want to thank you! With your foundation, and Iron Man, I want to tell you that you saved her life! My daughter chose to try to take the easy way out but survived. Thanks to Alexis and Iron Man and Sunny. She chose to get better. I want to tell you, Jim, because of your life's work she cannot wait to get back there. Thank you! Your horses touched her life. You both are gifts.

Some days, I remembered why I ran on a bit of sleep and the love of thirty-odd horses and coffee.

That was one of those days.

CHAPTER FORTY-SEVEN
SUNNY

Sunny was our baby.

Our first foal. Our first beginning. To this day, she remains the only horse on the ranch who was actually born on Tierra Madre soil.

When she was two days old, we turned her and Rain out into the arena together for the first time. Every horse on the ranch ran to the front of their stalls to look at the new baby and hollered at her in greeting. And Sunny shrieked with joy, echoing their neighs, and she bucked and kicked and reared and sprinted around the arena as fast as her gangly legs would go, her mother tearing after her, and the ranch was a symphony of rejoicing.

That moment set the precedent for Sunny's personality and all she brought to Tierra Madre: pure happiness and excitement at the prospect of experiencing everything life had to offer.

Her early months were spent romping, nursing, then promptly passing out in a milk-induced coma on the cushy, straw-covered floor of hers and Rain's stall. She knew only love from everyone around her. Being the miracle foal of a mare who was so nearly sent to slaughter, the love Sunny received from everyone who set foot onto the ranch was just short of reverence. It showed in the way she skipped toward people in eagerness when she saw them, thrusting her little face forward in hopes that somebody would offer scratches or give her something good to eat.

Like her mother, Sunny was pure mustang in body and attitude. She was a bay, with a white star in the middle of two inquisitive eyes that took in every detail of her surroundings. She was curious, playful, stubborn, and delighted with everything she saw.

We kept a breakaway leather halter on her so she could get used to wearing one from an early age. We were careful not to move quickly around her face and were gentle in attaching her lead rope when it was time for her to go out, lest she grow up head shy. We lifted her feet and scratched her all over so she would be used to human touch from the beginning.

All in all, almost from the very day she was born, we had begun the process of getting her used to being a horse.

She was already very good at being a horse. As a matter of fact, every horse is very good at being a horse.

But for Sunny, we envisioned a future that didn't follow the same path as that of the rest of the herd. The others had walked through our gates; she had been born within them. She would never leave through those gates, but retirement or recovery didn't befit her. She was a blank slate, a fresh start, and there were so many things she hadn't yet experienced that we wanted to show her. How to walk nicely on the right side of a human. How to pick her feet up for the farrier. How to be groomed. How to lunge at a walk, trot, and canter. How to back up and move around objects. How to wear a saddle. How-eventually-to be ridden and enjoy carrying a human on her back.

There was a catch. Around the time she was five months old, Sunny realized that she was both bigger and stronger than all of us, and she demonstrated her newfound discovery by engaging each of us in games of tug-of-war when we had her on a lead. Everyone's upper body strength improved drastically over those months and we all learned the tricks of walking a baby horse who was quite small but still had the strength of about three linebackers.

One Saturday when she was six months old, I was bringing her in from the arena and at the point where she would have walked into her stall, she stopped and absolutely refused to move forward. She only backed up. I tried changing directions, disengaging her hindquarters, taking the end of the lead rope to flick it toward her back end to try to encourage her to move forward away from it, and in no time at all she had pulled me back all the way to the field side of the ranch and I was no closer to getting her to move forward than I was in getting the Min to do backflips.

Hardly anyone was at the ranch; Jim had taken a bunch of the volunteers in to town for the annual Wild West Days Parade in Cave Creek, driving the ranch truck through the parade route with the Solids waving from the truck bed. But Bill was there, and he came running over to help. He couldn't get Sunny to move forward either. Eventually, he just turned her around and had her walk backwards toward her stall. I'm pretty sure the horses were falling over themselves laughing as she moonwalked away. Bill had no choice but to keep moving her backward until Sunny had sauntered into her stall butt-first with her head in the air.

More from guilt than anything, I told Jim about it after he and everyone got back from the parade. I was ashamed I hadn't known what to do.

"She's a kid," Jim said, chuckling at me. "She's a teenager who's been told she has curfew. Of course she's going to test us. She'll do it to all of us. We just have to convince her she'll have more fun with us when she's behaving."

We limited the number of people who handled her; it would be too easy for her to learn bad manners if consistency wasn't enforced. Only Jim, Bill, our ranch manager, and I were allowed to walk her. We had to be firm but gentle, clear with our direction, and quick to reward her with praise when she listened. I wrote a list of rules on the white board in the breezeway where I listed relevant news and reminders for the volunteers. Halter time = work time. No one was permitted to give her food or treats during training sessions. Nobody but me was allowed to touch her feet. If we trusted one of the Solids to move her from the arena to her stall, they were not to let her drag them places to eat food off the ground. We would use *these* methods of discipline, and not *these*. Just as children need boundaries, so do young horses. Especially young mustangs.

Sunny gave us all a run for our money. But there was not an ounce of nastiness to her, no irritability or confusion that might come from a young horse who simply doesn't know what's being asked of her. No matter how big she got, Sunny possessed a joyful innocence. Her acts of rebellion came from a place of true curiosity as she figured out her place in the world. Eventually, she learned that getting scratches, lots of praise, and the occasional treat were far more fun than playing tug-of-war. Eventually, she couldn't wait to walk with us anywhere and everywhere because she knew she was in for an exciting adventure.

When she was nine months old, I put a saddle pad on her back for the first time.

As was the case for most things I began at Tierra Madre, I had no idea what I was doing. But in my dumb, inexperienced head, I figured that if Sunny was going to be ridden someday, she had to get used to having things put on her back at an early age. And not only that, she had to get used to having things put on her back very gradually. I figured saddling up a horse wasn't a one-time deal that was only done when the horse was fully grown.

The first day, I brought out a white saddle pad-not nearly thick enough to be used as actual padding between a horse's back and a saddle-and showed it to her in her stall, where she felt safest. She sniffed it and I'm pretty sure she shrugged. So, I carefully rubbed it on her chest and her neck, moved it up to her withers, and eventually rested it on her back. She didn't even turn around to look at it.

I removed it, praised her repeatedly, and walked out of her stall. Jim had taught all of us to always end a lesson with a horse on a good note and to take things very slowly.

The next day, I put the saddle pad on her back again and left it there a bit longer. This time she turned around to look at it, sniffed it once or twice, then again looked straight ahead in utter indifference.

As we started doing this day by day, I played with her feet (or tried to, anyway, as it was something she hated for the first year or two of her life), backed her up, and moved her in circles. And around that time, we started working together for ten or fifteen minutes every morning in the round pen. Sunny was smart. She learned to lunge almost overnight, responding to my commands as I encouraged her forward with visual pressure from my raised hand or a lunge whip directed at her hindquarters. Eventually she responded to voice commands, and walked, trotted, and cantered according to my signals. She even knew when to stop and when to turn. She amazed me with her brilliance. I'm convinced she obeyed not from any eagerness to impress me, but to show me that she could, because she wanted to.

When Sunny had tolerated the saddle pad for a while, next came a bareback pad with a cinch. I put the bareback pad on her to no reaction, then fastened the cinch loosely around her girth, loose enough that it didn't even touch her. We walked for a little while before I took it off and praised her. Nonplussed, she nibbled at my hair in response.

Next came the saddle.

Once again, it was anticlimactic in every sense of the word. I'd built up to it so much that I was almost emotional the day I finally brought Sunny to the round pen and let her sniff the saddle I'd put in there. I figured if she was fine with it on the ground, then maybe she'd be fine with it on her back.

I was correct. Sunny couldn't care less about the saddle; far more interesting to her were the leaves growing on the mesquite tree that hung over the round pen. But when I'd convinced her to stand still and let me swing the saddle up over her, she didn't react. At all.

I'm pretty sure I laughed at her nonchalant attitude. I threw my arms around her neck and praised her again and again before I took it off. And the next day it stayed on longer. And the next, longer. And eventually I cinched it, tightening it a little more every single day until a few weeks later, it was tight enough for me to swing up and ride if I wanted.

But I didn't. Sunny was only a year old then. She was too small to bear the weight of a human. Horses' bones still develop all the way up to age six, and while different experts will say different things, four is about the average age for a horse to start being ridden seriously.

I didn't mind. Leading her around the ranch with a saddle on her back, showing her off, was one of the biggest prides of my life. I'm 100% positive that professional trainers could have done better and that I made all kinds of rookie errors. All I had other than basic horsemanship knowledge was love in my heart for Sunny and determination to finish what I'd started.

One crisp afternoon in November 2017, when Sunny was two and a half, I was sitting in the house with Lee getting work done. Jim was in New York for one of his biannual trips to visit Jean. When I walked outside at one point to do my every-half-hour check in on the herd, I saw Sunny alert in her pen, not napping like usual, but rather looking all around her. She whinnied when she saw me out of the house.

My head hurt from answering emails and typing up tax receipts and pulling numbers. I walked toward the shed row, Lee at my heels.

"You bored, baby girl?" I called out to her. "You want to do something?"

She whinnied again.

Grinning, I brought out her saddle and saddle pad, put them on the arena fence, then grabbed a halter. I brought her into the arena and let her romp around for a while before I saddled her up and put her halter back on.

She rubbed her head on my side. She did that often, by way of greeting. At two and a half, she wasn't as big as she would be as an adult, but she was pretty close, and I had to brace myself for how strong she was.

I took the lead rope off her halter and tossed it outside the arena. Then I turned my back to her and I held out my hand at the level of her nose, encouraging her to stretch out to nudge it, which she did. "Walk with me," I said.

And she did.

She followed me every which way around that arena, the entire space at her disposal but choosing-amazingly-to be right by my side. We turned and spun and backed up and moved forward again, me wading through the sand and she proudly wearing her saddle as she walked next to me, eyes shining and ears perked forward with interest.

And as the two of us just walked around the arena together, I suddenly realized that horse training isn't training the horse.

It's the horse training you.

Training you how to ask the questions correctly.

Training you how to interpret the answers you're given.

Training you how to respond to their language.

Training you to swallow your pride, to rethink your approach when something doesn't work.

Training you to be someone with whom they, prey animals, feel safe. Someone they trust. Someone they want to follow.

That afternoon as Sunny and I walked around the arena together, she at my side through her own choosing, the sky big and blue above us, it occurred to me that maybe-despite my immense ignorance when it came to horses-I was worthy of being trained by her.

And if this two-year-old miracle mustang filly somehow found me worthy of her confidence and trust, then I would find every way to live up to her image of myself, to be someone I never knew I could be.

At the very least, I would try.

As though sensing this newly formed commitment, Sunny nudged my side with her head again. And the happiness in her eyes made my heart soar.

CHAPTER FORTY-EIGHT
CORNERS

A few years before I began running Tierra Madre, when I was still getting my bachelor's degree, I visited the ranch after a particularly brutal college class and sat in the breezeway with Jim.

I was studying sustainability. Specifically, I was studying sustainability with a concentration of policy and governance in sustainable systems and a minor in political science. I was taking classes about poverty, famine, international development, global economics, political ideologies, human rights, and war. And anxiety was taking over my mind.

I wanted to be an activist. Someone who fixed things. Someone who swooped in to vanquish the evil and bring forth the good. To serve justice. To promote peace. But in learning the breadth of all the world's problems, so did I learn about my own inadequacy to find their solutions.

"There are so many bad things in this world," I said to Jim, who sat patiently listening to my rant of despair. "It's overwhelming. Sometimes I feel like I can't take it anymore. The problems humans are facing are so awful and on such a large scale. No one person can even make a dent. So if I can't fix everything, then what's the point in doing anything? How am I supposed to make a difference?"

Jim was quiet for a long time. He lit a cigarette and we both looked out into the arena. It was lunchtime, and the kids were contentedly eating in their stalls, heads buried in feeders.

"Well, that's just it," he finally said. "You *can't*. You can't fix everything. You can't solve all the problems on Earth. The world is too vast, and too complicated, for someone to up and fix the entire thing. You can't do it.

"But each of us has a small piece of it," he continued, gesturing around him to the horses, eating their lunches. "There are different corners of the world, see? And each of us has our own small corner to do whatever we can with to make better. And we all have that responsibility. We all have some part to play."

"You can't fix everything wrong with the world. But you can fix your corner of it." He looked at me. "*That's* how you make a difference, sweet thing. *That's* how you change the world."

CHAPTER FORTY-NINE
EVERY ONCE IN A GREAT WHILE

Tierra Madre is one of the few sanctuaries in Arizona. Every week we received numerous phone calls and messages and emails from people begging us to take their horses.

I always filtered out the requests. I forwarded most of them on to the head of our rescue network who connected horses in need to credible rescues all over the state. But sometimes, somebody slipped through the cracks and we welcomed a new horse into the herd-but only every once in a great while.

And the owners of the horses broke my damn heart. Black and white doesn't usually exist in horse rescue. Most times, situations were gray. That person lost their job. That person's husband just died. That person had a terminal illness. I found that most people only wanted the best for their horses and would go to hell and back if only to ensure the world for them.

That made it so much harder to say no. But 99% of the time, I said no. I had to.

The cold, hard truth was that we simply couldn't take in every horse needing a home. We'd go under that way. We'd have hundreds of horses packed into our few acres without the means to care for them. And that's why I loved our network of horse rescues. Even though we couldn't take every horse, we could still help keep horses out of the slaughter pipeline. We could still make sure that the horses went to safety.

There were so many situations, so many stories. And every once in a great while, a story sticks out.

For whatever reason, every single February, we got slammed with calls and emails and messages about horse surrenders. Just ten days in to February of 2018, I had spoken to at least seven different owners about nine different horses needing homes. One of those horses was named Annie.

Annie was in her early twenties, not rideable, and-according to her owner-lonely and depressed. Her owner, T, originally bought Annie as a riding horse and discovered within a week that Annie was sore and limping. She had been told by the sellers that Annie was in great shape and was so gentle a ten-year-old girl had used her for Gymkhanas and barrels and poles. Well, Annie may have been gentle, but it became clear that she was used to-and frequently anticipated-having the bit ripped out of her mouth by the way she fought T whenever it came time to bridle up.

Radiographs were done to see if a flare up of laminitis was to blame for her soreness, but a rotation of less than two degrees was found in both front hooves. Maybe the cold affected her arthritic limbs? Maybe her age was just showing itself? Who knew? But after consulting with a farrier and vet, and after seeing the soreness continue, it became clear that Annie was better off not being ridden anymore. And the next course of action would be to find Annie a home to live out her days with no responsibilities or expectations.

So in the middle of February, we got a call.

And as I talked to T about this horse that I didn't know, without reason or warning, something shifted within the unyielding voice in my brain that constantly screamed, "We already have enough horses!"

I couldn't explain it. But that barrier started to crack as I heard about how Annie was in pain, and had seemingly lived a life of serving others and how sad she was being on her own-

I told T that while Tierra Madre really wasn't in a position to take her horse, I'd find her someone who was. We'd been exchanging phone calls for a while when T told me she was terrified that if no one could take Annie, she would end up on the back of a slaughter truck.

Those words absolutely crushed me.

"T," I said, with conviction, "I promise you that will never happen."

Before we hung up, I requested some pictures and information I could send off to the network. Later, as promised, T delivered.

And I looked at those pictures.

And there was something about the way that horse stood.

Something about her face.

Something in her eyes.

Even as I sent off Annie's info, I thought to myself, "No one else will be

able to take her right now."

I thought to myself, "There's something else going on."

I thought to myself, "She needs us."

Even still, I pushed those irritatingly nagging thoughts away. Responsible. I had to be responsible. In February, our donations stalled. I had to think about feeding our other horses.

I was mucking Hudson's stall one morning a few days afterward when Jim came over. He usually came to check in before going out in the early morning, to confirm something we needed from the hardware store or to follow up on somebody's medicine.

"Has anyone from the network claimed the horses we got called about this week?"

I gave him the rundown. The two middle-aged Thoroughbreds were going to this rescue. The teenage Quarter horse was going to that rescue. A known private buyer was taking in the three-year-old Arabian.

"They're all spoken for and safe. Except for the one. Annie. The older lame mare up north."

Jim just looked at me. He knew how to read me better than anyone else.

"I just…" I tried to find words. "There's something about that horse, Jim."

He nodded. "Then what are you waiting for?"

Later that morning, I called T again.

"Has anyone reached out to you about taking Annie?"

"No. No one."

I told T we'd take Annie almost before she could finish speaking.

Right as I was on the phone with her, our therapeutic farrier pulled in to do that day's trims. And he, Jim, and I proceeded to talk for the next hour about her. We got Annie's vet on the phone and got the lowdown about her most recent x-rays. We made a plan.

Well, due to the logistics of getting a hauler to make a six-hour round trip drive from up north, arranging to get Annie here took about three or four weeks. And during that time of waiting, we suddenly, unexpectedly lost

Sweet Boy.

It was a devastating time for all of us. Sweet Boy was one of our cornerstones of the ranch.

But when he had joined the Great Herd, we had to move a horse from the shed row up by Sedona, to ease Sedona's broken heart over losing his dear friend. We picked Rusty. And the two geldings bonded almost at once.

And when Rusty had switched places, that meant another stall was open between Sunny and Buddy. One that would perfectly fit an older mare with arthritis needing some extra human attention.

Life has a way of making things fall into place.

As it happened, on the Sunday Annie arrived at Tierra Madre, I was standing in line at airport security in Cincinnati after attending my brother's wedding.

Jim texted me a picture and the volunteers started sending me videos and I started freaking out with joy there in the airport and later, when I was impatiently waiting to board my plane, I talked to Jim to hear about how well she was settling in.

She'd rolled. She'd dived into her food. She seemed reserved, but sweet. She was bigger than expected. She was beautiful. She was content. She was safe.

The second I got home Sunday night, I ran to my car and rushed over to the ranch. By the time I pulled up, the last rays of light had faded and night had settled in.

I walked up to the round pen, where Annie would live for a week or so in quarantine.

And after almost a month of talking about her, of seeing her pictures, of pushing away the growing feeling that she was somehow meant to be part of the Tierra Madre herd… there she was, silhouetted against the starry sky.

I walked in the pen with her. She was eating, but stopped and turned to face me as I carefully stepped around her and stood parallel to her body, as not to approach her too directly.

We studied each other by starlight, then I reached out to let her sniff my hand.

She was quiet, observing. She let me scratch her face briefly. She stood perfectly still in what I interpreted as acceptance.

And it hit me with inexplicable force that Annie's story was one of both good times and bad. That she'd had her heart broken at some point after many years of giving everything she had to humans. That arthritis was only some of the pain she'd experienced in her life. That Tierra Madre-a place filled with the most incredible, loving team of humans-was going to spend the rest of her life giving her the chance to just love and be loved.

After a beat, Annie took a step forward and rubbed her head on my shoulder.

Every once in a great while, forces out of your control and beyond your understanding reach across time and space to pull what is meant to be together.

The universe beckons to the unrevealed and whispers through the barriers.

And every once in a great while, you listen.

CHAPTER FIFTY
MY FAVORITE GIFT

Years from now, somebody might ask me, "What's your favorite gift you've ever been given?"

And I will say, "A traffic cone."

One hot summer day, I walked in the arena to halter Chance so I could bring him back to his stall, as usual. He looked up from what he was doing, saw me, proceeded to pick up a cone with his mouth, walked across the arena toward me, and dropped it at my feet.

Cones were among the most popular of playthings in arena, and Chance wanted me to have one.

Throughout the course of a day, little things like that happened that I tried never to take for granted. Even in the smallest, most ordinary moments lay something extraordinary.

Those moments may not have seemed significant at the time, but they were always the ones I looked back on and saw for what they were: instants that were seemingly nothing, but could turn into anything.

And even in those instants that were seemingly nothing… everything could change.

CHAPTER FIFTY-ONE
THE AUCTION

For nine years, I had heard all about livestock auctions. I learned about them my very first day at the ranch and spent almost a decade wondering about them. Instinct told me they were one of the most awful experiences in existence.

For many horses, livestock auctions are the stop before the slaughterhouse across the border. Horses with nowhere else to go often end up at these auctions where they are put up for sale by the county. They are taken in by rescues, bought by private owners looking for new projects, or-far more often-they end up with kill buyers, the people who sell them to their deaths.

I never thought I would go to one. Tierra Madre never attended auctions. If we did, we'd have hundreds of horses crammed onto our property and be bankrupt in a month from trying to feed them all.

But sometime in May of 2018, our friends at a rescue who managed the wild horse herds on the Salt River reached out to us and said that a number of wild mustangs had been rounded up in Sahuarita, just south of the Tohono O'odham Nation. The horses had wandered off their protected lands and into a neighborhood where one of the stallions had been hit and killed by a car. For their safety, the 22 wild horses were impounded by the Arizona Department of Agriculture and were being sent to a livestock auction. Per ARS 3-1402, the horses would be sold to the highest bidder.

Do we have room for one or two of the horses, and would we go? Our friends wanted to know. Since they monitored wild herds, they didn't have a local facility to care for domesticated horses, but they had a trailer they'd let us borrow. There were yearling colts, a stallion or two, a pregnant mare and nursing mares with their foals. And at that auction, where kill buyers waited, they would be in danger.

Mares and their foals?

Shit.

"Hell yeah," Jim and I said. "We'll go."

So on the first Saturday in June, Jim and I left the ranch at eleven, he driving our friends' trailer hitched up to his truck and me in my car, in case something should happen at the ranch and I needed to leave. One of the Solids stayed behind with Lee to keep an eye on the kids. The auction took place an hour from the ranch, in the southwestern outskirts beyond Phoenix, amongst pastures and farmland and desert that stretched to the horizon.

When we showed up to the auction at noon, it was hot, blazing hot. It would reach 112 degrees in the shade that day.

We parked and started walking across the barren dirt, blindingly bright in the sun. People were milling around the end of a long, skinny, rectangular barn that had an aisle running down the middle. There was a roof over the corrals but no walls which meant the sun beat down on the outer edges of the pens. Near the entryway were stalls of cows, and we could see horses in the middle area, but we walked around the entrance to the side of the barn to get to the other end, where we could see the crowd listening to an auctioneer.

Up front, near the auctioneer, was a labyrinth of twenty or thirty interlocking pens with gates that swung open or shut as needed to maneuver animals in different pens to the auction ring or else to create a walkway as needed. Inside them were goats and sheep, deafening with their cries and brays. Two bored-looking girls kept them moving in and out of the ring while the auctioneer sold them, rapidly, to the crowd.

We checked in at the registration table to get our bidding number. They asked for Jim's driver's license and had him fill out a form before explaining that the horses would be auctioned last, after the other animals.

"That might take a while," Jim said to me as we looked out at the hundred or so goats and sheep in their pens. "Let's go see the horses."

Rather than attempting to navigate the maze of pens holding the smaller animals, we walked all the way back up to the entrance of the barn and said hello to the cows before walking up the aisle to the midsection of the barn where the horses were. And as we walked through that barn, seeing the animals crying inside of them, sweat in my eyes and dripping down my face, the air so hot and the sun so bright that it seemed like the godforsaken land around us was burning, one thought kept running through my mind: we were in a living hell.

"That's the pregnant mare," I said, pointing to a pretty gray girl whose sides were bulging. Her stallion was guarding her closely in their pen. "And those guys down there don't look more than a year old."

"Yep, those are the yearlings," Jim responded as we looked over to a pen of four or five young colts, all arguing over food and throwing their heads around nervously. "Hi, kids. And these are the moms."

In four pens across from the yearlings and stallion and pregnant mare stood four mares with their foals. Other people were milling around us and I saw some eyes look us over uneasily. I saw t-shirts from well-known rescues and I understood. These were the people looking to save the horses, and they didn't know us yet.

"I kind of like these guys right here," Jim said, motioning to the mom and baby pair that was in front of us. I stopped and looked.

The mare was skin and bone. Her black coat was stretched over her protruding ribs and spine but her eyes were calm, though there was an apprehensiveness to her that I couldn't blame in the slightest. Her baby couldn't have been more than a month old. Unlike his mother, he appeared to be in perfect health as he had his mother's milk while the mare had clearly struggled to find food in the wild.

"Hi, guys," said Jim as we held up our hands, perpendicular to the ground. The colt stepped forward and nudged us. He was a bay, with long skinny legs and an inquisitive face. The black mare flinched a little and drew back. She was born wild, and wasn't used to be people.

Not yet, I couldn't help but think. "I like them too," I murmured, almost to the horses than to Jim. "She looks like she's been through some times."

"Yeah she does. She has a sweet face though. Don't you, baby face? And I bet you her son's a very nice boy. Aren't you, squirt?" And the colt nibbled at his hand in response.

We met up with our friends who had leant us their trailer and introduced ourselves to several other rescues. There were at least four of them represented at the auction and everyone had a game plan. This person was going to bid on the stud and pregnant mare. That place was going for two of the mares and their babies. We told each of the rescues we were going to bid for the skinny black mare and her baby. Word traveled. Everyone nodded at each other. It was an understanding. Everyone worked together. Everyone kept their eyes on the crowd that was with the smaller animals. Some of the rescues knew who the kill buyers were from past encounters and pointed them out to us.

The slaughter trucks sat parked around the barn, waiting. But they would leave empty. That was our mission.

We waited. We sat in the shade of the aisle running down the middle of the barn, gulping water. I'd brought a cooler full of ice and water which I kept in my car, and I was thankful for it as we all ran out of our own bottles midafternoon. We kept a close eye on all the horses but sat near the black mare and her baby. At one point, Jim saw them fishing for food in the dirt, glanced around the other side of the stalls at the bales of alfalfa laying around, and walked around the barn to get a flake. He came back and tossed it at their feet.

"Are we allowed to do that?" I asked, grinning, as the mare and colt scarfed down the food.

"I don't give a fuck," was his rejoinder.

Finally, finally, the auctioneer and his crowd came through the maze of pens and began to auction the horses. Our mare and baby were nearest to the entryway and would be one of the last pairs to sell. Jim and I stood guard over them protectively as we watched the rescues, one by one, claim each of the wild horses. I found out later that a kill buyer had ended up winning two moms and foals but a rescue had regrouped afterward, and went directly to the kill buyer to offer more money than he'd paid in exchange for them, and he accepted.

At last, the auctioneer came to our pair. Someone with a clipboard was next to him, as were ten or fifteen other people with bidding numbers. I looked out at them. Two of them had been pointed out to us as kill buyers and they were ready to go. Jim positioned himself directly in front of the auctioneer so he could see him.

"Start at twenty-five for the 927 pair, go for fifty, thank you sir, go for seventy-five…?"

Jim kept his hand in the air. The auctioneer was talking so fast I could barely understand him. The buyers next to the auctioneer, as predicted, kept countering. We didn't care. We would go up to a hundred, five hundred, and a thousand if we had to....

"One twenty-five," the auctioneer said, turning to the last kill buyer with his hand in the air and he nodded. The auctioneer turned to Jim. "One fifty?"

Jim nodded, keeping his hand up.

"And that's one-seventy-five," he said turning back to the kill buyer. "And two hundred?" he said to Jim who nodded. "Yes, I have two hundred."

The kill buyer put down his hand.

"Two hundred going once. Going twice... sold."

I let out a breath. Jim turned and put his hand on the stall bars, murmuring to the black mare and her baby. The rescues were smiling and turning their attention to the last group of horses. I was stunned. Not only had the auction moved so quickly, I couldn't quite believe we'd won the black mare and her baby for such a low number. And then I understood. The mare was so skinny that she wouldn't have fetched a big number from the slaughterhouse, who paid for horses by the pound. The foal, who couldn't be shipped over the border anyway, was worthless to the kill buyer, at least for a few years. So the kill buyer had given in at a low number.

Some time after we'd gone to the cashier's office to pay for our pair and before the horses were eventually in the trailer, we said goodbye to our new friends whom we'd worked with to save the entire herd. For a few minutes, a number of people were each talking separately to Jim and I in the barn.

One of the men who had been part of the crowd walking with the auctioneer came up to us and while I was speaking to someone else, he said a few words I didn't hear to Jim. They shook hands then he moved on to speak to me.

He was very neat, with a clean, tucked in shirt and white teeth, and he looked vaguely familiar.

"Hello," he said as he shook my hand. "Good to see you again."

"Hi," I said, thinking he must be with another rescue we hadn't noticed, or a private buyer. "Have we met before, then?"

"Oh sure," he said, and directly after he said his next words I got a sudden, alarming vision of myself pulling a lead rope out of his hands:

"I sold a pregnant mustang to you guys a few years ago."

Miraculously, though our pair had been among the last to be auctioned, they were the first to be released. We were anxious to get them home. Rattled by the continuous cries of the animals up front and dragging from heat exhaustion, we wanted to get the hell out of there as fast as humanly possible.

Jim backed the trailer into the entryway of the long, skinny aisle up the barn and opened it wide. Because the horses were wild and not halter broken, their pen was opened and the black mare and her baby were herded down the entryway and into the trailer. We shut the doors securely behind them and then, as Jim put it, we blew that pop stand.

Our friends who'd lent us the trailer followed us, and we drove in through our gates well after 6pm, close to seven hours after pulling up to the auction. Because of the wash separating the driveway from the round pen, we couldn't get the trailer close enough to it to safely release the mare and foal. But Jim backed the trailer up to the side gate of the huge turnout arena and we managed to turn the horses loose into it instead.

Then the question was how to get them from the arena's back gate into the round pen, where they would live for some time. Within our heat-exhausted brains we somehow concocted the brilliant idea to form an aisle way using our feed carts as panels, which were all of three and a half feet high and over which mare and foal easily soared when we opened the gate to the arena. They treated themselves to a lengthy self-guided tour of the ranch-inspiring a great deal of screaming from the rest of the herd-before we were able to chase them back into the big arena.

"So how about this," I said to Jim, after I'd slammed the gate shut and we all stood catching our breaths, "How about they stay there overnight, and we get panels tomorrow?"

He nodded. We were exhausted, and had no energy left for an alternative solution.

We dragged over an empty water tub and a feeder and proceeded to fill them with fresh water and alfalfa. After doing a few victory laps in the arena, mother and son calmed down and quietly began to graze. Bill came to feed the rest of the kids their evening snack, and so it was that as the sun was fading on the hot day, and I got in my car to finally head home, all the horses' heads were buried in their feeders, and everyone was at peace.

Two days later, we picked names.

Jim named the colt Jumpin' Jack Flash, after the song by The Rolling Stones, in commemoration of the colt's gallant leap over the carts we had attempted to use as a barricade. He became known as Jack.

I named the mare Journey.

Not only had I been listening to the band Journey on the way down to the auction, I thought it was a fitting name for a mare who had survived so much both in the wild and at the hands of humans.

Her journey, and that of her colt's, nearly came to an end at the auction that day.

But in a way, that auction was an ending for them both.

It was the end of scrounging for food in a dangerous area inhabited by highways and fast cars.

It was the end of fearing that mother and baby would be heartlessly separated.

It was the end of herded from one place to another.

It was the end of being unsure of what place to call home.

Ahead was the start of a life where mother and baby would be safe. Well fed. Well-watered. Given treats and a soft place to lay down at night.

Loved. Forever.

It was the end of one journey, and the beginning of another.

CHAPTER FIFTY-TWO
A FAVOR

A few days after the auction where we saved Journey and Jack, I was still recovering emotionally and physically. There was no way I could have known this at the time, but after that day, I would never be the same again.

After I'd arrived home that night after being in 110+ weather for 12 hours, I was sicker than I'd ever been in my life: skin hot to the touch, unable to get cool, vomiting, a splitting migraine, completely delirious. My husband spent hours patting my skin down with ice water, trying to keep me cool. Looking back, I'd drunk too much water and not enough electrolytes that day, and I should have gone to the hospital.

For days afterward, I could barely stand. I sat in a chair at the ranch and managed things as best as I could, pounding Pedialyte, thanking the universe my Solids knew what to do. I don't think I ever loved the volunteers more than in those days following the auction. They made me sit and brought me water and made sure I didn't lift a finger. In the afternoons, I curled up in bed and slept. But in the mornings, I dragged myself to the ranch.

Three days after the auction was Tuesday, and just like every other Tuesday, our vet and therapeutic farrier came out in the morning to work on horses. One of the concerns was Heighten, who had a problem with his hind left leg.

It wasn't the first time we'd had a problem with his hind left leg. In 2010, Heighten had broken his knee and was laid up for over a year. As a result, his knee was swollen to three or four times what it should have been due to the development of arthritic bone spurs, and while he wasn't in pain anymore, it was discomforting for him to have anyone touch his knee for an extended period of time. By default, he wasn't thrilled when anyone got anywhere near his bad leg at all.

This was a problem for us, because Heighten had developed dermatitis induced cellulitis in that leg the week before, and it required cold hosing, scrubbing, and sweat wraps-a significant amount of fussing. When we went in to wrap him each day, he walked off and gave us holy hell about getting near his leg. Getting the necessary wraps and medicine onto his leg with two or even three people was a challenge, and it required an immense amount of time, patience, bribes, and the uttering of some of our best swear words.

That particular day, Heighten had a checkup from our vet who told us he was progressing, but we still needed to treat the leg. But by the time we'd cold hosed and cleaned him and he was ready to be wrapped again, it was the end of the morning.

Jim had to go to a meeting, our therapeutic farrier and his assistant had another job, and our vet had another appointment. As none of the volunteers knew how to administer medical treatment to Heighten's leg, our vet offered to come back that afternoon to sweat wrap it for me.

"I'll be okay," I said with a smile, and everyone drove away. By that point it was past lunchtime, I'd made the volunteers go home, and I was alone on the ranch.

Slowly, I gathered the stuff. Schmoo, which was our name for a sticky concoction of gel DMSO and Fura-Zone. Gloves. Plastic wrap, which served as a protective barrier over the schmoo. Standing leg wraps. Polo wraps.

I dragged myself into Heighten's stall, beyond drained of everything I had. I knew what to expect. I had to wrap his leg, but this was going to be a battle to end all battles, and I had no strength to fight him.

I haltered him, threw the rope over the bars, then put my head close to his.

"Baby boy," I whispered. "I'm so tired. I have nothing left. I need to wrap your leg and I'm just begging you… please, please keep it still. Please. Please help me."

Heighten looked at me. I put my gloves on, picked up the schmoo, and took a step back toward his leg. I gently moved my hand from his hindquarters to his hock, then crouched down to apply the thick, gooey substance to his leg, starting from the lower half and working my way up. I waited for the fight, for the tugging and pacing and kicking and pulling.

Nothing.

As I slathered on the DMSO/Fura-Zone concoction, Heighten didn't move a muscle. He was still as a statue as I put the plastic wrap loosely around his leg, still as I pulled one standing leg wrap around the cannon and fetlock then wrapped the polo wraps around it tightly, and still as I placed another standing leg wrap over the hock and gaskin and secured it with another polo wrap. He didn't do so much as tremble.

When I'd finished, I stood up and put my arms around his neck, burying my face in his mane. I was shaking with exhaustion from those few minutes of work and clung to him for support. All the while he was calm, and I let my eyes fill with tears at this unanticipated favor.

"Thank you," I murmured into Heighten's mane. "Thank you, thank you, thank you."

He looked at me again, and his eyes were full of understanding. After a beat, he quietly turned and resumed eating his lunch.

I got kicked into the ground some days. Some days, I ran on empty and was pulled so thin in all directions that there was nothing left for me to give. The horses smelled weakness a mile away, and there were days I wondered if some people were the same way.

And then, once in a blue moon, out of nowhere, one of the kids caught my eye, nodded their head, and helped me out a little.

It was unexpected. It was very, very rare.

And when it happened, it was everything.

CHAPTER FIFTY-THREE
IF NOT US

Technically, horse slaughter is not illegal in the United States.

In 2005, Congress signed The Agriculture, Rural Development, Food and Drug Administration, and Related Agencies Appropriations Act into law. This law banned the use of United States Department of Agriculture (USDA) funding for salaries or expenses for the inspection of horses under section 3 of the Federal Meat Inspection Act (21 U.S.C. 603). By default, this led to the closure of slaughterhouses in the U.S., with three exceptions: two slaughterhouses in Texas and one in Illinois. The owners of those slaughterhouses found a loophole in the law, arguing that they could pay for their own inspections, and in early 2006, the USDA issued a regulation that permitted it.

Then in 2007, the U.S. District Court for the District of Columbia overruled this, issuing that it was illegal for the remaining slaughterhouses to pay for own inspections of horse meat. This closed the loophole that had permitted the slaughterhouses to remain open, and they were closed forever.

But horse slaughter itself, an act so inhumane and evil that even describing it is unthinkable, is illegal here only on that technicality. Further, the slaughterhouses in Canada and Mexico remain open and kill buyers in the U.S. continue to send unclaimed horses over the borders to them.

Thousands of horses. Every year. Thousands.

Before those last slaughterhouses were closed down, one of the (ridiculous) arguments for keeping them open was a question: "Where else will those horses go?"

Where else will those horses go?

If not to slaughter, where will those horses go?

How about this?

How about we save them?

How about we stop overbreeding them in every equine industry? How about we start regulating who can breed responsibly and who cannot?

How about we stop throwing them aside when they break down and can no longer be ridden or are older and need to be retired?

How about we hold owners accountable for their horses and ensure that those owners have the resources to care for them until the end of their lives?

How about we eradicate the need for kill buyers to make a living off of what they consider to be livestock?

How about we finally push the Safeguard American Food Exports (S.A.F.E.) Act (H.R. 961/S. 2006) through Congress, which would make it illegal to export horses out of the U.S. for slaughter?

How about we educate people on the plight that horses face?

How about we provide more funding to the rescues and sanctuaries across the country who operate on shoestring budgets and a scrap of hope that tomorrow they can keep saving horses, even if it's just one more?

The day I lost Sonora and I laid over her body and cried, I asked myself, *why would anyone do this?*

And I wish I could say that a shining realization came to me all at once, that I had an epiphany that cleared all doubt in my mind and gave me the answer in a single moment. The truth is, the nature of the equine rescue world is so hard and so complicated that the answers appear in glimpses. And in between those glimpses, I still ask that question.

But when I do, I look into our horses' eyes. And I know why.

We do it to see the look of relief on their faces when they walk off the trailer into the unknown and are faced with kind voices and gentle hands.

We do it to watch them tear into a flake of good hay or dive into a warm bran mash after months, years of being starved.

We do it to work with a medical team who fixes the fractured bones, the torn ligaments, the open wounds, while we fix the broken hearts.

We do it to watch them take off running as fast as they can go, mane and tail streaming behind them, after being locked in a small stall for so long.

We do it to hear them whinny with joy when their stall mate comes back from the arena or when the feed cart comes around.

We do it to feel the warmth of their lips on our hands when we offer them a treat and they munch it contentedly, at peace with everything under the sun.

We do it to watch the worry in their eyes disappear.

We do it for the new beginnings, the wonders of self-discovery, and the unbreakable bonds that form that cannot and will not be broken.

We do it for the look of peace in their eyes when they leave this world for the next, surrounded by love, feeling love, knowing love.

We do it knowing that the blessing and curse of life is that grief is the price we pay for love, accepting that no matter how short a life is, it is still a lifetime.

We do it knowing that the rescue world will kick us into the dirt again and again. But there is no telling how many more lives we can save if we can pick ourselves back up.

We do this. We save horses. We must.

Because if not us, who?

CHAPTER FIFTY-FOUR
DETAILS

The thin layer of frost on the ground as my tires rolled over the woodchips in the driveway.

The bite of the air on my face as I opened the car door.

The steam coming up from the manure dumpster, next to which I parked every day.

Lee there to greet me, tail wagging, ready to accept a few minutes of scratches and a small piece of my breakfast.

The crunch of dirt beneath my Ariats as I walked up to the barn, coffee and folders and snacks and laptop and gloves in my arms.

Bunnies nibbling on hay around the alfalfa squeeze or in the aisles or by the feeders under which the horses often dropped prime pickings.

Two of the horses in the turnout arena kicking up dust as they ran.

The way the first hints of golden light caught on the edges of the barn pillars, shadows sharp behind them.

The frost melting off the barn roof, droplets glistening as they fell steadily from the sloped edges onto the dirt.

The halters hanging to the left of the tack room door.

The precise order of the buckets placed on the counter in the tack room, from left to right: regular grain, salt, electrolytes, neigh-lox, low-starch grain, psyllium.

The mash buckets resting on the rack above the counter, two yellow, one blue, the rest white.

The way I had to shake the whiteboard pen to get it to work so I could write down that day's tasks. The recognition that the volunteers were so good that really, I didn't have to anymore.

The horses' heads buried in their feeders as they finished breakfast–or drooping down as they dozed off-secure in their stalls, well fed, well kept, well loved.

The birds awakening and chirping.

The warmth of the sun on my face as it finally broke over the horizon.

The stillness as I stood in the breezeway, alone, broken only by the sounds of contented snorts from the herd or the creak of a feeder or the swish of a tail.

The peace washing through me at the sound of my own breathing, my own heartbeat.

And then-

The familiar rattle of the chain on the gate, ringing out as the first of the volunteers started to arrive, creaking as it opened, singing:

You're home.

You're home.

You're home.

CHAPTER FIFTY-FIVE
ONE MORE THING

It was an evening in early December of 2018.

I was doing math. I hate math. I especially hated math then, because I didn't like the numbers I was seeing.

I had pulled our financials to start prepping for my annual report for the board of directors. I compiled one every January to showcase where all our money went and from where it had come. How much went to food and medical care and farrier work and facility upkeep, etc.

And in comparing that year's numbers to the numbers of the last two or three years, I observed two main things: one that was good, and one that concerned me.

Our revenue was increasing. We had more donors than ever, had retained more of them from the year before, and fundraising had been a great success that year. We were moving in the right direction in terms of retaining individual donors as well as being creative in obtaining other sources of funding through community partners and targeted campaigns. Naturally, we had room for improvement, but the revenue looked good.

But our expenses for 2018 had increased too, and the total was just high enough to take the shine off the great success of fundraising that year. It was odd, because our spending seemed to be fairly consistent over the past few years. The labor category, however, had risen as we gained a few more employees who worked five to ten hours a week-a donor relations manager, a volunteer coordinator, another ranch manager-and it was now a threat to the financial stability of the ranch.

In scrutinizing that year's expenses, it was obvious to me that our total could not be repeated in the years to come. Long-term financial sustainability was my mission and it had been for years. We couldn't dip into Jim and Jean's emergency fund over and over again. Something would have to change if we were going to continue operating into the future. Idiocy, after all, was doing the same thing over and over and expecting different results.

We were doing everything right. But given the competitive climate in which we operated-one where we still struggled to obtain funds-we still had to keep our expenses as low as we could.

The ranch would be better off long-term if a significant chunk was cut annually, a low five-figure sum if possible. More growth would come of it in the next few years. More stability. To expect to raise that much more in the coming years, given our history of fundraising, was an absurd and unrealistic fantasy.

And as I stared and stared at my screen on my laptop, I realized that there was one very easy way to cut a portion of our expenses without slashing necessities like food and medical care and farrier work and facility upkeep. One expense could be cut *so* easily, to enormous benefit to the horses.

One expense.

I closed my laptop. Stared blankly into space. Sunk into my thoughts.

The ringing silence in my room was overwhelming.

Maybe it wouldn't be so easy.

The ranch was doing better than it had in years. The volunteers were exceptional. We had a board of directors, managers who knew the complicated rhythm of the ranch back to front, an Excel spreadsheet full of updated medical information for each of the horses, a schedule for their farrier visits. I had color coded folders for our receipts, for god's sake. I had established systems for everything.

By that point, it had been over nine years since I first walked into Tierra Madre, over four since I took charge of the organization, and two since I had been named executive director. I had overseen four benefit fundraisers, attended three Homes for Horses Coalition conferences, managed two ASPCA Help A Horse Day events, and had one hell of a time remembering the vast number of fundraising campaigns and program initiatives in between.

We had outreach operations, a foot in the world of equine rescue networking, and the expertise to apply for grants and create more partnerships within our community.

The ranch may not have been a brick house just yet, but the foundation was up and the concrete had been laid.

I had the dance down. It was a part of me. How could it not be a part of me?

Then, from the confusing cascade of thoughts and emotions that went through me that night came a curious one: that maybe-just maybe-there was another place for me, somewhere, that existed beyond the front gates, if I were forced to look.

If.

But then, another thought. Another emotion, one that tore me apart.

The horses.

I needed them. I would always need them.

As I sat that night with my numbers, the truth of what needed to be done crashing through me, I realized that they no longer needed me. But for them, as executive director, I could do one more thing.

~

Originally, the plan was to be executed gradually.

I talked to Jim about my decision the next day, showing him the numbers, voicing the concern. Offered to stay on as a part time, volunteer executive director for a little while. Listed the responsibilities that I could see being carried on by the current staff and volunteers. Named a few that I would be willing to do on a volunteer basis.

There was ringing silence when I'd finished. There was no argument, no show of defiance or outrage. The numbers spoke for themselves.

"What will you do?" said Jim finally. "Where will you work?"

"I don't know," I confessed. "I want to work for a nonprofit. But I don't know where yet."

I don't remember what else was said, if anything. There was nothing else left to say.

It took the better part of a week for Jim to come to terms with my decision, which was fine, given I was still coming to terms with it too. A week later, after I again brought up my desire to be a part time, volunteer executive director, Jim quietly rejected my offer.

"You're not going to have time," he said. "You're going to need all your time for another job, whatever that may be down the road."

My heart broke at his words. But I knew he was right.

Instead, we decided, it would be more feasible to find a public relations director. Someone to continue building Tierra Madre externally on a part-time basis in a predetermined timeframe and for a fraction of the cost it would take to keep me as a full-time employee. The rest of the work would be disbursed to some of the Solids and some of the board, though small parts of it-sorting through rehome requests, pitching in with fundraising ideas, grants research-I would carry on as a volunteer.

We talked to Jean. Showed her the numbers. Shared the plan. She was devastated, but agreed that for the financial stability of the ranch, my decision was the way forward.

"You know something," Jim said one morning as we sat in the house scheming for the ranch's future, "you could run a legitimate nonprofit someday. A big one. I can really see it."

"You know I'll never leave this place," I said, trying to smile. "You're stuck with me. Ever since the day I drove through those gates and tried to park in the wash."

Jim chuckled then looked at the ground. "I thought you'd last a week. But here you are."

I foresaw around two months of transition. Two months of slowly transferring my tasks, of showing the others my ways and plans and ideas, of slowly ending my era. I thought something like two months would be realistic.

The worst part was telling the volunteers. People cried. I had trained all of them, taught all of them (and been taught by them in turn), had been through so much with each of them. We had become more than a group of people running a ranch. We had become a family.

"Who's going to be executive director next?" someone asked one morning the week of Christmas, as we all stood in the breezeway after feeding the kids their lunch.

"No one," Jim said shortly before I could say anything. "No one will be. There is only one Alexis."

When January came around, I was actively job searching-a fascinating, intriguing new venture for me-while transferring my wealth of knowledge about the ranch to different people. This person would continue heading the events. That person would continue with volunteer management. Another person would manage donor relationships and keep sending the thank yous and receipts. That one would continue running the equine experiential coaching program. This one would be the ranch manager on Mondays. That one would continue overseeing the ranch on Saturdays. I would always be on hand, of course, to help. I wasn't really leaving, I kept telling myself. I would always be around to volunteer, even though I would be starting another chapter elsewhere.

Passwords. Email addresses. Receipts. Waivers. Excel spreadsheets. Reports. Contacts. Everything had to be transferred, everything had to be written down. As tired as I was in those final days, I figured I didn't have to rush the transition while I found a new job. I had plenty of time to stay on and help. And after all, more time job searching was more time I could spend just being with the horses.

Then, in mid-January, about a month after I had made my decision, I saw two pink lines on a test that changed my world forever.

And ranch life as I had known it for the last four years suddenly came to an end.

CHAPTER FIFTY-SIX
THE GATE

Every ranch has its seasons.

The first thing I did at Tierra Madre was convince Jim that my leaving immediately was the right thing to do, as not to take any more paychecks. After all, I said, it had been a month already, and who knew when I would find another job? I would stay on as a volunteer and continue to help with the transition and, of course, come by a few times a week to play with the horses. But the time had come. We shouldn't draw it out any longer.

Such was his trust in me that it only took a short time for him to reluctantly agree. Only then did I drop the bomb. He looked thunderstruck.

"You should have opened with *that*!" he exclaimed, and pulled me into a hug.

We decided the end of that week would be my last official day. Jim supported me completely, knowing my fear of getting hurt and losing the baby. "Besides," as he reminded me, "getting hurt around horses is a matter of how bad, and how often."

At my request, he swore not to tell a soul, though I think he may have said something in private to Bill because the rest of that week, the two of them subtly made sure I didn't lift any hay bales or handle any of the crazier kids. To take one more thing off my shoulders, Jim contacted the board of directors himself to tell them I would be stepping down effective immediately.

My last day came. Jim wrote a beautiful post on Facebook in tribute to me, telling our donors, supporters, volunteers, and friends all over the country who knew me that I was surrendering my post as executive director in exchange for that of a volunteer in order to pursue the next phase of my career. It was my time to fly, he said to them, and all their love would be the wind beneath my wings.

There was truth to what he wrote, because I had meant every word about it being my time to go. But nobody else knew the real reason why I was leaving so suddenly. And that's how I wanted it. I wasn't ready to share with the world that I would soon be bringing life into it. I was starting to fight morning sickness, and it was all I could do to fend off the volunteers-albeit with gratitude for their devotion to me-who were alarmed to hear my two-month exit had been suddenly shortened.

That last day didn't feel real. It was all a blur to me. So many emotions were tangled together and pulling at each other all at once. The volunteers left at the end of the morning as usual and I started the walk around. It normally took me fifteen minutes or so. That day, I don't remember how long I spent checking things, but it was longer than fifteen minutes.

I picked up fallen hay from the ground and put it back in Sunny's feeder, topped off Guess's water, brushed hay out of Hudson's eyes, re-wrapped a hose, scratched goop off of Tater's eyelids, and rubbed Jazz's nose. I offered Sedona a piece of alfalfa from the hay shed, kissed Rusty's face, gave Chianti a few scratches, and moved Spencer's feeder away from the fence where River waited to steal some of his food. I double checked Studley's chin for any signs of fly bites, whispered a few words to Oliver and M'Stor, waved at the Min who was getting started on a nap, and lingered by Chance's stall for a while, just watching him eat peacefully.

I made sure the dinner mashes had been made correctly and the tack room door was shut and everything in my office had been put away. I stood in the breezeway by my whiteboards that I had written on every day for the past four and a half years and looked out at the shed row and the field to see heads in feeders, the horses utterly content.

Jim waited until I was ready, then-as we'd always done-I walked to my car and he to his truck so we could drive out the front gates together, he headed to the grocery store and me to my house.

I got to the gate first. As usual, I opened it, drove through the threshold, then steered off to the side to park and get back out so I could go back to shut it. I got to the gate just as Jim drove up, his window down. He put the truck in park.

"Well," he said. And we were silent.

"I'll come by Saturday if I'm feeling okay," I said, "to say hi. And to give Chance his mash."

He nodded. "And your job interview? The one you were telling me about? That's lined up for next Wednesday, you said?"

"Yep. At two."

"Good."

Overhead, at the edge of the property, the Tierra Madre flag waved. A bird flew over it and landed in one of the mesquites by the garden. Somewhere in the distance, one of the horses let out a long, contented snort, indicating that he or she was about to drift off to a nap.

"It's just weird, you know?" I said finally. "This is all I've ever known. Since I graduated college for the first time, this job is the first grown up one I had. And now it's like... I'm going into the world, and...."

I trailed off. I didn't need to finish. Jim smiled at me, complete understanding in his eyes. To this day, no one can quite understand what I cannot say like he can.

"It's a big world outside these gates," he said, truck engine running. "It's time you go explore it."

When he had driven away, I stood there for a long time, hesitating to close the gate.

I don't know what I was waiting for. Closure, maybe. Someone to either pull me back through the gates or push me through them.

And as I stood and stood and waited for a sign that it was time to leave, it occurred to me that the first time I had opened the gates to Tierra Madre nearly a decade before, I hadn't felt anything at all.

Now, I felt everything. A deep ache in my heart. A lightness I couldn't explain. Searing fear. A lurching thrill of possibility. Love so strong and overwhelming it nearly took my breath away as I looked beyond the trees in the wash at the horses in the barn, the field, the shed row stalls. How did I not notice until then just how many beautiful trees were in the wash?

A lump in my throat, I looked up the driveway. Our welcome sign stood off the dirt road by one of the palo verde trees near the gate. It read:

WELCOME

All sizes

All colors

All ages

All cultures

All sexes

All religions

All beliefs

All types

All people

SAFE HERE

Safe here.

Something in my memory stirred.

This place does something to you.

The wind picked up then, rustling the chain on the gate. I smiled. The sound was so familiar to me, so engrained in my subconscious, that there was only one thing I could do in response.

I cast another look out toward the horses, walked across the threshold toward the road and my car, then turned around.

The chain rang out one last time as I closed the gate.

EPILOGUE
CIRCLES

Two years later

When I return to the ranch now, I often get there before sunrise.

The florescent light still shines in the tack room. Spiders still weave their webs in the corners. And the whiteboards still contain the feeding regimes, medicines, and farrier schedules, all of which change every single day-though there are a handful of things written on them that are still in my handwriting.

Gone are the days of mice nests, which disappeared forever the day someone dumped two cats over the fence and one of them-a black female Jim named Mystery-stuck around. She's since made mice-catching her personal mission, which she does in between prowling the ranch and sleeping on Jim's chair in the house.

There's a new hay shed along the north fence, just outside M'Stor and Min's shared pen, and it holds an entire squeeze of alfalfa that's kept safe from the elements with its four tarped sides. There are a handful of new carts, new halters, and a new misting system for each of the stalls. And some of the stalls hold new horses. One by one, as the kids each join the Great Herd, they leave behind a chance for one more life to be saved. And there are always horses needing to be saved.

The rhythm constantly changes, just as it should.

When I return to the ranch now, I park where the other volunteers park, collect my things, and walk up the driveway to the barn. And when I'm there early enough to be walking at dawn, I look toward the east at the light growing brighter and brighter on the horizon. The morning's rays illuminate every last detail of the ranch-the grooves in the dirt, the jagged curves of the woodchips, the shine of the aluminum stall bars-and set the ripples of the sky aglow.

Sometimes, as the sun breaks, I see a flash of red.

And my Sonora is there in the brilliant, golden light spilling from the horizon.

Beside her is Rain. And Moosie. And the dozens of horses who have called Tierra Madre home over the years and who now run joyfully in the Great Herd. And as they gallop, they pull the sun across the sky.

Jim is usually in the tack room, preparing medicines, or talking to Bill in the breezeway. He tells me everything that went on that week: vet visits, new medicine regimes, anything new and exciting. At some point during the morning, we sit down for a while and just catch up. We talk about everything from fundraising ideas to each of the kids and how well they're doing. Sometimes there's a grant opportunity to be discussed, or some news in the equine rescue world. A few times, I've brought my daughter to meet him and everybody else. Soon, she'll be old enough to toddle around the ranch on her own, and I hope with all my heart she'll fall in love with the horses like I did.

Throughout the morning, I pitch in with the chores and chatter with the volunteers and spend time with each of the horses, savoring every second I get to walk them, groom them, and be in their stalls with them.

And when the activity has died down and I've made my rounds, I go to the tack room.

I pick a bowl, fill it with bran and grain, and mix it with water from the sink, like Jim showed me all those years ago.

I stir it up into a mash, then I carry it out into the golden morning and set it on the ground a little away from the barn, across from the field. There's a halter swung over my shoulder, like old times, when I ran around the ranch doing a thousand things at once.

But I'm not running anymore. In fact, once I put the mash on the ground, sometimes I stop for a moment and just look around.

Breath in, breath out.

And then, as I turn and begin my walk up the hallway on the field side, I hear a nicker coming from the other end.

Chance is always ready to go.

"Hey, you," I say as I enter his stall. He puts his head into my halter and lets me fasten it. Then he waits exasperatedly as I give his face a quick kiss.

"I missed you this week," I tell him as I gather the lead rope in my hands. "Let's go get a mash."

He always steps forward eagerly.

I love mashes, he says.

Away we go, and we don't look back.

When I return to the ranch now, I always ponder how when we look back at our lives, and want to share our stories, we always want to tell them in a linear fashion. A clean, straight line, with a beginning, a middle, and an end.

But the truth is, there is no line. Our stories-our lives, our experiences, our thoughts and our hopes and our dreams-they are circles.

They expand and they shrink, they rise and they fall, they move through both light and shadow. They are complex and they are infinite. One end curves away and another beginning emerges.

The next turn is there, laying in the dreamlike haze between being awake and asleep, in the silence that contains the echo of an ended song, in the beat just before the sun peeks above the horizon to emit that first glow.

And the next turn is waiting, sure as the darkness that falls when the day is done, and sure as when tomorrow comes, the sun will rise again.

ACKNOWLEDGEMENTS

So many people have been a part of the Tierra Madre family-my family-over the years. To name each and every person is a monumental task, but I will do my very best:

First and foremost: to the volunteers, the individuals who graced Tierra Madre at some point during its lifetime and without whom we could not have thrived: Bre, Leika, Stephanie, Kendra, Holly, Claudia, Cristina, Marti, Tracy, Morgan, Adolfo, Sarah, Josh, Shana, Denise, Marcia, Bonnie, Kathy, Leah, Casey, Angela, Julie, Susan, Christine, Andy, Victor, Paige, Judy, Carrie, Tom, Leslie, Nanci, Daisy, Lynn, Brandy, Jean, Amanda, Shirley, Linda, Chandra, April, Sonya, Tahora, Michele, Cheryl, Andrew, Mackenzie, Angie, Lilly, Lyla, Didi, Ken, Dana, Kari, Pat, Ashley, "Iron" John, Kathi, Amy, Denae, The B family—John, Jenni, and Payton—Sam, Debbie, Marianne, Nancy, Carin, Rebecca, Kevin, Vivian, Katie, Brad, Laura, Michelle, Georgeta, Samantha, Marta, Torie, Anne, Sandy, Monika and K, Shiann and A, Nicola, the M family—Carolyn, Joe, and Chloe—Shelly, Jim, Donna, Philip, Paige, Hannah, Alissa, Kenzie, Amber, Kelley, Erin, Cathy, Jeremiah, Lee, Helene, and many, many more whose names I may have forgotten over the years but whose faces I never will. Thank you for being a part of my life and more importantly for being a part of the horses' lives. I love you all.

To our donors, partners, and dearest friends: I hope you know the impact of your contributions. Thanks to you, Tierra Madre has carried out its mission for more than fifteen years and has saved dozens of innocent lives from the slaughter pipeline. Thank you from the bottom of my heart for your support. As the saying goes: "Saving one horse won't change the world, but it will change the world for that one horse."

To Jean Gath, who has been there for Tierra Madre every step of the way since its founding, and who continues to be a force behind the ranch's operations. Jean, thank you for your unconditional support, your enthusiasm for our mission, and for always believing in me.

To Dr. Anastasia Keyser, who I look up to immensely, who taught me horsemanship and patience, and who humbled me every single visit with her determination, intelligence, and kindness. Thank you for your huge heart, your words of wisdom when I needed to hear them, and for loving every horse you meet with everything in your soul.

To John Samsill, who taught me more about hoof care than anyone, answered my thousands of questions with patience and enthusiasm, encouraged my founding of Sonora's Cure, and took care of our horses' hooves with expertise that I haven't seen before or since. Thank you for your genuineness, our many long talks, and for being one of my favorite people.

To the many others who provided services to us and our horses: the incomparable Dr. Rollins, Dr. Gryl, Dr. Thomasson, Dr. Shields, and all the other vets who graced Chaparral Veterinary Medical Center; Brian and Scott; Jim "the woodchipper", and the teams with G-Farms, Scottsdale Livestock, Dynamite Horseman Supply, and Karsten's Ace Hardware. Thank you for your compassionate service and fierce commitment to both horses and their humans.

To the incredible organizations to whom I look for inspiration and whose people I admire fiercely: Jennifer at Healing Hearts Animal Rescue and Refuge; Curry at Triple R Horse Rescue; Soleil at Arizona Equine Rescue Organization; the Team at Equine Voices Rescue and Sanctuary, Simone and Debra at the Salt River Wild Horse Management Group; Cindy Gendron and so many others at the Homes for Horses Coalition including Tinia Creamer with Heart of Phoenix Equine Rescue and Elaine Nash with Fleet of Angels. Thank you for being advocates for horses, for extending a hand to help others, and for making strides in shoes I someday hope to fill.

To my husband, Alex, who has supported me through absolutely everything from the day I brought him to Tierra Madre for the horses' approval after we started dating, who attended every fundraising event, who put up with mud and hay being tracked into the apartment every day for years, who understood when I raced out at night to an emergency and all the days I'd be gone from dawn till well past dusk, who talked me off ledges and lifted me up in my darkest days, and who above all knows my heart and shares it unconditionally with the horses. Alex, I couldn't have done any of it without you by my side. Thank you.

To my hermano Abel who I love dearly, a true gentleman, the hardest worker I've ever known, and without whom Tierra Madre would simply not exist. Thank you for being a calm voice of reason in all and any storms, for being strong like bull always, and for loving the horses so well.

To King John, Solo, Suze, Bentley, Venture, Jericho, Kiss, Charlie, Min, M'Stor, Slayer, Little Rusty, Tarzan, Sweet Boy, Sedona, Moosie, Ted, CharlieHorse, Guess, Bella, Jani, Heighten, Hudson, Mr. Steve Vai, Akira, Mistah Lee, Little D, Rusty, Chance, Iron Man, Hollywood, Cadence, Studley, Chester, Nibzie, Bourbon, Buddy, River, Jazz, Spencer, Sonora, Marvel, Chiquita, Wild Bill, Danny, Chianti, Rain, Sunny, Tommy, Abuela, Oliver, Annie, Journey, Jack, Tally, Blaze, Birdie, Sweet Lorraine… and Mike and Lee and Mystery (and to the kids before me: Mr. Bernie Rivers, Winston, Dawnie, and Little Bird Sing Pretty). Each of you is a beat of my heart. Thank you for my second chance.

And finally, to Jim Gath….

Thank you.

Thank you for everything.

All is well.

ABOUT THE AUTHOR

Alexis Roeckner Ferri was born in Scottsdale, Arizona and was raised in the outskirts of Cave Creek. Between the ages of 12 and 15, she lived with her family in three different cities in California and one in Florida before moving back home to Arizona.

At 17, Alexis came to Tierra Madre to fulfill one hundred hours of community service for a graduation requirement for high school, but by the end of her first day, she knew she was never going to leave. She received her Bachelor's Degree in Sustainability from Arizona State University in the spring of 2014 then following a summer of volunteer work at Tierra Madre, she was appointed the Ranch Director in October of 2014. In January of 2017, she was promoted to Tierra Madre's Executive Director.

During her years as Director, Alexis implemented a foundational structure including the creation of the first active Board of Directors, volunteer orientations, donor development strategies, fundraising initiatives, and policies and procedures that are followed by volunteers to this day. She worked with numerous community partners to form programs that benefited the ranch's growth and oversaw the name change to Tierra Madre Horse *and Human* Sanctuary. While running the ranch, she earned a master's degree in nonprofit leadership and management, also from ASU.

Alexis is currently working on a project called Sonora's Cure, which she envisions as an informal coalition that empowers horse owners and farriers with resources about the causes, signs, treatment, and prevention of laminitis. She additionally works as the Development Manager for United Cerebral Palsy of Central Arizona, a nonprofit organization that provides programs and services to individuals with disabilities. She also runs her own candle making business, Ferri Light Candles.

Alexis lives in Phoenix with her husband Alex and their daughter Aurora, two cats Gypsy and Theon, and dog Lucy. She loves road trips, coffee, and Kenny Loggins.

Alexis is on Tierra Madre's Board of Directors and returns to the ranch every week as a volunteer, fundraiser, videographer, and a maker of mashes.

www.ingramcontent.com/pod-product-compliance
Lightning Source LLC
LaVergne TN
LVHW011911080426
835508LV00007BA/337